THE HALLS OF
THE FISHMONGERS'
COMPANY

Fishmongers' Hall as built 1668–71 (terrace altered 1790), drawn just before the riverside block was demolished in July 1827, showing construction of the coffer dam for the new bridge-abutment, at low tide, and in the background the tower of St Michael Crooked Lane, demolished 1831. Watercolour by E. W. Cooke (later R.A.), original $8\frac{1}{2}'' \times 11\frac{3}{4}''$, Guildhall Art Gallery, City of London.

THE HALLS OF
THE FISHMONGERS'
COMPANY

An Architectural History of a Riverside Site

by

PRISCILLA METCALF

PHILLIMORE

1977
Published by
PHILLIMORE & CO. LTD.
London and Chichester

Head Office: Shopwyke Hall,
Chichester, Sussex, England

© Fishmongers' Company, 1977

ISBN 0 85033 243 5

Set in Intertype Baskerville
and printed in Great Britain by
The Compton Press Ltd.
The Old Brewery, Tisbury, Wilts.

Foreword

There is nothing like the London livery companies in any other capital in the world. Yet this book is the first serious architectural history of any of them. This makes it important not only for today, but also for the future. Moreover, Dr Priscilla Metcalf writes so easy a style that her reader may well be deceived at first, unaware until seeing the ample notes that he has here the result of several years' first-hand research conducted by a scholar with a rare intuition of where finds can be made. Dr Metcalf could indeed base her work on a wonderful wealth of documents, written as well as drawn, and so the story unfolds itself: a freehold plot of ground facing the Thames and facing London Bridge, a hall built in the sixteenth century, an extended hall of immediately after the Fire, a classical building of 1831–5, and so on to the most recent adjustments, with the gilded barges and 'The Shades', and finally to the men behind the buildings.

NIKOLAUS PEVSNER

Contents

List of Illustrations

PHOTOGRAPHY

K. Bruce: Pl. 5*b*, 8*b*, 18, Fig. II; S. B. Bolas: Pl. 17;
J. R. Freeman & Co.: Frontispiece, Pl. 1, 4, 5*a*, 8*a*, 9, 10,
12–15, Fig. III–VI; Bedford Lemere: Pl. 19, 20 22*a*, 23*a*;
J. R. Pantlin: Pl. 22*b*, 23*b*.

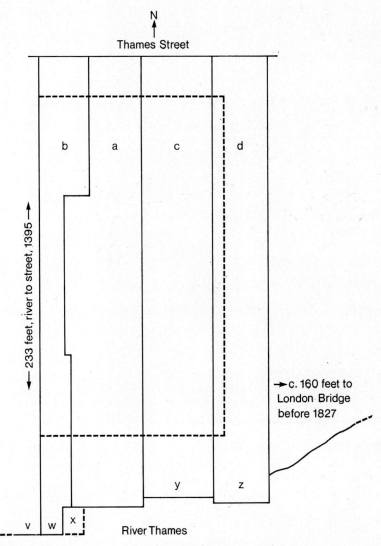

Fig. I The ground before the Great Fire, including wharves, yards, water-stairs, and overbuilt alleys, but drawn with irregular boundaries straightened. (*a*) Walworth-Askham site, Fishmongers' Hall from 1444. (*b*) Pepper Querne site, defined 1395, added to *a* 1573–81. (*c*) Nun's Head site added to *ab* after 1666. (*d*) Flower de Luce site added to *ab* after 1666 (east boundary = parish boundary). (*v*) The 'stone house' next door *c.* 1525–1666. (*w*) The 'little wharf' defined 1395, so called 1525, part of Hall shoreline 1975. (*x*) Approximate site, Walworth's water-tower mentioned 1395, and of Hall pump and cistern before 1666. (*y*) Dyehouse 1592–1666. (*z*) Former Stockfishmongers' Hall, rebuilt 1618. Vertical broken line: Hall's east boundary since 1827. Upper horizontal broken line: setback of present Hall since 1832 (any change in 1667–8 unknown). Lower horizontal broken line: Hall's present south front, minus terrace. Shoreline straightened (except at *w*) 1668, 1828. (A series of medieval waterfronts west of Hall, excavated 1975–6, projected less boldly into the river than *v* and *w*, both possibly wharfed out by Walworth.) From (very) rough diagram by author based on deeds of 1395, 1525, 1641, 1652, and drawings of 1667, 1828. Compare Pl. 2–4, Fig. VII and Summary on p. xii.

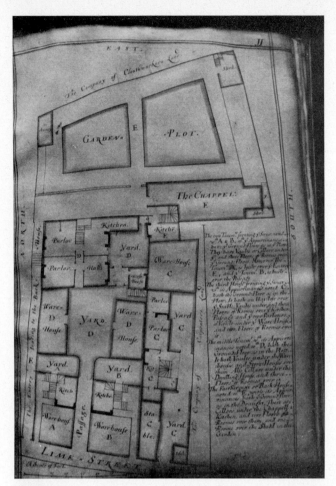

Fig. II Plan of the company's garden and Lime Street houses, later Nos 44–7, from planbook by William Leybourne, 1686, at Fishmongers' Hall. (p. 42)

Fig. III Note of survey by Edward Jerman, 1667, in Fishmongers' Company Ms 5857 at Guildhall Library.

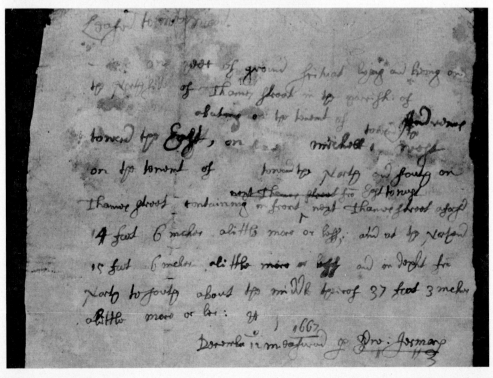

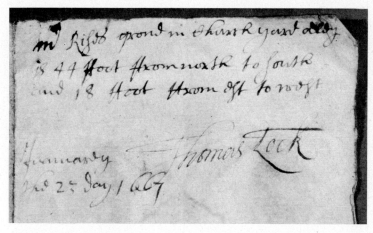

Fig. IV Note of survey by Thomas Lock, 1668, in Fishmongers' Company Ms 5857 at Guildhall Library.

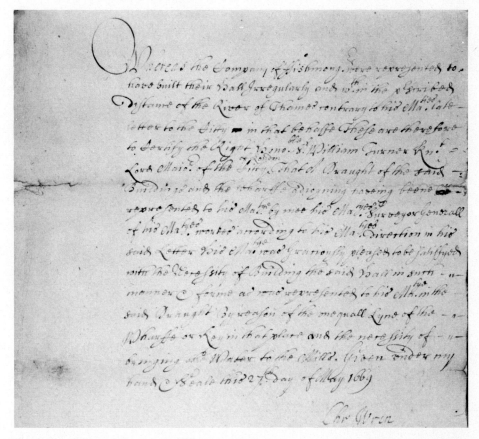

Fig. V Royal licence allowing the Fishmongers' Company to continue building the Hall within less than 40 feet of the river, signed by Christopher Wren as Surveyor-General of the King's Works, 1669, counterpart in Fishmongers' Company Ms 6762 at Guildhall Library.

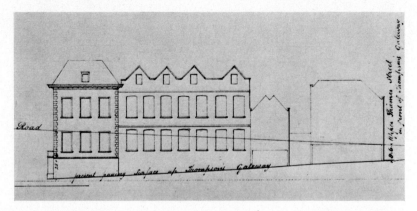

Fig. VI Profile of roofs, from east view of Hall drawn by Richard Suter, 1826 (in relation to bridge-level as then supposed), in Fishmongers' Company collection at Guildhall Library.

Fig. VII Plan of the north approach to the new London Bridge in relation to the old Bridge, Fishmongers' Hall, St Michael Crooked Lane, and other properties, drawn by William Knight, published in William Herbert, *History and Antiquities of the Parish of St Michael Crooked Lane*, 1831.

Plates

Frontispiece. Fishmongers' Hall, 1671–1827

Between Pages 28 and 29

1. Plan of early fifteenth-century livery hall on Old Fish Street Hill.
2. Views of the Hall from Southwark in the mid-sixteenth century.
3. Views of the Hall from Southwark in the early seventeenth century.
4. The ruins of the Hall after the Great Fire.

Between pp 76 and 77

5. Plans of the post-Fire Hall, as proposed and as built.
6. The Hall river-front about 1700.
7. The Hall river-front by 1753 or before.
8. William Daniell, view of the City and London Bridge in 1804.

Between pp 116 and 117

9. Henry Roberts, drawing 1831 for the south front.
10. Henry Roberts, drawing 1831 for the east front.
11. Plan of upper floor showing ceilings, engraving 1836.
12. Henry Roberts, drawing 1831, longitudinal section.
13. Henry Roberts' office, details of main staircase compartment, 1834.
14. Henry Roberts' office, drawing for chimneypiece, 1834.
15. Henry Roberts' office, details of fittings, 1835.
16. The banqueting hall as decorated by Roberts, engraving 1861.

Between pp 164 and 165

17. The main staircase in 1896, before changes of 1898.
18. The banqueting hall as hospital ward, drawn in 1914.
19. The banqueting hall in *c.* 1920, as redecorated 1898.
20. The Hall and the wharf from the Bridge in 1914.
21. The neighbourhood from the air *c.* 1923 and from the river in 1904.
22. The court drawing room in war and in peace.
23. The court dining room in war and in peace.
24. Upper Thames Street in 1920.

Preface

For three years spent in preparing this book I thank the Fishmongers' Company and the members of its court, especially a committee composed of Sir Leslie Farrer KCVO, Mr J. G. Phillimore CMG, and Mr J. V. G. Mallet, and Mr Eric S. Earl the Clerk, who have continuously shown faith in the enterprise even when the going was slow : there was little writing to show for many long months among the company's manuscripts until the third year of my appointment. I owe this totally unexpected commission to a kindly grapevine among architectural historians that suggested my name, but Dr A. E. J. Hollaender, when he was Keeper of Manuscripts in Guildhall Library, must be credited with the initial suggestion that such a book should be written and it was a pleasure to start work on the records under his care. Originally it was thought that the book might concentrate on the history of the present building, but when it was seen how much could also be winkled out of the records about previous Halls, I was allowed to follow my bent in treating this as a history of the site, a piece of ancient ground swarming with life and buildings.

Along the way, there have been extremely helpful people whom I am glad to thank : especially at Guildhall Library, Mr Christopher Cooper and his assistants in charge of manuscripts, Mr James Howgego and Mr Ralph Hyde in charge of prints, maps, and drawings, Mr Donovan Dawe and Mr Thomas Shaw and their assistants in charge of printed books, both in the old and the new library premises. One is glad to remember the old lofty reading room, even with its occasional eccentricities (in what other great library in the world could one have had a request for a book returned with 'Dinner in Crypt' written across the slip?). And at the Corporation of London Record Office under Miss Betty Masters there is always a friendly welcome. At the Victoria and Albert Museum, I was helped by Mr Michael Darby on Owen Jones drawings, and by Mr Robert Charleston and other members of the Ceramics Department with information about various forms of glass. The R.I.B.A. Library, the London Library, and the National Monuments Record have been helpful as always. Anthony McIntyre, while a student at the Architectural Association, did some research on the life and work of Henry Roberts which he shared with me, and I thank him for allowing me to quote him. Dr Timothy Wood, a member of the livery, kindly sought out and sent me the recollection of the Hall in 1914–18 quoted in the last chapter. And Mr P. A. Bezodis of the Survey of London supplied useful references.

Three busy architectural historians have been good enough to read certain chapters : Sir John Summerson, Curator of the Soane Museum, Mr John

Newman, Lecturer at the Courtauld Institute, and Dr J. M. Crook, Reader in Architectural History at Bedford College. Most of all I thank Sir Nikolaus Pevsner for reading the whole and for encouraging me when I needed it.

At the Hall, where the staff have been most kind, observing the life of the place has helped me to understand its records and its surroundings: working in the courtroom among old paintings of the river while remnants of London's river traffic moved past, on quiet summer days with the cathedral bells sounding over the water, or, on foggy winter days with mists swirling outside as if the Hall were a natural outcrop of rock. When the ground itself lies beside a world-famous Bridge, and when a series of historically interesting people and several distinct periods of architecture have been concerned in a neighbourhood affording continuous evidences of urban change, what more could an urban historian ask? The company's records afford many other evidences than I have used, for the history of commerce, of fisheries and fish-markets, of charity and education, for example, and they have been, are, and will be mined by other kinds of scholars. But it seems appropriate that the owners of this unique site have commissioned this particular kind of book. I've learned far more than there's room for.

P.M.

December 1975

A Summary

SITE I: ground probably *c*. 62 feet EW by *c*. 186 feet NS (excluding wharves but including two tenants' houses) between Thames Street and the River Thames; that is, the western half of Site II. Domestic and commercial premises of perhaps *c*. 1350, officially Fishmongers' Hall from 1444, rebuilt probably 1520s/30s (riverside block) and 1570/80s (great-hall block). Major repairs 1639, 1660. Destroyed by fire 1666.

SITE II: including Site I with addition of two plots east of it, in all *c*. 123 feet EW by *c*. 185 feet NS (excluding terrace and uneven wharf, but including six tenants' houses). Building designed partly by Edward Jerman 1667–8, partly by Thomas Lock 1669 with outside advice (from Robert Hooke? Peter Mills?) or aided by Edward Peirce. Built 1668–71, part occupied 1669. Alterations and redecoration by John Gorham 1788–91. Demolished 1827, 1830 during rebuilding of London Bridge.

SITE III: same as Site II minus 20-foot strip on east side; that is, it includes all of Site I and most of Site II (allowing also for east basement-area, setback from Thames Street, and embankment extending wharf). Building designed 1831 by Henry Roberts. Concrete bed laid 1832. Carcase built 1832–3, interior completed 1834, occupied 1835, decoration completed by Roberts 1840. Redecoration by Owen Jones 1865; by John Dibblee Crace 1898 according to advice 1894 from George Frederick Bodley; and by Harry Stuart Goodhart-Rendel 1926. Partly gutted by fire in air raid 1940. Reconstruction and redecoration 1943–53 by Herbert Austen Hall in collaboration with Sir Edward Gillett.

See Fig. I opp. p. viii.

PART ONE

THE GROUND BY
FISHMONGERS HOLE

'Fishmongers 3 hallis, whereof one ys at Oldefysche stret in seint Nycholas Colde abbey paryssh & a nother of them ys in Stok-fyshmonger row in temstrete, & in ye paryssh of Seynt Myghell in Croked lane, and ye thryd of them is in bryggestrete in seynt Margaret paryssh & all these 3 hallys longe to the fishmongers.'

> Harley 541 f. 225v, ?1483–5: papers used by John Stow.

'It is agreed and appointed that all Assembles of Courtes aswell for the good politique gurding and ordre of the same crafte . . . shalbe holden kept and used in the place comonly called the Fishmongers halle in the parisshe of Saint Mighell ny Croked lane of London and not in any other place.'

> Article 4, agreement of January 1514, Company Book of Ordinances.

CHAPTER 1

Why These Buildings Are Interesting

A BUILDING is not a static thing. Little processes of decay and renewal go on as long as occupation goes on, as every householder knows – processes that are patterns in little of complete destruction and rebuilding. Where one site has known every degree of decay and renewal for centuries, and where records survive from six of those centuries, you have the materials for history. The few City livery companies still standing in their old places and still in possession of their records are, by their very nature as continuous institutions, uniquely able to testify to City building-history – and not only from long standing on single sites but from long ownership of other City freeholds, ancient legacies and investments. And of course these networks of property imply networks of craftsmen, tradesmen, tenants, neighbours, lawyers, and above all committees, hatching and patching the bricks and mortar of their estates. So a true history of the City of London will require a mosaic of histories like this. Of any city or town or village this is true; how much more is it so of the centre of a nation's commerce as it was becoming a world-centre. The building-history of one City of London site can contribute to the main stream of urban history. Such a site represents more than itself.

Since the sixteenth century, Fishmongers' Hall has stood out in views of the neighbourhood of London Bridge, the old front door to visitors from the Continent. When Elizabeth I went down-river by barge to meet Drake at Deptford, and still when Charles II rode in over the bridge to claim his kingdom, the Fishmongers' battlements and lanterned hall-roof reared up beside them. On the terrible Sunday morning in 1666, while battlements and roof collapsed, armfuls of valuables were slung into a barge by the glare of the Great Fire, rescue as was fit coming by river (for it is on record that the lighterman came asking reward for it afterward). The new Fishmongers' Hall and Wren's Custom House were after the disaster the riverside's first buildings that could be called architecture. The post-Fire Hall during its century and a half of existence drew the eyes of many artists as part of the setting of the Bridge against the skyline of Wren's spires. When one more total destruction of Fishmongers' Hall was required for the re-building of the Bridge, the winning architect in the competition of 1831 thought the site presented 'such difficulties as are rarely found in Combination with equal Advantages for the display of Architectural taste'. This narrative is a little more than building-history : on such a site, the Thames too is a theme. For, among City company halls, this one, constantly conditioned by River and Bridge, sits at an opposite extreme from, say, that of the Merchant Taylors' entirely private architecture, conditioned though that may be by the human rivers of its bounding streets. Other companies, the Watermen, the Vintners, and the Dyers, gradually drew back from the waterside, which in any case they never confronted so grandly as the Fishmongers did. A riverside situation can imply far more than a nice view, it means an active relationship with a tidal river. And always the inhabitants of crowded waterside buildings, before and after 1666, were uneasily aware of their vulnerability to certain facts of crowded waterside life – to flood and fire, to damage from traffic by land and by water, to the quietly insidious effects of shifting ground and the damp beneath, and always the ancient watercourses bringing downhill the incessant tide of human waste. Here, as in Holland and Venice, waterside buildings depended on humble wooden piling, and if the foundations laid upon the piles were badly made, tidal floods spawned hidden forces of rising damp, until the virtues of concrete were discovered.

Another background theme, necessarily muted in a book with so much material, is the ancestry of the architectural profession. Through these records stalk the craftsmen – makers and measurers and menders of buildings – whose story, where it can be plucked out of anonymity, is part of the history of the slowly emerging professions of architects and surveyors. Long before architects emerged socially, some master-craftsmen could be fairly grand in the world of the City: in the eighteenth century Charles Easton served as Master of the Masons' Company and John Price as Master of the Carpenters' Company while they were employed by the Company of Fishmongers, who in the previous century referred to men even of the stature of Edward Peirce and Edward Jerman as 'workmen' and only late in the eighteenth century invited the company surveyor to dinner.

The company's small but interesting collection of architectural drawings, deposited in the Guildhall Library, provides only piecemeal evidence for its architectural history before 1831. There are several reasons for this. Not that earlier surveyors and craftsmen didn't make drawings: they did, but most of those vanished after use, dog-eared and pricked into holes, worn out in the workshops. Drawings that did survive tended to be alternative designs unused, or furnished especially for the company's court to consider and the Clerk to file away. Until the eighteenth century, drawings chiefly kept were plans. Elevations, or 'uprights', had less significance in the medieval City, whereas a plan – or platform, 'platt' or 'plot' – represented ground-cover, property. Such drawings were regarded as working documents like leases, not as evidence for the 'handwriting' of draughtsmen, certainly not as works of art.

Three main architectural periods concern us. The first buildings for which there is visual evidence were late medieval, a riverside range probably of the 1520s–30s and a great hall probably of the 1580s; with some Stuart shoring-up and embellishment these Tudor structures stood until the Great Fire. The next group of buildings were a late Stuart mixture of certain medieval features clung to by a merchant society and new features modelled on the latest courtiers' houses;

the showpiece riverside range of 1669 was a sophisticated late example of what
has been called artisan mannerism. With a drastic late eighteenth-century over-
haul this group of buildings lasted until 1827. The present Hall, combining the
old group of spaces into a single building with warehouses below, dates from that
late Georgian/early Victorian period, the reign of William IV: with the livery
hall, in the Greek Revival style then fashionable, deftly placed on a commercial
substructure that relates back, via the Palladian style, to ancient Italian town-
houses, especially those of Venice, with water access on one side and land access on
the other. Grounded in the uses of waterborne commerce, such a building symbolizes a whole city's past. The livery hall's separate access from the bridge-approach
is part of the building's bond with the Bridge. Now, the Hall has dual importance
as the sole survivor of quality from an important piece of town-planning and as
one of the rare examples in English cities of a large free-standing Greek Revival
building.

The field of architectural history ranges from architecture unencumbered by
neighbours and other urban nuisances (e.g. the country house) to architecture
encumbered, steeped in the urban brew; its practitioners range from ivory-tower
specialists ignoring environment to slum-and-suburb specialists ignoring art history. It might be all too easy to become so involved in reasons for the shape and
uses of a town site as to exclude the architectural forms upon it: the real fascina-
tion lies in seeing how far a building is shaped by its makers' ideas of style, how far
by its physical environment and the economic climate, and how far by the functions it serves. These halls have housed a particular set of functions, the regular
meetings of the 34 members of the company's court, composed of six wardens and
their assistants, in courtroom and committee rooms, with reception rooms for a
steady stream of guests and of organizations related to the fishing industry, as well
as the traditional great dining-hall seating several hundred members of the livery,
in a building ready to receive royalty or pensioners while accommodating the daily
business of a trade-supervising, charity-dispensing, property-owning body run by
its chief permanent officer the Clerk and his staff. It would have been interesting
to compare and contrast Fishmongers' Hall with buildings abroad such as those of
the *scuole,* or craft fraternities of Venice. Yet it may be better first to concentrate
on circumstances peculiar to the City of London, where – so far as I know – no one
series of livery halls has been the subject of full-scale architectural history before.

Sources for the first buildings here that we know anything about include certain
drawn or engraved views of the riverside, combined with deductions from charters,
deeds, and comment in surviving minutebooks and account books – for where
repairs were made or neighbourly differences had, a good deal emerges from such
records: sometimes one can almost hear men talking, even a few women. For the
post-Fire Hall there are fairly full records for the exterior from construction to
demolition; for the interior there is much written evidence but almost no remaining visual record. As for the present Hall, sources for site, design, construction
and decoration are unusually full, thanks to an administration that has thrown
little away. We can give, too, a more reliable history than before of the wine vaults

let out to tenants of the Hall's cellars between 1680 and 1830, and the origins in the 1740s–50s of the famous Shades wines tavern there, not roystered-in by Tudor or Stuart royalty as mythology has it.

The site of the present Hall represents the core of the fourteenth-century Stock-fishmongers Row, the combined ground of three medieval sites with a sliver from a fourth mostly given up in 1827. The east boundary has fluctuated most, as the Bridge has come closer and closer. The Hall's west boundary (until 1975) has remained precisely the same for about four centuries, and the strip that formed it was defined in the fourteenth century. This old party-wall boundary was an affair of close living, ancient lights, and mutual irrigation, the 'Mary Ann behind' of city life (borrowing Lutyens' phrase, 'Queen Anne in front and Mary Ann behind'), an unlovely and, until Fishmongers' Hall Street was made in 1889, an unseen borderline. Now, with rebuilding west of the Hall beginning in 1975, the border shifts farther westward. For the Hall's north frontage on Thames Street and the lettings to generations of tenants there until 1831, there is plenty of documentary evidence. The south boundary was and is the river, its shoreline varied surprisingly little since the sixteenth-century views were drawn and indeed, it would seem, in certain dimensions cited in 1395.

This is a biography of a site. As yet, no full and serious history of the company itself has been written. Inevitably some writers down the years have indulged in thoughtless repetition of unsifted myths about the early halls, so a good deal of time-consuming sifting has had to be done. The contents of these buildings take a lesser place, though the genesis of a few splendid fixtures and fittings is given, along with the general flavour of decoration and furnishings, and movements in taste including five stages in the decoration of the present building. The company barge, as occasional outlying seat, receives attention; as does the Lime Street garden house with its links to the office of the King's Works during the Surveyor-ship of Inigo Jones.

The City, sometimes, is fond of pointing to evidences of continuity. This ground is a good example. Officially the company has owned the core of it since 1444. Before that it seems to have been occupied by the company's trading ancestors at least since the thirteenth- or fourteenth-century development of Stockfishmongers Row, or, since fish-merchants first put out their wharves and sorted their wares here. Occupation has continued, except for the years 1666-9 and 1830-5, when the company perforce met elsewhere – yet demolition and rebuilding are a form of occupation. There was partial wartime disuse towards the end of 1939 and after the air-raids of September 1940 until June 1941. Of the three heroic periods of coping with destruction by fire, bridge-building, and war – to which can be added a fourth period of enduring the latest bout of bridge-building – at least it can be said that the rebuilding of the Bridge in 1825-31 allowed for planned withdrawal and renewal, the last war brought only partial destruction, and the latest bridge-works caused no more than discomfort and inconvenience. But even from the Hall's first, worst, and totally unexpected destruction in the Great Fire, not only was a gallant and orderly recovery made, all things considered, but the chance was seized to make a bigger and entirely different building. Again in 1831, there was no question of clinging to old building-forms. Ancient institutions can be infinitely adaptable. Naturally after 1940, when the Hall was only crippled, the existing building was restored. On the other hand, with expansion to the neighbouring site on the west, imitation is not in order, while preserving a proper deference in the matter of scale.

The present Fishmongers' Hall, like Wren's surviving church towers (where we can still see them), is one of the few firmly fixed points of reference left in a panoramic view of the Thames shore. The scale of the latest bridge is entirely different from that of the structure with which the present Hall was so carefully designed to be in keeping. A new value has accrued to the Hall in this matter of 'keeping'. not only in the everyday sense of determined possession and maintenance, but in the old English sense of human and natural arrangements 'in keeping with' one another, that is, with a more humane and civilized scale of building-values than measure the monsters rising around it. Life was not always humane and civilized in the Hall's early days, though the scale of inhumanity has changed too – but we are talking about architecture. This is the story of one waterside piece of ground and the series of buildings with which it has been encrusted, prime specimens of the layers fertilizing that ancient archaeological site, the City of London.

CHAPTER 2

The Circumstances before *c.* 1525

FISHMONGERS HOLE was a local term for the deep little bay on the upstream west side of the medieval London Bridge. In the late fourteenth century, Henry Yeveley, King's Mason and distinguished architect, parishioner of St. Magnus, and associate of Chaucer and Sir William Walworth, owned land at 'Le Hole'.[1] In 1769, Fishmongers' Company wardens suspecting the rowers for Doggett's Coat and Badge of some knavery ordered them to bring their boats to Fishmongers Hole for inspection.[2] Part of the strange landscape of the river-bottom emerged at low tide: in 1738 rumours of foul play in the Doggett race put it that 'most of them had assistance from their Friends to help them over the Sand Bank' – the upper lip of the Hole. Yet at low tide in front of the company's wharf there was no long beach such as Hollar's drawings show at Westminster. When, in 1650, a water-carpenter was instructed to set 'before this Hall . . . two or three steps whereby people may go in and come out of boats at low water', there was apparently a brief mud slope there, like the barge-bed now visible at low tide. About sixty yards east of the Hall gate, an ancient drain known as the Gully Hole, redolent of East-cheap's meat and fish stalls and household debris, lay open at the edge of Thames Street from which a horrid stream ran down to the river at what had earlier been called Oystergate, near the waterworks established at the bridge in the sixteenth century.[3] What the Gully Hole contributed to the water drawn up there seems to have been questioned by nobody, for the water-supply was regularly rinsed by the force of that 'violent roaring tide' through the narrow bridge-arches that Shakespeare, out of daily familiarity, made into a figure of speech.[4] Sir John Rennie was to describe the medieval Bridge as standing 'upon a hill' with valleys either side of it about thirty feet deeper than the bridge-foundations because of 'the great fall and scour produced by the contracted waterway'. 'I was obliged to build', he said of the Bridge of 1825–31, 'in the deep hole above the old bridge.'[5]

The London Thames in the sixteenth century was a clear and fishful river: 'fat and sweet salmons [are] dailie taken in this streame'; and 'the water of itselfe is very cleare', said William Harrison in 1577, telling too of the 'infinit number of swans dailie to be seene upon this river' despite its traffic.[6] For 'two thousand wherries and small boats' maintained three thousand watermen 'through the cariage and recariage of such persons as passe or repasse upon the same' – so that,

The notes for Chapter 2 are on pp. 184–6.

at every set of public river-stairs, clusters of watermen waited like cab-drivers for custom. And there were 'those huge tideboats, tiltbotes, and barges', bringing passengers and provisions to London from the countryside up-river. When, in the seventeenth century, the Fishmongers' Company sent coal by river to its alms-houses at Bray and received timber by river from its woodlands there, the barge journey – above the tidal reaches horse-drawn from a towpath – could take nearly a week each way.[7] (Still in the nineteenth century coals were bought for Jesus Hospital in the port of London for delivery 'into a West Country Barge alongside the Ship', e.g. in August 1867.) Most building-materials for the Hall, stone, bricks and roof-tiles as well as timber, will have come to Fishmongers' Wharf by barge. There were other cargoes on the river. Prisoners bound for the execution-block at the Tower might be rowed silently past at low tide on their way to Traitors' Gate, or livery-company barges with escort of trumpet and drum put off from Old Swan to accompany the Lord Mayor to Westminster. At night less pompous music, out of wherries homeward bound from the stews and theatres of Southwark, crept by on the waters. But when the tide was running, the cataracts at the Bridge drowned human sounds. In the 1660s Pepys enjoyed the excitement of shooting the rapids by wherry ('had a good wash').

The narrow highway on the Hall's other doorstep was full of human noises. Narrowing the width of Thames Street between the housefronts were jutting upper storeys and shop counters, with no separate footpaths. In the late sixteenth century, City streets scaled by old usage to pedestrian and packhorse were in-creasingly invaded by 'carres, drayes, carts and coatches, more than hath beene accustomed', complained John Stow, as the same streets are now invaded by lorries.[8] Thronged with porters, horses, beggars, pedlars, apprentices, and all the less daring wherry passengers footing it between the water-stairs either side the tide-race at the Bridge, Thames Street was much 'pestered with Carts' laden with coal, wood, beer-casks, manure, and goods from the quays. In 1584, for example, below-bridge by the Custom House, there was Porter's Quay, a property of the Fishmongers' Company, serving the French trade and coastal trade; and just east of the houses clustered by Fishmongers' Hall was Bussher's Wharf, owned by Thomas Carter, fishmonger, a quay where pitch, tar, flax, iron, timber and fish were landed, all generating traffic in the neighbourhood.[9] Great personages rode through the din of Thames Street, as when Wolsey in 1516, proceeding from Westminster to Greenwich, landed at Three Cranes wharf to avoid the Bridge and 'rode upon his Mule, with his crosse, his Pillars, his Hatte, and Broad seale caryed afore him on Horse-backe through Thames Streete, untill he came to Billingsgate, and there tooke his Barge again', as described in Stow's *Annales*. From the skirts of medieval Thames Street various little belongings have found their way to the London Museum – knives, a pewter spoon, an elaborately moulded prick-spur, a carpenter's axe, daggers. Violence was never far away; every private yard-entrance and cartway needed a gate to shut, preferably with a wicket like a side-hung cat-door for swift single entry on foot. At one end of Thames Street the turrets of the dreadful Tower, today just visible from the site

of the old Hall gate, were partly hidden by oversailing garrets and thick atmosphere between. For, even though Thames water was still clear, the air was smoked
by multiplying chimneys, commercial and domestic. And near the floating swans
lay reeking rubbish-heaps awaiting removal in dung-boats attended by scavenging
birds hovering overhead. The contrasts in daily life were very great.

   This waterside jungle grew on ground that did not exist when the Romans came.
Thames Street, sometimes called 'the Cradle of the City', is thought to have
started as a waterside track at the foot of slopes we still know, but steeper, below
Cannon Street and Eastcheap (although recent rediscovery of a Roman riverside
wall makes the early existence of Thames Street a question). Gradually there
began to accumulate between ancient track and river an alluvial foreshore,
rammed down and propped up to make landing-places. A well-boring in 1834
beside or in the cellar of the present Hall at a point four feet above high water
found 'made ground, black boggy soil, and peat' to a depth of 27 feet before
reaching the 'valley drift' layers of sand and gravel above the London clay.[10]
Such ground needed bolstering against the eating action of the river. Remains
from a wharf strengthened by elm piling, found in the twentieth century just
north of Upper Thames Street opposite the Hall, marked a possibly second-
century shoreline there. Just south of the street a somewhat later embankment,
formed by massive oak and chestnut piles, was found ten feet below the surface
under the south abutment of the London Bridge dry arch formed in 1830, and
roughly on a line with the present north front of the Hall. And since 1974 a
whole series of wharf-remains have been uncovered west of the Hall.[11] Historians
have long been aware (though only now confirming by systematic excavation) that
a process of wharfing-out the shore into the river apparently went on in and after
the Anglo-Saxon period as trade flowing into London from abroad needed ever
more wharves and warehouses. The seeming mystery of the siting of the medieval
London Bridge, at what was later the river's widest point thereabouts, is explained
when we realize that the wharfing-out either side of it went on after it was built –
hence the receding shore between Hall and Bridge before 1825. Once that Bridge
was finished in 1209, the tides straining through its nineteen narrow arches became forced and unnatural. Against high spring tides, periodically flooding the
riverside warehouses, wharf and floor levels at the waterside were gradually raised,
and so the pitch of the foreshore slope was slowly trimmed up between street and
river. Before 1666, ground-floor level at the street was apparently first-floor level
at the waterside, over a wharf-level basement all too near high water. By 1816,
Fishmongers' Wharf had been raised seven steps above at least part of the basement floor of 1669. And by 1830, Thames Street at the Hall was ten feet and the
Hall wharf three feet above average high tide.[12] On plan, the shoreline mapped
after the Great Fire was apparently set in the medieval period, although obscured
in pre-Fire views by overhanging structures at the water's edge : one deed of 1395
and a rough plan of 1667 for the Fishmongers' ground confirm the outline the
views suggest.[13] Propping up the riverbank, which went on even after the civil
engineer replaced the water-carpenter, was part of a London marine merchant's
life, as a need for fences is for farmers.

The Thames north shore at certain angles of its twisting course can have an almost seaside intensity of weather. The Hall's south-southwest-facing front receives the full force of prevailing winds, so that, for instance in the seventeenth century, its window-glass needed protective 'skreenwork'. When, during the centuries of the medieval Bridge, the partially dammed river froze over in certain hard winters, life beside it could be less a jolly frost-fair than a dark time of pent-up shipping and sewage, though the greater depth of Fishmongers Hole would not have frozen solid. Always, when the tide was unleashed again, there were eddies here against the current, making the company's water-steps in bad weather so near the old Bridge dangerous to use, and silting up mud against the jetties so that certain late views of the post-Fire Hall show grassy banks outside the river wall (Frontispiece). Still in 1833 a drain-mouth was stopped up by 'accumulation of Mud & Sediment in front of the Company's Wharf' caused by a neighbour's jetty 'which prevents the flow of water in the usual & ancient Manner'.[14]

London's first reliable maps were suddenly provided when desperately needed after the Great Fire. John Leake's map of the surviving skeleton of City streets shows the common alleys and a few semi-private cartways, but gives only a partial sense of the long narrow ribbons of pre-Fire property between Thames Street and the river.[15] Each separate strip once had its own passage to its own wharf and privy. Such strips of ground, over two hundred feet long, might be of any width between ten and forty feet, the side boundaries and passages, like the common lanes, taking a slightly wandering downhill course. A similar shore-side density once existed at Great Yarmouth, Brighton, and Deal. Urban plots in general tend to be long and narrow : a fairly typical London house-lot today, including the back garden, might measure one hundred by twenty feet. But there was nothing else in London quite like these strips on the south side of Thames Street where much of the business of the port of London was carried on before the wet-docks were built. Each strip, from the shop or counting-house on the street to the wharf at the bottom of the slope, was filled with living, stabling and warehousing accommodation 'promiscuously disposed' (as later surveyors loftily described such premises) among sheds and yards, with an overbuilt entry beside the shop for porters, packhorses and sometimes carts removing newly landed goods craned out of lighters. With growth of London's trade and population in the sixteenth century, such a site under single occupation lent itself to subdivision and subtenants, in spite of royal and civil attempts to forbid the increase of 'indwellers, inmates or undersitters' (i.e. lodgers) and so the dangers of plague 'amongst those multitudes'. The multiplication of subtenants on such narrow sites inevitably led to ill feeling over use of the passage from street to wharf. Access to this shared private way was supposed to entail 'free liberty of ingresse, egresse, regresse way passage and repassage for this Company's assigns, tenants, servants and workmen dwelling in any houses adjoining to fetch carry and recarry wood water and other things to or from River of Thames to go and pass to and from the stool or privy there for their easement and to go return and pass to and from the Thames for their recreation' etc., as a company lease of 1593, for example, recited the old formula for parts of the Nun's Head ground next door to the Hall –

a shared access that caused the waterside tenant there in 1602 to complain of 'great and common resort through his house to the waterside'.[16] The biblical repetitions of London's legal prose over the years seem to echo the flux and reflux of the river.

'On the South side of Thames streete', said John Stow in 1598, 'about the midway betwixt the bridge foote and Ebgate [Old Swan] Lane, standeth the Fishmongers hall, and diverse other fair houses for marchants.'[17] The Hall and eight houses formed the south end of the parish of St Michael's Crooked Lane. Until 1830 the church rebuilt after the Fire stood about 130 yards from the Hall up Miles (St Michael's) Lane, just below Little Eastcheap and the site of the Boar's Head tavern (see Fig. VII opp. p. ix). After 1830 the parish was absorbed in that of St. Magnus Martyr. The church of St Magnus, until then *juxta pontem* and now cut off from the river by warehouses and from the Bridge by Adelaide House, has lost its proud position beside the old City gateway from Kent and the Channel ports. Until Rennie's bridge was begun, Magnus Corner, where the traffic of Thames Street met the traffic of Fish Street Hill, was known to every traveller from Dover and every rabble-rouser in town ('Up Fish Street! down St Magnus Corner!"). Along the mile-length of Thames Street between Tower Wharf and Puddle Dock there stood before the Fire nine churches, with twenty more a few yards off. After the Fire six of the nine were rebuilt, of which two remain and the tower of a third, and those still standing nearby have been revealed now that the narrow old street has been so greatly widened. For believers inhabiting the riverbank at Fishmongers Hole before the Fire, the bells of All Hallows the Great and the Less, St Lawrence Pountney, St Martin Orgar, St Michael Crooked Lane, St Margaret New Fish Street, and St Magnus Martyr made a ring of sound, echoed from belfries a few yards beyond, and re-echoed beyond those, in the City's square mile of a hundred parishes.

So much for the setting. Now for the ground on which successive Fishmonger Halls have stood. Before the ancestral fish-merchants' ground in Thames Street was secured for a permanent meeting-place of the whole trade, the Fishmongers and the then separate Stockfishmongers had separate meeting-places in each of their several market areas of Old and New Fish Streets and Thames Street.[18] Those in New Fish Street (Fish Street Hill) we know little about, and may have consisted of separate tables at the Star Inn, subsequently owned by the combined company. One in the Old Fish Street area we do know something about, the premises referred to in the sixteenth century as Old Fishmongers Hall, when as Stow said it was 'one great house now letten out for rent'. This stood on Old Fish Street Hill, also called Labour-in-Vain Hill – running down toward the wharves from the fish market east of St Paul's – at the corner of Five Foot or Fye Foot Lane, about midway between the churches of St Nicholas Cole Abbey and St Mary Somerset in the parish of St Mary Mounthaw. We know something about this building because it was leased to the Glaziers' Company from 1612 to 1653 for their livery hall: the Fishmongers' records contain a ground-plan marked 'The Glasiers Plott' (Pl. 1), apparently the plan referred to in Fishmonger court minutes for March 1618 when the Glaziers were making alterations upstairs; and the Glaziers' records contain a schedule of fixtures of 1601, when the place had been let to a private tenant.[19] With its three-foot external walls, bands of five- to seven-light windows, hall screen, and odd plan – with the kitchen beyond the parlour, off the head-table end of the hall, and a warehouse in the traditional kitchen space off the screen end – the drawing of 1618 shows the building as it existed after it was 'letten out for rent'. But the plan does presumably tell us that the dining hall where part of the company met in the fifteenth century measured 44 by 24 feet (roughly the size of the court drawing room now), similar in size to certain fifteenth-century Oxford college halls and country manor-house great halls. Four tenements were built on the whole site after the Great Fire, that on the site of the dining hall becoming in the eighteenth century the Rummer Tavern, later No. 9 Old Fish Street Hill, and all were taken over in 1865 by the Metropolitan Board of Works when it was driving Queen Victoria Street through this neighbourhood of lanes. So the site of Old Fishmongers' Hall lies in or near the south carriageway of that thoroughfare, just southeast of Wren's church of St Nicholas Cole Abbey: that and his tower for St Mary Somerset are the only fixed points left for medieval site-finding purposes hereabouts, for the rebuilding of the City after the Great Fire changed the medieval road system very little, whereas Victorians and post-Victorians have changed it very much.

What might be called the core-site in Thames Street (Fig. I*a*) was secured for this company representing the whole trade soon after the company had obtained a new charter from Henry VI in 1433 – the first in the company's long series of charters to stipulate that all members of the craft – fresh-fish, saltfish, and dried-fish dealers – should be one body, a federation actually achieved only a century after 1433.[20] The core-site had been occupied for almost a century before 1433 by four fish-merchants in succession, three of them Lord Mayors, prominent men in the City – John Lovekyn (d. 1368), Sir William Walworth (d. 1385), and William Askham (d. 1415) – the property passing in each case from former master to former apprentice.[21] Lovekyn may have been one of the early property-developers on the south side of Thames Street and is said to have rebuilt the parish church of St Michael's. Walworth, as everyone knows, slew Wat Tyler; and besides, he was an outstanding man of public affairs, a considerable property owner, and collector of a large library. Askham apparently enlarged Walworth's house, thereafter usually referred to as Askham's great tenement. The last individual holder of the site seems to have been Thomas Botiller (or Butler) from whom it passed in 1432 to a set of trustees, just as the company was applying for the new charter.[22] During 1435–7 a series of trusts and wills were arranged to secure this ground from royal interference under the law of mortmain: the City manoeuvre known as a 'testamentary devise'. There were two carefully staged interlocking bequests, that of Henry Preston (proved 1438) and that of Lord Fanhope (proved 1444). Preston was a rich stockfishmonger who, also in concert with Fanhope, secured for the company its property in Lombard Street and Gracechurch Street. John Cornwall, Baron Fanhope, K. G., second husband of Henry IV's sister Princess Elizabeth, was a more interesting figure, neglected by the *Dictionary of National Biography* but resurrected elsewhere.[23] Long after his death in 1443 the Thames Street property secured in his name was glibly referred to as his house, the 'Hall in Thamysestrete of the gift of the Lord Fanhope', but it is now accepted that his separate will of 1437, proved in 1444 ten months later than his last will of 1443, was a testamentary device and that he himself never lived in the great tenement in Thames Street. He fought at Agincourt, and in 1433 was created Baron Fanhope (Drayton's Agincourt ballad rhymes him with 'ran up'). His agreement with the Fishmonger trustees was made in 1435, his wife and their two children having by then died. He himself was buried in a chantry chapel he had founded at the priory of Black Friars, part of the later site of *The Times* newspaper. Here masses were to be said for his soul and the souls of his nephew Henry V, his late wife Lady Elizabeth Lancaster, their son John and daughter Constance, 'late Countess of Arundell' – celebrations for which he bequeathed the annual sum of forty marks (£26.13.4) due from the Fishmonger trustees – joint ground rent of Askham's great tenement and the Lombard Street/Gracechurch Street site. There must have been anxious moments a century later, after the dissolution of the monasteries, when this ground rent escheated to the Crown until the company was able to redeem it. In the 1630s a hereditary friendship between the company and the Earls of Arundel was briefly revived, apparently stemming from the short marriage in the 1420s of John Fitzalan VI to Fanhope's daughter.[24] But when, in the nineteenth century, it became legally necessary to distinguish between properties given to the company in trust for charitable uses and properties bought by the company for its own corporate uses, it was decided upon the highest legal authority that neither Fanhope nor Preston was a 'principal benefactor' of the company.[25] They gave nothing, they simply lent their names to a tissue of useful fictions. And so, in successive buildings, the Hall has stood its ground while some of the old props laboriously assembled to shore it up legally have, as it were, washed away with the tide. Yet still underneath the firmer foundations that the nineteenth century was able to put down, lie the slowly accumulated assumptions – such as the basic one that this site is worth having – on which older plans were founded. The names of Fanhope and Preston are part of the Hall's history.

The great tenement's western border was carefully defined in a deed of 1395, when Lady Walworth's executors sold off a long thin irregular piece of ground there (Fig. I*b*) which became part of the Hall site after it was got back during 1573–81 by another testamentary arrangement.[26] In 1395 an unusually full set of dimensions were recited for this strip, showing that the executors, and Walworth before them, had reserved considerable ground from it for the main site. Site *b*, with the streetside house called in the sixteenth century the Pepper Querne, narrowed down behind the house to a strip leading to a 'little wharf' (*w*) under a *hautepas* or platform projecting into the river beside Walworth's water-tower (*x* at the upstream end of his main wharf) and leaning against the stone wall of another wharf next upstream. The Pepper Querne tenant's right of way to his little wharf was to be perpetuated: running through or beside the cellars of both pre-Fire and post-Fire Halls, it forms the site of the cartway threaded through the present building to the waterside. The 'little wharf' projects today at the upstream end of Fishmongers' Hall Wharf : part of the company surveyor's office has been sitting on it lately. Sites *a* and *b* constituted the site of the Tudor Hall destroyed in 1666. Sites *c* and *d* were then added to the Hall site, which thereafter consisted of sites *a-d* until 1827. Site *c*, at the sign of the Nun's Head, was apparently built upon by Walworth's contemporary Simon de Morden, with the widest street-frontage of the four and the usual maze of great tenement, warehouses, wharf and water-stairs. It came officially into company possession by purchase and bequest in the names of two members of the company's court in the 1590s and was until the Fire divided among three tenants and their lodgers.[27] Site *d* at the sign of the Flower de Luce, also by the late sixteenth century divided among three tenants, included Old Stockfishmongers' Hall (*z*) at the water's edge, and apparently came with the possessions of that company.[28] Most of site *d* was given up in 1827 for the new Bridge. The jog in the shoreline between the Hall and Nun's Head wharves remained until 1828. The present Hall site consists of sites *a-c* and a sliver of site *d*. We, being visually used to twentieth-century plot-sizes, find it hard to imagine those long, narrow, swarming sets of premises on the Hall ground now. They formed the heart of old Stockfishmongers Row, mentioned by that name in the company's charter of 1399 from Richard II.[29] Romantic nineteenth-century historians who thought every medieval shop or warehouse with a distinguishing sign was a tavern, instead of seeing the sign as combined trademark and equivalent to a street number, have invested Stockfishmongers' Row with a row of taverns, but that is not what these premises were.

From 1444 on, and perhaps unofficially before, Askham's great tenement was Fishmongers' Hall. In the troubled years before 1485 there was probably little money for wholesale rebuilding, so that Askham's dining hall had to last, with patching, until well after 1500. But at least on this comparatively commodious site it provided a meeting-place worth all the legal devices of the mid-fifteenth-century documentary exercise, a more attractive prize than little old Stockfishmongers' Hall or the rooms on Old Fish Street Hill could afford. To make the Walworth-Askham site the one and only meeting-place, however, took years of debate, especially between the years 1504 and 1536. The first new building was put up there during or very soon after that period, as the following history suggests.

In January 1504, Henry VII took over control of the livery companies to the extent of requiring their ordinances to be submitted for approval, with an eye partly to their control over prices in their trades or crafts.[30] From 1504 on, this company's wardens evidently lived through stirring times, none more so than Thomas Knesworth, alderman from 1503, Mayor in 1505–6, briefly imprisoned and heavily fined for resistance to royal agents in 1506, master (prime warden was the later title) of the Fishmongers' Company in 1508 when its charter was confirmed and its ordinances newly drawn up; but Knesworth was never knighted, as his will shows, though the myth that he had been was in full swing by the end of the century, a posthumous unofficial knighthood.[31] In July 1508, when the company's charter of 1433 from Henry VI was confirmed by Henry VII, the new version reiterated the rule laid down in 1433 that fishmongers 'and all others of the same mystery' were to be one body. Early in October 1508, the company's ordinances submitted for royal approval (received in February 1509) included the corollary that all should meet at the one Hall. But already by September 1508 the stockfishmongers – like their product more stiffnecked than the rest – had walked out and re-formed their own company in their old livery hall nearby. What the actual situation among them had been since 1433 is even hazier now than it was probably allowed to be until 1508. Henry Preston who with Lord Fanhope had helped to secure the Hall for the whole trade, had been a stockfish-monger; the premises had been the core of Stockfishmongers Row, an area which had, however, been open to all fish-dealers since the charter of 1399; an amal-gamation of fresh-fish, saltfish and stockfish men had apparently been the aim of men of good will on all sides ever since. But crossing the t's and dotting that i's of it seems to have been put off while times were hard; only when civil peace seemed assured and plans for the future possible, was definition called for. Contention may have arisen in 1508 over proposals to rebuild on the main site, entirely abandon-ing the old separate halls. Until then, separate meetings had probably continued with only occasional joint dinners in Askham's great hall. In other words, one assumes, during the years before these men fell out in 1508, their fathers and grandfathers never quite fell in.

In May 1512 attempts to urge the stockfishmongers back into Fishmongers' Hall for joint election of wardens brought such complaints in defence of 'their ancient liberties and the custom of their own craft' that the court of aldermen decreed an immediate meeting of both parties at Guildhall. There, no doubt after private diplomacy, representatives of the whole trade elected wardens together. Knesworth was there that day: the diplomacy and the urge to consolidate had first taken practical form during his wardenship. Six months later in October 1512 twenty-four delegates met at Guildhall and agreed to be thereafter one mystery or craft, an agreement spelled out after a further year of debate in articles of union submitted at Guildhall in January 1514. Meanwhile, Knesworth had died in June 1513, and his last will (and also a separate will, or device, of 1511) showed how he and his trustees had been accumulating property for the newly consoli-dated company. These lands included the wharf property later called Porter's Quay, on which part of the present Custom House stands, and the Star Inn, just north of the future site of the Monument to the Great Fire, and other valuable ground. In the long memory of the company, Knesworth was to have a special place, splendidly commemorated in silver in the eighteenth century.

Yet the good will wore out soon. Early in 1522 a new separation took place which lasted until 1536. Two joint accomplishments of the years before 1522 were mentioned afterwards: a rebuilding of the company's chapel at the parish church of St Michael's Crooked Lane, stipulated in 1514, at the joint cost of both parties; and the granting of joint arms by the College of Heralds, though not of course used between 1522 and 1536 (and the merman and mermaid sup-porters were officially added only in 1575). If any building was done at the Hall before 1522, not a word survives to prove it.

The years 1522–36, however, could have been propitious for construction, even though the Fishmongers' Company – by now with more income from rents – again lacked stockfishmonger funds. Discreet property development might be a desirable mode of investment in times such as these : in 1522 the City was called upon to advance large sums to the Crown for invasion of France, the livery companies had to surrender their plate, and individuals were forced to testify before Wolsey's deputy as to how much each was worth in money, goods and jewels. To a spirited corporate society, investment in building for the society may have seemed advisable and the Fishmongers' riverside block may then have been begun. Certain stockfishmongers were also busy, in 1523–5 buying up land including the narrow site called the Pepper Querne and, since that can have been of little corporate use by itself, possibly the ground upstream of it, projecting farther into the river (Fig. I*v*) – ground that was a thorn in the Fishmongers' west side until they were able to acquire it in the nineteenth century, although as we have said the Pepper Querne strip in between became available much sooner.[32] One slight clue to a Fishmonger building begun before rather than after the reunion of 1536 may be the roundel of painted glass, now inserted in one of the present courtroom windows, bearing the arms of fishmongers only, without stockfish emblems, in a style peculiar to the time of Henry VIII.[33] Possibly relegated before the Great Fire to one of the almshouses founded in the seventeenth century, it went out of the company's hands at some time and was bought back in 1930. Possibly it came from some church window not consumed in the Great Fire. Or possibly it now looks out over the Thames for the second time, but that is all one can say. Meanwhile, men of good will brought the stockfishmongers back into the fold in 1536, where an indenture summarizing past separations and new intentions was entered at Guildhall in May. Views of the Thames shore taken in the early 1540s (next chapter) seem to be the first visual records of their meeting-place.

The outlook from Fishmongers' Hall then was like that on a lake or harbour, the medieval Bridge with its load of houses giving a sense of enclosure to this reach of the river. Today there remains only one ancient fixed point, one witness to all that has taken place at Fishmongers Hole since the 1420s : the tower of St Mary's priory church, later St Saviour's parish church and now Southwark Cathedral.[34] The tower's stonework has been restored, but bells were hung in its bell-chamber in 1424. The hour bell's sweetly tinny tone still comes over the water to the present Hall. Riverside ramparts of warehouses have never obscured the upper stages of the tower where view-makers like John Norden in the 1590s and Wenceslaus Hollar in the 1630s climbed up to take sketches for panoramas that tell us so much, and so little, of pre-Fire London. Norden even placed a little figure of the artist on top of the tower, waving a pair of dividers. (Wyngaerde in the 1540s, the earliest known viewmaker here, however, chose to draw the shore by the Hall from a point east of the Bridge.) St Mary's tower has overlooked and overheard Tudor river-pageants, the Great Fire and the Blitz, the renewals of London Bridge, the railway invasion that hemmed the church in behind, and always before it the ebb and flow from the sea. Now we look at the Hall the viewmakers saw.

PART TWO

THE HALL BEFORE 1666

'On the west side of [Bridge] ward, at the north end of London bridge is a part of Thames streete, which is also of this warde, to wit, so much as of old time was called Stockefishmonger Row, of the stockefishmongers dwelling there, downe west to a water gate . . . now the olde swan, which is a common stayre on the Thames. . . . On the South side of Thames streete, about the midway betwixt the bridge foote, and Ebgate [Old Swan] lane, standeth the Fishmongers hall, and diverse other fair houses for marchants.'

John Stow, *Survey of London*, 1598, reprint 1971 of 1603 ed., I. 213.

CHAPTER 3

Buildings and Repairs, *c. 1525-1666*

ON 26 JUNE 1592 (when surviving minutebooks begin) six 'worshipful persons', newly elected wardens of the company, sat with their assistants in the court parlour overlooking the Thames. The Master or Prime Warden was John Porter, the company's tenant of the two ancient wharves combined since 1582 as Porter's Quay. The fourth warden was William Thayte or Thwaites, whose only memorable act, though prosaic enough, was to stand surety four years later for a company tenant, his neighbour the host of the Mermaid Tavern in Bread Street: tavern talk on renewal of leases may have been reflected in Hamlet's subsequent tribute to fishmonger honesty. William Penyngton the Renter Warden, if he was son to William who died in 1592, was uncle to the future puritan M.P., Lord Mayor and friend of Milton, Isaac Penington, who as Lieutenant of the Tower was to conduct Archbishop Laud to the scaffold.[1] Isaac in his day was to sit in this parlour with fellow-wardens more royalist, some of them, than he was – but loyalty to one's livery company submerged political differences. Meanwhile, despite such evils of City life as plague, famine, and royal borrowing, the company minded its own business. During Elizabeth's reign, only one Fishmonger served as Lord Mayor, John Allot in 1590; whereas in a similar period two centuries earlier there had been ten Fishmonger or Stockfishmonger mayoralties, held by seven men of whom three served twice. John Stow, gathering information for his pioneering Survey of London, published in 1598, irritably reproached the Fishmongers for being 'ignorant of their Antiquities' when he enquired about the company's past. (Perhaps he ought to have suspected that, until 1594, the company was treating with agents of the Crown 'for certain concealments',[2] property of religious origin about which it had to be reticent: the history of a City company's estates was a purposeful blur for the fifty years after Crown confiscation of Church property and related religious trusts began – threatening, we may remember, the Hall itself.) In the 1590s City merchants' minds were much on the present. The Spanish Armada was then so recent that Walworth's heroics of two centuries before, even the company's unifying years two and three generations before, must have seemed prehistoric. Adventurousness was being spent in commerce: from the 1570s, for example, English ships were increasingly busy in the Mediterranean,[3] carrying out woollen cloth, tin, lead, and barrels of preserved

The notes for Chapter 3 are on pp. 186–8.

fish – with the last, exporting preserving-skills perfected for the fast-days of the old religion for the fast-days of still-Catholic countries – and the same ships returned to London River with wines, spices, silks, and the travellers' tales that Richard Hakluyt was carefully recording. The minutes of this company's court meetings, during the 1590s as later, were mainly concerned with its members and pensioners and property and regulations for the sale of fish. The room they sat in – called parlour then, not courtroom – lay partly where the present courtroom lies, as nearly as one can tell without the existence of contemporary maps or plans. The company's Clerk since 1579, Roger Glover, lived on the Hall premises and so continued until his death in 1624.

That almost no repairs were made to Hall buildings during the 1590s – only a furbishing of the great chamber over the parlour – suggests that larger works had taken place within that generation. The presence of very little plate in the treasury, according to an inventory recorded at election-time in 1592,[4] also suggests large and recent building-expenditure together with continuing loans to the Crown. There were no almshouses to maintain until St Peter's Hospital was built at Newington south of the river in 1618, and then Jesus Hospital at Bray in Berkshire begun in 1623, and finally the almshouses of 1651 at Harrietsham in Kent. Until after 1600 there was no private company barge; earlier, for the annual river procession accompanying the Lord Mayor to Westminster, barges were hired – with an extra one for water pageants charged with fireworks and staffed with mythic figures in gilded buckram. In 1501 a garden off Lime Street had been bequeathed for the company's recreation, the Hall ground having no space for trees or bowling alleys. In the years before the Great Fire, as indeed until the nineteenth century, most of the worshipful persons lived within stately walking distance of both Hall and garden, or within short rowing distance of the Hall's water-stairs.

By the time continuous (surviving) records begin in 1592, the principal building construction of the pre-Fire Hall – even discussion of the bills for it – was over. The main pattern of structures, until1666, was set – structures in the plural, for the pre-Fire Hall was a group of buildings, separately conceived and erected. No documents date these buildings. Sketchy panoramic views of the 1540s record the existence of riverside block, and later views show a steep-roofed great hall behind it. Clues from architectural style are not much help for the riverside range, because certain forms in fashion in the 1440s, when the premises became the official meeting-place for the whole trade, were still (just) in conservative fashion in the 1540s. Pre-Elizabethan views (Pl. 2) are vague about the hall behind, but room for the one shown in seventeenth-century views (Pl. 3) was only securely available from 1581, and by 1592 its construction was a thing of the past. No pre-Fire plan exists; any craftsmen's drawings that survived the craftsmen's use of them must have perished in the flames. But a rough idea of the premises can be derived from certain title deeds, City views, and evidence picked out of orders, payments, comments and complaints buried in minutes and accounts: a jigsaw puzzle lacking many pieces.

A history of the building crafts in the City has yet to be written. Supervision of repairs and rebuilding on this company's estates was the province of a renter warden, ever since if not before Knesworth's will stipulated that 'one honest man of the clothing' (liveryman) should be elected not only to receive the rents from properties bequeathed therein but also to oversee and pay for their repair. By the 1590s this was performed by a 'renter's clerk'. A certain member of the court, perhaps retired and hard up, asked for that job in 1593; it was agreed, he would look to all necessary building and repairs, reserving to company use any timber, bricks, and nails left over, and would be paid £6.13.4 a year. Three years later, he being 'very ancient' the reversion of the post was granted to an Edward Jennings, who succeeded in 1598. The first appearance in these records of the title 'company surveyor' was applied to him: in 1600, 'Edward Jennings the surveyor' brought a note of money laid out in repairing some houses; in 1605 'Jennings the Company's surveyor' being dead, the job was divided between the company's two beadles 'within their several precincts', the one in the Old Fish Street market area, the other in that of New Fish Street (Fish Street Hill). For years thereafter the two beadles received the extra annual allowance of £3.6.8 apiece as 'Surveyors of the companies reparacons & buildings' in addition to their main job as market-inspectors. Anything concerning the Hall itself, however, was dealt with by a committee of the court. As for supervision of workmen, a directive was given in 1643 that was to be forcibly repeated after the Fire, that master-craftsmen should 'come themselves & begin the work & direct their servants what to do & oversee them twice or thrice a day at the least to see them perform their work as they ought to do.' Many of the company's principal craftsmen were responsible men of position in their own livery companies, but they spread themselves thin sometimes.[5]

In the 1590s the company had its appointed company carpenter, but called much less often on the services of a mason except for repairs to existing stone buildings or wharves. Until earlier in the sixteenth century in London, these had been the chief building crafts. By the 1590s the company also had its master-bricklayer, whose craft had risen to importance in London. In 1647 the court increased from 18*d.* to 2*s.* 6*d.* per day the pay of the company carpenter and the company bricklayer for 'attending upon views' (building inspections), without any mention of the company mason. When in 1602 the company plasterer – often an important medieval figure as finisher of stonework – was angry at no longer being asked to come along on the annual view of company property, 'he was thought unfitt . . . and full of wordes', although they continued to employ a plasterer for interior work. When a company tenant at Broken Wharf laid a brick foundation for his tenement in 1593, that seems to have been nothing new, for Gresham's Royal Exchange of 1566 is said to have been built on brick foundations. A city surrounded by brick-clay used bricks for major buildings well before that, as for the Lambeth Palace gatehouse of *c.* 1495, the gatehouse and Old Buildings at Lincoln's Inn, and other Inns of Court. Most of the 118 houses (as of 1666) that contributed their rents to the company's income and charities must have been of timber construction on cellars of stone or brick.[6]

This livery hall had no gatehouse, such as the lawyers' Inns and large private mansions had. To the passer-by in Thames Street, where houses were cheek by jowl, only 'great lanterns' and probably some heraldic ornament distinguished the company's gate. The lanterns, renewed in 1654, were required by a City law dating back to 1416, that householders should light their doorsteps at certain times – apparently the first municipally-induced street lighting in any city. A wicket was made in the gate in the spring of 1600. In 1647 a bell was hung in the entry, presumably with bell-rope outside: there had been complaints from the neighbours of loud knocking on the gate in the night (the porter in *Macbeth* must have had a long entry to traverse). The 'long entry' here, so called to distinguish it from the basement entry off the wharf, and because it was almost eighty feet long, must once have been the approach – overhung by the upper storeys of the street-side house – for packhorse and porter to Walworth's wharf. The minutes mention neither horses nor stables on the pre-Fire premises: if the Clerk, the only official in residence, had kept a horse there we should have heard about it, such were the court's objections to hay and other 'Combustible stuffe' in the Nun's Head stables next door, and references to dunghills had a way of creeping into the post-Fire minutes.

The streetside house with its kitchen yard had apparently been for letting ever since, with great hall and wharf behind, it had been secured for the company in 1444. In the records we have, this front house was never referred to by name or as having had a name, as the Pepper Querne and Nun's Head either side of it were in the sixteenth century. A lease of 1474 shows that the house by the gate was then let to a group of stockfishmongers.[7] By 1605 the most recent leaseholder was a haberdasher subletting to a grocer, so the ground floor was either warehouse or shop, Thames Street tending always to wholesale rather than retail dealing. A tenant in 1608 tried to assign his lease to a vintner, but the court getting wind of the prospect that the house was to be converted to a tavern, 'which they do not think fit', refused consent and on the petitioner's repeated request desired him 'to get a tenant of some other trade'.[8] (So much for imaginative historians of jolly tavern-life on the Hall premises then.) During 1730–91 there was to be a tavern there beside the Hall gate – Jacobean waterfront taverns may have been tougher, or Georgian wardens less puritanical or more anxious for the rent – but one everyday reason for the earlier prohibition is clear from the lease of 1474, when the tenant was denied access to the river via Fishmongers' Wharf and told to use the wharf next door, a facility that by 1608 was bedevilled by rows among the Nun's Head tenants. A tavern dependent for supplies on drays unloading casks beside the Hall gate in the tumult of Thames Street as it was then would have been a nuisance. There were also problems of drainage. The tenant by the time of the Great Fire was Ralph Trattle, a member of the court who was to become Prime Warden in the summer of 1666, a circumstance that eased matters for the company after the disaster, on his boundary at least.

The long entry sloped gently 'from the wickett towards the streat to the stair-foot ronnynge up into the hall', that is, to the courtyard. The entry was repaved in 1600 with Purbeck stone, not the Purbeck marble of church interiors but a grey limestone, 'such stone as will bear weather' blowing in from the courtyard; there was a 'sink hole' near that end of the passage over the drain from street to river. The paving was jointed 'with Tarris' or tarras – perhaps an early instance in England of that mortar made of volcanic rock imported from the Rhine region especially for waterproofing use – for the company's coal cellar also lay underneath. In Stockfishmongers Row such private entries seem to have developed in pairs, with party walls between. Next to the company's entry ran the less manicured passage at the Nun's Head. In 1649, with unpaid soldiers roving the streets, the court worried over security : 'Whereas there are old turned pillars in the wall between this Company's Hall Entry and the passage on the east side thereof . . . which is a dangerous place for thieves to break into this Hall, the Court is of opinion that said pillars should be taken away and good iron bars put in place thereof so close that neither man nor boy may creep through.' And so a smith inserted 'iron bars in the entry windows'.[9] Turned pillars could mean wooden balusters as of the balustrades of galleried inns, or ornamental wooden columns set in unglazed openings on a high base. Such an open wall between two separate entries seems odd if it existed before the Nun's Head was firmly in company hands, that is before 1599, and no reference to its installation thereafter remains. The covered way or secular cloister was a common medieval link within groups of buildings under one owner. The scant evidence here is tantalizing and makes us wish we knew more of Tudor architecture in the City of London.

The ceiling of the long entry near the courtyard end was, for over twenty years, a sore point. Overhead was a larder 'where the Cooke powdereth his meate', that is, salted it with a lavish hand, there being no refrigerators. In 1630 the court ordered that 'the walls of the long entrey . . . shoud be mended & some course taken that the moistnes of the wall wch happens in rayney weather by reason of the Salt Peter . . . might not be so offensive. . . . for that it oftentimes drops downe upon their Cloths [clothes] as they come along the entrey'. Ten years later, 'Ordered, a good Powdringe tubb lyned with leade to prevent the spoylinge of the Tymber under the Larder flower [floor] and the droppinge of brine into the Entrey', though brine in lead sounds lethal to meat. By 1645 it was felt that the meat-powdering operation really must be moved, possibly to the oven-room (splendid idea), but only in 1647 was a convenient spot partitioned off for the cook in a cellar under the service wing, where he was to keep all his pans and implements, with only dry provisions henceforth in the old larder where 'so much of the lathes & seeling under same room [were] spoiled by salt water Bryne and other moystures'. Eventually the lead-lined salting tub became, for better or worse, a kitchen water-cistern.[10]

This end of the long entry abutted on the Hall service wing, one wall of the kitchen being weatherboarded in 1645 after brine from the larder spoilt the plasterwork. The main steps to the great hall – stout stone steps needing no repair, apparently – will have been in the courtyard, or middle yard. Repairs in 1660 to 'rails, bannisters & posts on the east & north sides of the middle yard' may suggest a separate flight of wooden stairs along the east wall of the yard against the

Nun's Head warehouses, leading to the Hall's galleried upper service wing on the north side of the yard. The term 'middle yard' was a set phrase on long urban sites, as for a company tenancy in Leadenhall Street of messuage, middle yard, and garden; at the Nun's Head in 1594 a new stool was installed in the middle yard, presumably over the drain running from street to river.[11] The underlying watercourses that drained the Thames banks, after a rainstorm and after a fashion, can be better defined when we know the premises better. As one entered the yard, the great hall loomed up on the right, and the parlour block lay ahead, closing off the yard from the river.

The parlour range stood three storeys high (on the riverside at least), crowned with battlements concealing a low-pitched roof. On plan it contained mainly three large spaces, one on top of the other, connected apparently by the newel staircase indicated by a turret-lantern in some views made before the great hall was rebuilt. The foundations of this building rested on subterranean timber piling, 'the foundation standing upon piles' endangered during floods in 1642. The ground floor was the 'great cellar' lying beside the wharf. (The undercroft of the Bishop of Winchester's great hall on the opposite shore lay similarly parallel to the river at ground-level then.) Storage space for wine, beer and oil would be near to delivery from the river, and 'paved for wine or oil' (smooth enough to roll casks on) like the fair cellar under the parlour of Thomas Cromwell's house taken over by the Drapers' Company after 1540. A passage through the Fishmongers' wharfside cellar was protected 'with deal boards to keep the walls from breaking' after the tidal floods.[12]

On the first and main floor overlooking the river was the 'great parlour'. Before the Fire there was no reference to a separate courtroom by that name, but abundant references to court meetings held regularly in this parlour. Only a 'lobbey' lay between it and the head-table end of the great hall when that was rebuilt, with an 'inner' buttery for the court's refreshment and an office for the Clerk nearby. Above the parlour, the 'great chamber' seems at first to have been left unfinished. In 1595 'much speech was used' on the question of making it 'fit to receive gentlewomen at any time of assembly' by installing a chimney (fireplace), a floor, and new stairs there. The room was given its own privy or 'house of office', probably in the thickness of the wall at the east end over the sewer from street to river. Over the chamber lay the 'great leades' or lead-covered roof, with warlike parapet (no longer requiring 'licence to crenellate' and purely decorative). Stow described the fifteenth-century rebuilding of Ludgate prison with 'faire leades to walk upon well imbattailed, or for fresh ayre'. Whether or not anyone walked for fresh air beside the Fishmonger battlements, the Clerk was regularly paid twenty shillings every two years for brooms bought to clean out the gutters 'after great raines or snowes'.[13]

And so, in elevation such a London building – with double access to street and waterway – had the proportions of a similarly placed urban building in, say, Italy, not from direct influence but for similar reasons. The Fishmongers' waterside storage floor was not unlike the 'sea storey' of a Venetian merchant's house, their parlour floor was a *piano nobile*, with a lesser chamber floor above – a pattern resulting from like needs and minds in a mercantile-marine society. This was the building the first viewmakers saw.

Of the four views drawn between *c.*1540 and *c.*1640 (Pl. 2-3) that seem more reliable than the few others known of the pre-Fire City, the two earlier ones show the Fishmongers' riverside block as three windows wide and the two later ones show it as four windows wide. This seems to confirm what may have happened before, during and after the new great-hall range was interlocked with the parlour range. Until building was completed there, probably in the early 1580s, ground behind the Pepper Querne's 'little wharf', at the upstream end of the parlour block, would have been needed for delivery and stacking of building-materials. Great precarved roof-trusses, such as we know the dining hall was to have, could not be taken through the parlour block's cellar. Extension of the parlour block thereafter, so far as the ground floor was concerned, simply meant enclosing and vaulting over the Pepper Querne tenant's old right of way. Upstairs, 'the inner buttery next the parlor door' – 'inner' as being for the court's own use – could be added or enlarged with the new fourth window on the riverfront. And the space before the parlour door, called the lobby in the seventeenth century, will have led to those 'stairs to the leads' or roof, moved to the new west end that was endangered by a neighbour's lack of fire precautions in 1645. For the parlour in the spring of 1646, 'two sun dials' were ordered to be set up 'in the glass window of this great parlor next the East', that is, the easternmost window on the river, farthest from any shadow of the projecting building next door. Painted-glass sundials were briefly fashionable in the seventeenth century, though the metal stylus often proved too heavy; the Pewterers' and the Weavers' Companies each had one after the Great Fire, while an early pair in London were two oval ones in Laud's Tower of about 1635 at Lambeth Palace, one in a south window and one in a west window. Two are also known to have been placed in the commissioners' room of Wren's Custom House after the Fire.[14] But why, at Fishmongers' Hall, two in one window? one numbered for morning and one for afternoon? or simply panache with two lights to fill? In 1654 John Ogilby the scholarly publisher brought the court a copy of his translation of Virgil, for which he was given £10, and four years later the wardens caused a small desk (for placing on a table) to be made 'for the book called Virgill . . . or any other books to be kept therein that they may be ready to be seen & read by any Wardens & Assistants at meetings here' – the nucleus of a library.[15] In summer or during repairs at the Hall, courts might sit at the garden house off Lime Street; some committees met at taverns, in one of the private rooms, as many a parish vestry did. Pepys attended weekly meetings of a Royal Fishery commission at Fishmongers' Hall in the autumn of 1664, probably in the parlour.

Other apartments in this building may have included the company armoury, kept away from ground-floor flooding and from kitchen hearths, possibly on the chamber floor. Stacked with arms and ammunition in presses to keep them 'upright', the armoury was a source of disquiet in May 1640, when the Prime Warden

Sir John Gayer was arrested and gaoled for a few days with three other aldermen by order of the King for refusing to list the inhabitants of their wards able to lend £50 or more to the Crown. (Seven years later, after City opposition to the parliamentary army, when Gayer was Lord Mayor, he was deposed and imprisoned by the House of Commons; first and last, toward King or Commons, he was a man of the City.) Four days after his release in 1640, nervous court members protested against his borrowing of headpieces, swords and muskets from the company armoury and so setting a precedent that might bee of evell consequence', for 'what use of them may bee required . . . in regard of the unquietnes and trobles of the tymes cannot bee knowne'. By 1642 the livery companies were being officially required to lend arms to the parliamentary forces.[16] If, by 1666, grenades and match held a generation before were spent, so much the less fuel for the Great Fire; gunpowder, as we shall see, was stored in the garden. The survival of most of the riverside block's walls in September 1666, until purposely demolished thereafter, suggests there was no explosive material here then.

A brief enigma of the early 1660s was the short existence somewhere at the Hall of a 'long gallery', just as the one at the garden was being let off to a tenant, a joiner bringing tables (and possibly wainscot?) to it from the garden. This may have been a light wooden structure added, during large building-repairs in 1660, to the roof of the parlour block which would have afforded a length of about sixty feet within the battlements and access from the staircase to the leads from the chamber floor. If so, no views remain to show it, with a fine Thames prospect and a short life before it.[17]

The Clerk's office, which seems to have been behind the parlour, overlooking the yard, was an interesting survival. Called 'the office or Chaple' (in 1639), it may have been originally, in this building made just before the Reformation, the court's private chapel, 'the Chapel at the Hall' where in 1606 a committee of wardens met to deliberate while the yeomanry attended service at 'the Company's Chapel' at the parish church. At some time after the Reformation, the east end of the Hall chapel apparently became the treasury; workmen inspecting 'the Greate Wall . . . Eastward' in 1660 found cracks 'in the Treasury Roome'. The silver was kept here between dinners, and from 'the Iron Chest in the Treasury', where the altar had been, several hundred pounds would be disbursed to workmen during large repairs at the Hall. In 1631, presses and boxes were made 'for leases, writings and books lately inventoried & taken into the Treasurie, which may otherwise be spoiled & eaten with Ratts & Mice'. The treasury was already partitioned off and locked up when a new methodical Clerk, John Lee, arrived in 1639 and asked for another partition 'through the middle of the office or Chaple with deal boards & shelves . . . for the safe keeping of books & writings remaining with the Clerk [current ones not yet filed in the treasury] . . . & more private & better dispatch of Company business'; that is, an inner office for himself and an outer office for his clerks. These 'two little rooms where the Clerk & his servants write & keep the books' were in 1658 'ceeled with lathes to keep the dust from falling upon their books & writings' : that sounds like decaying stone vaulting, of some powdery stone

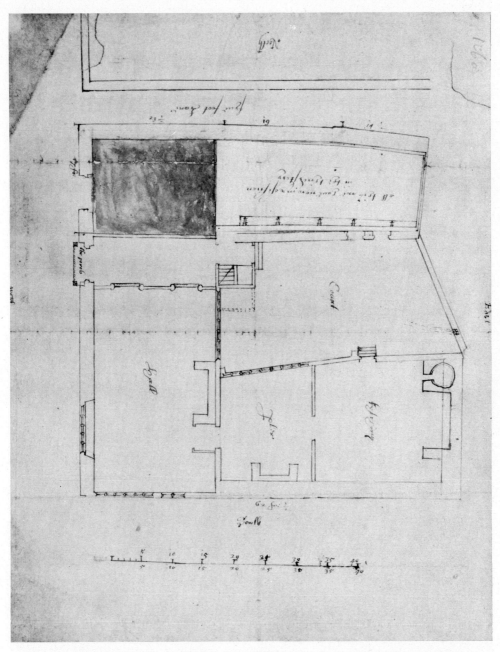

Pl. 1 Plan of medieval house on Old Fish Street Hill, occupied as one of the Fishmongers' livery halls in the 15th century. Drawing 1618, when occupied as Glaziers' Hall, with warehouse-space at top (p. 12). Pen and wash on paper, 13″ × 10½″. Fishmongers' Company collection, Guildhall Library.

Pl. 2 Views of the City from Southwark, showing the Fishmongers' riverside block and wharf in the mid-16th century (p. 27). (*a*) Drawing by unknown artist *c.* 1525–40 (detail). (*b*) Drawing possibly by Antony van den Wyngaerde, *c.* 1544 (detail). Both, Sutherland Collection, Ashmolean Museum, Oxford.

Pl. 3 Views of the City from Southwark, showing Fishmongers' Hall and wharf in the early 17th century (p. 27). (*a*) View by John Norden 1600 (detail), from facsimile in Guildhall Library of engraving in Royal Library, Stockholm. (*b*) View by Wenceslaus Hollar engraved 1647 (detail): portion showing Fishmongers' Hall probably drawn in September 1639 (p. 36). Guildhall Library.

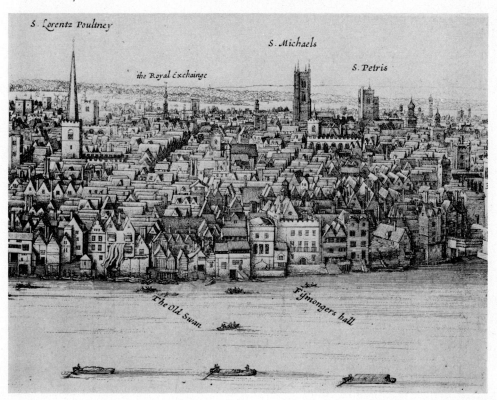

Pl. 4 The ruined City after the Great Fire, engraving (detail), view by Wenceslaus Hollar 1666 (Hind catalogue no. 19), showing shell of Fishmongers' riverside block and that of 'the stone house west of Mr Trattle's' (pp. 17, 1863²). Guildhall Library.

like chalk, of which the infilling of medieval vaults, between the ribs, was often made. In damp situations, especially when flavoured with coal-smoke, chalk might well 'shed' after a century or so. In 1660 part of the treasury was 'added to the rooms where the Clerk keeps this Company's writings for a lodging room for his servants in respect of the straitness of room in his house', that is, for his clerks who were paid by or apprenticed to him.[18]

The Clerk's 'house' where he and his family and maidservants lived – large enough for a bachelor chaplain, no doubt – was over the office, and their kitchen was below the office in the cellar, probably the former undercroft of the chapel. According to the parish register John Lee's wife was having a series of daughters in the 1650s; this family had a wainscotted hall and a chamber over it – all clustered at the rear of the court's great chamber, apparently, and looking north on to the courtyard – rooms 'malloncholly & remote' from their kitchen. The kitchen was worse, according to complaints of 1626, its floor flooded by every spring tide, its plaster decayed, with little daylight and no oven so that the Clerk was 'constrained to make bold with his next neighbours'. In 1631 he was allowed to make a little parlour out of part of his coal-store under the court parlour, apparently overlooking the river. Similarly in the eighteenth century the Clerk's quarters were to be extended from crowded inward-facing rooms to the riverfront, and the size of a Clerk's family remained architecturally relevant until 1889, when the family ceased to live on the premises. The beadles, before the Great Fire, did not live at the Hall, nor is there any reference to a porter's living quarters there.[19]

The verbal tradition of the office that had been a chapel, together with the graphic testimony of the earliest views, date this riverside block in the pre-Reformation period. Loyalty to the 'Fishmongers' Aisle' or chapel in the parish church of St Michael's Crooked Lane, with its tombs of eminent fishmongers and stockfishmongers, continued after the Reformation. In 1648, 1650, and 1652 there was no biennial election sermon there, but from 1654 the sermon continued to be preached at St Michael's by one of the moderate nonconformists favoured by the company;[20] beforehand, chancel, pulpit and pews were 'made clean & decent for that day'. But the old gold-embroidered 'burying cloth' or pall – one of the prime examples of late *opus anglicanum* – was brought back to the Hall treasury in 1656 for safe-keeping, which ensured its survival ten years later.

A chief function of the riverside block seems to have been that of safe-deposit or strongroom, for the company's wine, its money, title deeds and other private records, its gold and silver plate and perhaps its arms and armour, all grouped around its private meeting-place in the care of a resident custodian with a household of his own, all concentrated within a cubic area apparently smaller in every dimension than that of the Hall's riverside wing today. Now to the hall block that was keyed into this building. The parlour floor will have set the level of the great hall floor, within a few steps.

Whenever the Middle Ages may be said to have ended in England (with Bosworth Field? the Reformation?), three sorts of institution went right on building themselves late-medieval open-roofed dining halls: the two Universities, the Inns of Court, and the City livery companies. Even if we had neither Hollar's 'long view' (Pl. 3b) with its tip-of-the-iceberg view of the Fishmongers' dining-hall roof, nor the random jottings thrown up by eighty years or so of use and maintenance, we would still have some general notion of this traditional room. As it is, we know quite a lot about it. On plan it lay north-south, its long walls to east and west with courtyard beside it, the high table at the south end with the parlour block behind it, and a service wing at the north end abutting on the street-side tenant's back yard. The north end of its cellar may have been underground. Our clues derive from dinner preparations, building repairs, and Hollar's view.

These testify to a steep tiled roof with a lantern on top and a hammerbeamed frame within, buttresses along the sides and chimneys along the west side, an undercroft with the Pepper Querne passage from the little wharf tunnelling through, and a flight of steps before the hall door or porch in the yard. Inside there was wainscot with attached benches at the high-table end, and probably also along the side walls below high windows. There was a 'compassed' (curved bay) window in one side wall, probably on the courtyard side, and a cupboard for display of plate on the other, paintings of St Peter and St Dunstan on the upper end wall above the high table, and a door to the parlour lobby near that end, a music gallery above the other end and service wing beyond it with the great kitchen on the north side of the yard. There are no clear references to a screen, or to a hearth, or to a raised dais, but what is taken for granted and never needs repair may never be mentioned in such records as these.

As for the size of this great hall, we may guess that the ever-present strength of precedent was operating after the Fire when a plan (Pl. 5a) was drawn at first for a hall 60 by 30 feet. (For comparison in the London area before the Fire, there were the Abbot of Westminster's hall at 52 by 26 feet, Gray's Inn hall 69 by 35, Crosby Hall 70 by 28, Merchant Taylors' hall 93 by 43, Hampton Court hall 97 by 40, Middle Temple hall 101 by 40.) For a large livery dinner the Fish-mongers' dining hall overflowed, as in 1614 when 'the yonger lyverey . . . sete downe in the parlor', or in 1617 when 176 were served in the hall itself while 80 more were fed in the parlour, or, as they called it eleven and five 'messe of meat'; for traditionally in this company it was '16 persons to a messe' for a big dinner (the Inns of Court still serve four to a mess, or set of serving-dishes, so perhaps the ratio of legal to mercantile feeding was four to four-squared).[21]

Some of the chimneys Hollar shows along the west side of the great hall (Pl. 3b) may date from a kitchen originally in the undercroft. (By 1663, hearth tax of thirty shillings meant fifteen hearths at the Hall altogether.) Thomas Cromwell's mansion that became Drapers' Hall had winding stairs 'from the kitchen into the hall' and on urban sites basement kitchens might not be unusual. The slope of the Fishmongers' site is suggested by the expression 'upp cellar'' used for the space where the cook's wet-larder was fitted into the 'north west corner . . . under the buttery', next to the Pepper Querne tenant's entry. The tenant's passage, wide enough for carrying his goods domestic and commercial through the hall under-croft from the waterside, will not have married well with a kitchen there. The main problem must have been the cellar's insufficient ventilation for great roasting hearths and boiling cauldrons. At any rate, there was considerable new building with ovens and chimneys in 1605, and that is probably when the great kitchen was erected as an extension of the service wing on the north side of the yard, on ground-floor level where it suffered from high tides backing up the drain, as apparently all the yards and cellars here did. The company cook, who did not live in and who catered to other employers as well, himself provided the movable instruments of his trade : his brass pots, cauldrons, spits, dripping pans, basting ladles and trays were mentioned in 1653. Fixtures were another matter : a brazier was paid in 1657 'for a copper caldron' for the 'furnace in the kitchen', or boiler.[22]

A carved mermaid weather-vane was poised on 'topp of the Lanthorne' astride the steep tiled roof, a carver being paid twenty shillings in 1640 for making a new mermaid, presumably of painted and gilded wood since he was carver not metal-worker – unless he simply carved a model for a brazier to work from (nothing in the accounts for that) as Edward Peirce was to do for the dragon on St Mary-le-Bow after the Fire.

Inside, the nature of the roof structure is suggested by the need in 1639 to renew two 'hamerbeames' and rivet their accompanying 'long posts . . . pendoll posts & brases'.[23] The great series of English hammerbeam roofs from Westminster Hall of 1395-9 to Hampton Court hall of 1531-6 was extended in London by a lesser series for certain Inns of Court between 1556 and 1581, to which the Fish-mongers' roof may have been related. The only clue to a music gallery/screens passage formation at the north end is an order of 1660, 'the scaffold in the Musicke Room to be made handsome and strong', that is, the floor of the musicians' loft. That the new dining hall built after 1666, within a fashionable exterior, was to hold to the old gallery-screen form at one end (even though a more modern cantilevered gallery all round was to be grafted on to it) implies that the pre-Fire Hall had its screen.

The great hall's 'compaste wyndow' will have been a half-cylinder bay window the full height of the side wall, near the head table. Such a 'compassed' window, that is, laid out on plan with a drawing-compass, seems to have been rare in the sixteenth century save for the one in the Great Watching Chamber at Hampton Court of the 1530s and one or two in Cambridge, such as that of *c.*1595 made by a London mason for Sidney Sussex College hall, which means that the Fish-mongers' window, mentioned in 1594 and presumably part of the construction of the 1580s, must have been an early non-royal example. Rounded bays became more numerous in England after 1600. In 1605 a committee was appointed to see about adding a 'compast wyndow' to the Fishmongers' parlour – presumably to its only windowed side, on the river, where the company glazier will have pointed out the risks of wind pressure, or else to the east side (too close to the Nun's Head dyer's chimney), and we hear no more about it.[24]

The 'Cubbord of Plate' during the 1590s-1630s was opposite the compass window; by 1660 it was 'at the lower end of this hall', perhaps in the centre of the screen. A 'brasse Laver' or washbasin, to which a founder fitted 'twoe brasse Cockes & a washer' in 1657, was fixed somewhere 'att the lower end of the hall' in some wall convenient to the water-pipes between a pump on the wharf and the

kitchen. In 1600 the high table washed hands in older style, dismissing the butler
for 'not providing water to wasshe at the high table . . . at the last great dinner
here', although a parcel-gilt basin and ewer formed part of their meagre supply of
plate in 1592. As for seating at high table, there was the 'benche side' and the
'forme side'. A bench can imply fixture to wall-panelling (for example, a schedule
of fixtures annexed to a lease might include 'a back of waynscott with benches').
Some special joinery will have emphasized the prime warden's seat. More comfort
for the form side at high table arrived in 1624 when an upholsterer supplied chairs,
and in 1627 it was noted that Thomas Baldwin, Comptroller of the King's Works,
with the Chamberlain of London, two parsons, and three upper wardens, sat 'on
the outside of the table on the Cheires'.[25]

'Tapestrye-hangings for the hall' were borrowed, as in 1624 when a fresh
salmon was given to 'Mr Curselleis' (also Corsellis, Corcelys) who 'doth usually
lend verry faire hangings to hang their hall at every election dinner without any
payment'; in 1613 Lucas Corseilis, merchant, had taken a company lease of the
Star Inn on Fish Street Hill, at the entrance to London from the Bridge, a prosperous position.[26] His Flemish-sounding name – recalling the opening of the Mort-
lake tapestry works in 1619 and the importing of Flemish weavers by the King –
suggests a possible source for the Star Inn's hangings.

And there were other ornaments here, at once gorgeous, barbaric and touching:
the pageant figures, like elaborate stage properties of stuffed and painted cloth,
ready for the next Lord Mayor's show on land or water. When a member of the
Fishmongers' Company became Lord Mayor, as Sir John Leman did in 1616,
new figures were commissioned and then certain ones were kept 'for an ornament
in Fishmongers Hall', to quote the scroll commemorating the pageant contrived
for the company in 1616 by Anthony Munday. Munday was apparently much
influenced by Inigo Jones's masques, perhaps especially by an Inns of Court
procession in 1613 in honour of Princes Elizabeth's marriage. The Fishmonger
show included a 'King of the Moores, gallantly mounted on a golden leopard, he
hurling gold and silver every way about him' with attendants in feathered head-
gear reminiscent of Jones's masquers in 1613 and of the American Indians that
entered European art in the late sixteenth century from travellers' drawings made
on expeditions to Florida and Virginia. And the Fishmongers had a great chariot
drawn by pairs of mermen and mermaids with bodies like sea-monsters: two
extra barges needed to carry the 'meirmen & meirmeades' alone, so they were not
small. Heraldic fantastic scenes even more marvellous were accompanied by a
monster dolphin, 'a fish inclined much by nature to musique'. These creatures
were carried 'upon the water first, and afterward marshalled . . . on land',
forebears of gilded wooden figures on the company barge in the next century and
similarly transferable at the water-stairs to be borne or dragged like idols to
Guildhall. Between pageants, one nineteenth century historian imagined them,
without naming any source, dangling from the great hall roof – possibly from the
hammerbeams that needed mending by 1639.[27]

Inigo Jones was one of the distinguished men who came to dinner in this hall.
In the early 1630s during the period of friendliness with the Earl of Arundel, 'as

my Lord's predecessors were free of this Company & he a well-willer of same', the Earl's arms were placed in the parlour 'where formerly set up & now quite defaced'. (It would have helped to date this building if we knew which predecessor's arms were first placed here, those of the tenth earl who died in 1524 or those of the eleventh earl who died in 1544). This revival of good will inherited from the fifteenth century may have related also to the interest of the Earl's son Lord Maltravers in fisheries. Both came to dinner in June 1632, and again in December 1633 when they 'came thither by water' with a noble company that included 'Mr Inicoe Jones Esq. Surveyor General of the Kings Majesties workes', and 'in the Great Parlour they took oaths as free brothers [honorary freemen] of the Company'. Again in November 1634 came Lord Arundel, his two sons, and 'Mr Indico Jones' to dinner. (A building-development in Lothbury designed around this time by Inigo Jones for Lord Maltravers was to influence post-Fire building in the City.)[28] And some fishery connection may have brought about the company's friendship with John Rushout, sworn honorary freeman in June 1631 and occasional dinner guest until 1652 : a native of France descended from the de Rouhault family, he settled in London as a merchant in the time of Charles I; his descendants bore the title of Lord Northwick between 1797 and 1887. In 1654 his executors came to present a great standing salt left to the company in his will : a splendid piece of silver, parcel gilt, that experts date to that year, made in Amsterdam by Jan Lutma, the friend of Rembrandt who etched Lutma's portrait about this time. Very sophisticated the great salt's coiling dolphins must have looked on the head table during the grey years of the Commonwealth. In November 1651 Oliver Cromwell and his officers had dined at Fishmongers' Hall. By April 1660 it was General Monk (soon to be Duke of Albemarle) who was chief guest 'with all his field officers both horse and foot'; Pepys noted that Monk ate with all twelve of the great livery companies that spring. In December 1664, John Evelyn recorded that he and fellow-commissioners for care of the wounded in the imminent Dutch war, with the governors of St Thomas Hospital, came to 'a great feast' here.

Not only men but women came to dinner, especially in the earlier years recorded. At first it seems puzzling to find the Clerk in 1596 bothering to mention 'some Gentlewomen in frenchoods at the high table'. The headdress called a French hood, according to historians of dress, was in fashion mainly between 1530 and 1580, continuing to be worn unfashionably long after; we associate the English variant with portraits of Queen Mary I who died in 1558.[29] Therefore these ladies at high table in 1596 must have been somewhat ancient and honourable, like wearers of 'Queen Mary hats' in the 1950s. In the early seventeenth century at election dinners a group of 'the wyves & widdowes' of the company would sit, 'very disorderlye' sometimes, at one of the side tables.

Occasionally the great hall had other uses. During famine in 1596, certain livery companies were required to store cargoes of rye and wheat brought into port from Amsterdam until granaries, in addition to those on the Bridge, could be provided; and the Fishmongers allowed a corn merchant to 'lay so much as the parlour and hall will conveniently hold, other rooms fit to lay corn in the Company has none' (the great chamber having just been decorated). In 1642 a silk merchant who sat on the court, Henry Austen, was given leave 'to bring his silk that was wet at sea into this Hall to dry . . . [with] use of the hall, the parlor, & the chamber over the parlor'. Austen's was not an unusual case of the patrimonial process as time went on, whereby some took up their fathers' livery membership without taking up their fathers' trades: in 1659, for instance, a list of sureties gave 'vintner, by trade a hop merchant', 'joiner, by trade a dyer', and so on.

For the materials of these buildings we have only hints. For the parlour block, bricklayer and mason together reported in 1660 on the state of the east wall, cellar vault, foundations, sewer, and treasury wall above. Stone battlements, probably on this building, were mentioned in 1632. The shell with 'great vault' or undercroft left standing in 1666 and drawn by Hollar (Pl. 4) looks likely to have been stone, though temporarily secured with old bricks. For the great-hall range, a mason investigated a neighbour's complaint against the lower courses of its buttresses in 1635, but a bricklayer-and-tiler repaired its walls, chimneys and battlements in 1639: probably there was a stone undercroft with brick upper walls as in the Middle Temple. The collapse of the great timber roof in 1666 left no recorded shell beneath, and no sixteenth-century building-accounts survived the flames. Lasting less than a century, the hall block proved expensive to maintain.

For, in the summer of 1624, the court observed that the great hall 'sinketh and is weake'. Fifteen years later, after the matter had disappeared into committee twice, something was done about it. The initial observation may have been made by the practised eye of the Comptroller of the King's Works, who had just been there for dinner. Thomas Baldwin (c.1568-1641), in fact, outside his official capacity, was actively supervising for the company during 1623-8 the erection of Jesus Hospital at Bray, which he had designed (bringing in 1623 'a plott of his devise').[30] Possibly there was a family connection between Baldwin and William Goddard, deceased member of the court and founder of the almshouses. The old-fashioned style of Jesus Hospital (the scene of Frederick Walker's painting *The Harbour of Refuge* in the Tate Gallery), for someone in official circles in the 1620s, was doubtless due to delay, while the will of 1609 was contested by relations and subject to the widow's life-interest. Goddard probably approved the design in his lifetime. Baldwin was a bit touchy about it, reacting to criticism after the alms-houses were finished, 'for that some aspertions (as it seemeth) were cast upon him, hee haveing the orderinge of it' – and indeed his comptrollership (since 1606) of the royal building works, equal in eminence to the position of his colleague Inigo Jones, must have involved him less in building-design than in administration. That this cannot have troubled the company is shown by their inviting Baldwin in 1628 to place his own arms in the east window of the almshouses' chapel along with the arms of King, company, and founder – all replaced by new glass in 1878. (Baldwin referred to the five lights of the chapel window as 'crotickes', a word derived from a form of the word 'grotesque' used for compartments or panels of ornament: only occasionally do these minutebooks pierce the barrier between us and such long-dead technical vernacular.) No payments were ever made to Baldwin except for building-expenses or alms to be dispensed at Bray. He was simply a friendly adviser to the court of this company, from the day of the election dinner in 1614, when he was made an honorary freeman and his wife (Goddard's daughter?) also sat at the high table, until at least 1639, when in May 'in respect of the pains & care that Mr. Baldwin has always had of the hospital at Bray & of his love to this house in giving them a buck yearly, a firkin of sturgeon is to be sent him'; and in August, while discussing reconstruction of the wharf-wall at the Hall, Baldwin 'did promise to move' the Surveyor General on the company's behalf for some Portland stone from the royal quarries (but see p. 46). He was also, by implication, consultant in the matter of the company's new garden house.

So in 1632 when debate arose about 'strengthening' the great hall, 'some of opinion it might be done with iron bars & others of contrary opinion', Baldwin was entreated to advise. With one of his royal works craftsmen and the company's men he inspected the roof, decided to inspect again with the tiles off before considering 'whether the lanthorne should stand or come down', and then we hear no more for three years – few committee minutes survive from the seventeenth century. Presumably when Baldwin's colleague the Surveyor General dined under the Fishmongers' hammerbeams in 1633 and 1634, the more than un-classical irregularities overhead provoked no comment. In April 1636 repairs were referred to committee, but no expenditure resulted and dinners were held as usual, though without guests in that summer of plague. The whole question lay dormant until the election of an energetic Prime Warden, Alderman John Gayer, who seems to have acted as one-man building committee (the rest acting as chorus) throughout heavy repair works in 1639-40, doubtless in the same self-confident spirit with which he had escaped from a lion in Africa and afterwards founded an annual 'Lion Sermon' at his parish church of St Katharine Cree to celebrate. That this period of having the builders in also coincided with the arrival of the much-respected Clerk, John Lee, at midsummer 1639 meant that we have better records than we otherwise would, though not in modern detail, of the work so dangerously deferred.[31]

Work began in the spring of 1639, and by the end of the year about £850 had been paid to seven craftsmen, much of it on the great hall and about £280 to the master carpenter Richard Wade.[32] (He was to be Master of the Carpenters' Company in 1645, and a tenant of the Fishmongers' from 1640 in Old Fish Street, where he built tenements in Middle Row.) In August 1639 he and John Turnor the bricklayer, Alexander Meriam the mason, and Abraham Stannion the plasterer sat with a court meeting held, away from builders' dust and scaffolds, at the garden house in Lime Street to consider whether the great hall roof needed iron cross-bars or not. Wade described what he had done in words that suggest how unsafe the sixty-year-old oak frame had become: he had made two new hammerbeams, one either side and mended the rest, inserted new 'reson peeces' (wall plates) where the old ones had decayed, tied the roof together with iron bolts and stirrups, riveted with iron bolts certain long posts (wall posts) that were split, and shored up with 'skrues' the 'pendoll posts & brases' (pendants and braces) 'to their places where they were first framed' – that is, the whole set of trusses that braced one another from wall to wall and gable to gable, bearing the weight of rafters, tiles, and lantern, must have been ripe for collapse. Gayer brought in two outside experts to inspect the work and find the roof safe, Anthony Jerman the City Carpenter, who was also the Goldsmiths' Company carpenter for their recent new Hall, and Thomas King (masters of the Carpenters' Company in 1633 and 1642 respectively).

To the same meeting Alderman Gayer posed a question about renewal of 'outer grates' on the parlour windows, that is, grilles or window-guard railings (not balconies), 'whether for safety & ornament it be better to keep them or to pull them down & set up new grates . . . & the workmen [the four master craftsmen present] said that those outer grates as they now are will be a footing or scaffold & means to help a knave to enter [doubtless thinking of the fire ladders kept in the entry below], & are like an old prison window & undecent for a hall', in fact it would be 'far more safe & decent without them'. So after 'mature deliberation' it was agreed to take them down and have 'strong locked bars' placed inside. Those 'grates' appear in Hollar's long view (Pl. 3b), etched only in 1647, but he is thought to have been making drawings for it between 1636 and 1642. Supposing that this order of August 1639 to remove the grates was carried out within a month or so (the accounts are not that specific) may help to date Hollar's drawing for the section of his view in which they appear. He also leaves the wharf-wall entirely vague, without its distinctive battlements visible in older views: the wharf-wall was being partly demolished in September for rebuilding, with battlements, in October 1639. So far as Fishmongers' Hall is concerned, his drawings of the Thames shore just west of London Bridge probably date from the late summer or early autumn of 1639.[33]

A charge (undated) was incurred in that work at the Hall, presumably before certain craftsmen were paid : 'Paide unto Edward Jerman Surveyor for mesuringe the Masons worke the playsterers Joyners Carpenters & Painters worke 30s' (at his later rate from this company, three days' work). So here in 1639 or 1640 was the first appearance of the man who was later to become the company's first professional surveyor, recommended perhaps for this measuring-job by his father. The Jerman family were a brief dynasty of City carpenters, Elias and Richard and Anthony were all taking apprentices in 1604, Anthony serving as City Viewer until his death in 1650, and his sons Edward, Hugh, and Roger were all carpenters : Hugh died young, but Roger (died 1678) did a good deal of work after the Fire. Edward was taking apprentices by 1632 and in 1652 paid a fine for release from serving as a warden of the Carpenters' Company. Before the Fire he served successively as City Carpenter, City Viewer, and City Surveyor, and he succeeded his father as surveyor to the Goldsmiths. In April 1654 he was appointed company surveyor to the Fishmongers' Company, and from 1662 he was managing the felling and selling of timber from the company's woodlands at Bray.[34]

As to the company carpenter, between 1654 and 1660 there were small payments for work in London to Thomas Lock. In the spring of 1660 came larger payments to an older man, and from 1661, after one abortive tender in June, Lock was off the books until just after the Great Fire; we know that he was employed on Horseheath Hall in Cambridgeshire between 1663 and 1665, with interesting consequences for the next Fishmongers' Hall. Lock (usually Locke in the company records, but signed Lock by himself), a generation younger than Jerman, was a freeman of the Fishmongers' Company – his father and brother, both bakers, served successively as company cornkeeper during much of the century, when storage of grain was still one of the civic duties of livery companies.[35] William Lock Sr was made free by service (very likely to the previous cornkeeper) in 1621, his two sons by patrimony in 1655, which doesn't tell us who Thomas was apprenticed to. The work Thomas Lock did for the company before the Fire was slight, but his work on the Hall afterward, and his nuisance-value, were considerable.

Jerman's employment by the company in London before the Fire was slight too – the frugality of life under the Commonwealth saw to that. Jerman's fees as company surveyor were fixed in 1655: for inspecting and reporting on company buildings he was to be paid five shillings per half-day or ten shillings per whole day – four times the half-crown awarded the company carpenter in 1647 for each day spent in that way. Although Jerman never acted as carpenter or in charge of carpenters for this company – he was above that by 1654 – now and then the pre-Fire minutes refer to him, as to them, as a workman. Although ready to defer to Jerman's judgment, neither the mercantile nor the clerical mind had yet noticed any social distinction between estate surveyor, supervisory master-craftsman, and working artisan.

Large repairs to the Hall at the Restoration were not referred to the company surveyor. A devoted prime warden or renter warden backed up by a building committee and separate arrangements with craftsmen were preferred there, although Jerman was already supervising formal tendering to his own design and specifications by single craftsmen dealing with their own subcontractors elsewhere on company property. The Hall repairs of April to June 1660 have a joyful sound. There had been a decade of 'moderate' dinners during the Commonwealth, with complaints from younger members (when it was the yeomanry's turn to provide dinner) of deadness of trade, greatness of taxes, dearness of provisions especially wine, and hard times in general. Now, while court meetings were held at the garden, great works went on at the Hall under the 'extraordinary care & pains' of the renter warden, John Hayne, a wealthy scrivener who had once been apprenticed to a Clerk of the company and whose son-in-law was to handle company law suits in the Fire Courts after 1666.[36]

In these repairs, so much expense went for timber – £324 paid to two timber merchants – one suspects this was what led the company to turn to its own woodlands at Bray, both for use and for income, from 1662. More beer seems to have been provided for (perhaps more) workmen in 1660 than in 1639, when the wardens had parted with a total of £2.1s.10d. on several occasions of viewing the

work; according to the building-accounts in 1660, a brewer delivered beer to
the Hall to the amount of £10.8s.6d. (the Navy paying 18s. per barrel in 1662,
according to Pepys' latest editors). There was an unitemized payment of £30 to
three masons, one of whom was John Colt, probably Le Sueur's one-time assistant
carver, of the family of the sculptor Maximilian Colt: there may have been
repairs to tomb carvings in the company chapel at St Michael's. Interior redecoration at the Hall in this royal spring season required (in round sums) the services
of William Rider 'for carving worke' (£133), 'Vanbeison glass-painter' and
Samson Allen glazier (£46 between them), Nathaniel Pollard painter 'for work
& materials done about this hall' (£154), Walter Dole goldbeater 'for leafe gold'
(£27), Thomas Kemble colourseller 'for colour' (£10), and 'Marke Garrett limner
for work at this hall' (£114) – that is, Marcus Gheeraerts IV, perhaps partly for
a royal portrait (to replace one ordered 'by some skilful workman' in 1635, certified 'taken away' by 1650), partly for new saints above the high table. The
materials from Dole and Kemble will have been used by Garrett, since Pollard included cost of materials in his charge.[37] Designs for 'leafe gold' and 'colour' here,
like heavy orders for silver trumpets from the royal castles, were an outburst from
austerity. The Hall was burnished just in time for its destruction.

CHAPTER 4

The Great Parlour in the Garden

FROM 1501 UNTIL 1661 the Fishmongers enjoyed a garden, about ten minutes' walk from the Hall, with a 'parlour' in it. A garden room or enclosed gallery can be a delightfully civilized piece of minor architecture, a cross between an ephemeral summer-house and a small villa. In grand gardens once it could be a banqueting house, for dessert with a view, or on hunting estates a lodge *cum* elevated grandstand. The London version – when central London still had domestic gardens in it – could be a long gallery on stilts, raised above the dampness of the earth, facing south to catch the sun in winter or north to trap the coolness in summer, at any rate with its back to the house or garden wall and its windows opening on the garden itself, a wholly private place with a view of trees and bowling alleys. Sometimes its staircase wound up to the roof, or leads, where one could walk for fresher air. A parlour in a London garden can perhaps be read into Chaucer's Troy, which was really medieval London, in *Troilus and Criseyde*.

In 1501 Richard Knight bequeathed to the wardens of the Fishmongers' Company 'all his Great Garden with a Parlour in the Same Garden' and they were 'to keep and Repair the great Garden to and for the Recreation and Disport of themselves'. This with the 'great house Tenteryard and Six Tenements' on or near the east side of Lime Street which he also bequeathed to them had lately belonged to John, fifth Lord Scrope of Bolton, and his forebears. Presumably the great house, an old mansion once called Tiptoft Inn, was the one lying back from the street with a courtyard and warehouses in front and a large garden behind (Fig. II): that garden combined with the garden of the tenement next southward seem to have comprised the 'great garden'.[1] The company let the houses to tenants without this garden, which the court and sometimes other members of the company enjoyed as intended for more than a century and a half. The garden was reached from Lime Street by a long private passage (138 feet long from street to garden gate, where the west arm of Fenchurch Avenue is now) along the north side of the old mansion, and the garden walls bordered other gardens behind houses in Leadenhall Street, Billiter Lane, and Lime Street. It was large for a town garden, measuring approximately (in 1686) 70 feet along the north wall, 144 feet along the east wall, 117 feet along the south wall, and 167 feet along the rear of the houses, or roughly one-third of an acre, enlarged in outlook by the

The notes for Chapter 4 are on p. 188.

presence of other gardens on three sides of it. That area north of Fenchurch Street was rich in gardens still on Ogilby and Morgan's map of 1677. The Great Fire only scorched the edges.

In 1592, when surviving minutebooks begin, Widow Garland the Fishmongers' garden-keeper was held responsible for sundry disorders there such as the 'common drying of clothes' and bowling by strangers 'for great game' contrary to the orders of the alley. To an official enquiry from the Lord Mayor in these years just after the Armada the company certified that its full complement of 1200-weight of gunpowder was kept 'in the garden house'. The keeper, who cannot have been squeamish, seems to have lived in the garden house then; in 1596 the court decided it should not be let, even to the garden-keeper, but retained for company use and pleasure, and those applying for the job of keeper in 1600 were told that 'no one may dwell there'. The keeper's job included 'new making the bowling alleys', gravelling the walks, planting herbs and fruit trees (pear, mulberry, cherry and walnut), and chasing apprentices out. There was a well, with a pump, and watering-pots for the keeper. At the southeast and northeast corners were two 'small buildings at the ends of the alleys, [one] where the powder lies, and the other coming out of Mr Owfeild's garden': a pair of two-storey Elizabethan gazebos apparently, each with one room up and one down; in the former the gunpowder was kept upstairs, and into the upper room of the latter, one of the wardens was allowed to make a door from his own 'leads or gallerye' at the bottom of a garden behind his house in Billiter Lane. The plan of 1686 shows an aviary in that corner; in the 1650s gunpowder was still kept in the other corner (marked 'shed' in 1686) whence thirty barrels of it were stolen in 1631. The 'garden house' in which the keeper had lived was apparently on the southwest side, attached to the rear wall of one of the houses adjoining the medieval mansion.[2]

There was talk in 1617 of moving the garden house to the north side of the garden with 'a gallery built there along', but nothing came of it. An existing gallery was large enough for a summer court dinner in 1620. In 1630 the Prime Warden spoke disparagingly of 'that part of the building at their garden house which stands out upon posts in the garden to the great disfigurement of the garden', and produced 'a draught which he caused to be made for the frame of the said gallery', that is for a new one also of wood. But his term of office was almost up and his successor had better ideas. Thomas Laughton or Langton was then having the medieval mansion rebuilt for himself (with the almost un-heard-of term, for a company lease then, of ninety-nine years from 1632). Apparently he had some quiet advice from Thomas Baldwin, who was helping to arbitrate a party-wall dispute there at the time. The upshot was that on 20 September 1630 'Mr Carter a Surveor brought a plott for the Gallery which the Company intended to build at their garden in Lyme streete & had £3 given him for his paines'. There are no building-accounts to give his Christian name, but this was probably one of Baldwin's colleagues from the King's Works office: perhaps Francis Carter, although he made his will nine days later and died in November; his son Edward Carter, not then in the King's Works, was to succeed

Jones as Surveyor General during the Civil War, and there was a brother William of whom less is known.[3]

Laughton (or Langton), at this point in London planning history, will have been building his house with a brick exterior, although the ground had been measured for him in 1628 by Richard Wade the master carpenter. The company had already had sufficient experience of the powers of the King's Commissioners for Building in 1623 when a tenant's plans for repairs at the Star Inn were frustrated by the Commissioners' insistence on complete rebuilding with (external) brick or stone, and in 1624 when the company could not authorize even a new building in the suburbs, on a garden plot adjoining St Peter's Hospital, without permission.[4] Apparently Langton had been enabled to obtain some of the prized royal stone for himself, probably a fairly small quantity for stone dressings, and apparently with some left over early in 1630 (a year before the new gallery was begun) when the court directed him to make 'a faire gate of Portland Stone' at the entrance to the garden-passage from Lime Street 'with a door and wicket to it', appearance unspecified. That is the maddening thing about references to the gallery or 'great room' built in 1631 at the garden, designed apparently by a man in Inigo Jones's office and obviously prized by the court: the only specifications for this 'stone building and pillars there' give its dimensions and interior treatment, without description of its outer appearance. The exterior design having been handed down from on high, as it were, the Clerk felt no need to enter the details of it in the minutebook. Carter's elevation may have been very plain; no view of it has survived, only block plans. The structure itself lasted until 1735. We know of no payments to craftsmen in 1631, nor any orders for stone, but the details we do know are interesting.

The total cost was to be £700 including glazing, it was to be 66 feet long 'from out to out' with a 'breadth within' of 20 feet, a ceiling-height of 15 feet 'and a roof over it', and the floor was to be eight feet above the ground, that is, supported by the stone pillars, like a market-house above a low open ground floor, or like a certain colonnaded garden wing at Arundel House, modernized by Jones. An apse-like projection on the block plan of 1686 may represent the buttery and 'house of office' with 'small vault' (specified as 20 by 15 feet) below. The connecting kitchen was part of the old garden house behind, of two storeys and garret. The great room was to be paved with Purbeck stone and wainscotted twelve feet high with pilasters of wainscot, a 'Portal of wainscot with one door thereunto' (a wooden doorcase with a single-leaf door), the three feet of wall above the wainscot 'done with Playster of Parris' (a plaster frieze above the panelling), and the 'seelinge to be fretted with lyme and heire' (a plaster fretwork ceiling). There is no reference to a fireplace or chimney, except a 'furnace' probably in the kitchen for hot water, and a chimney renewed in 1638 was probably on the kitchen wing. Presumably all was finished by the end of 1631 at the estimated cost, since no protests arose over 'extras' or delay. The inner space of about 60 by 20 feet made it a 'long gallery' in the late-medieval sense for indoor strolling in bad weather. It could have had, say, six mullioned-and-transomed windows on the long east side toward the garden. No 'artisan-mannerist' carving of stone pilasters, pediments, or balustrades that one might expect is mentioned. For £700 perhaps one could not have the simulated courtiers' style that, for example, shaped the Carpenters' Company's 'great room' of 1664.[5]

For almost thirty years the new garden parlour, furnished with tables, stools, and cushions, served as an extenson to the Hall. In 1644, 'Mr Alderman Penington having been chosen Governor of the Turkey Company & his own house inconvenient for keeping their courts . . . requests the liberty of the Garden House, those who would come being civil men', unanimously granted; foreign trade must go on even in wartime. The next year, the bowling alleys were not made up 'in regard of the troubles of the times & the great disorders & abuses complained of there', but the keeper and his wife were to attend daily to open the gate 'for any of this Company to walk and recreate themselves', and the keeper was warned against being 'taken drunke' again. Trees continued to be planted. In 1645 paintings of SS Peter and Dunstan were laid 'in some by place in the garrett' (over the kitchen), to be brought out of hiding in 1660. During the Commonwealth one bowling alley was prepared for freemen of the company playing with their own bowls. And doubts arose in 1655, whether to dispose of the garden 'in regard the yearly value thereof is wholly lost & the taxes & charges of keeping the same are very great' – the pressure on all green spaces in cities. In 1659 the question was raised whether it would be in keeping with Knight's will to build 'two or three fair houses there', as better than 'to suffer it to be used in such disorderly manner as of late it has', contrary to the donor's intent: the Leadenhall markets just west of Lime Street will have attracted disorder nearby. In 1661, the court being satisfied by learned counsel that they might lease the garden, and urgently in need of money to pay for Hall repairs, offers for a lease of the existing building and garden were entertained. That of Henry Boone, barber-surgeon, a company tenant in Leadenhall Street offering a £650 fine 'and two good fat bucks', with £4 annual rent for a fifty-one year lease, was accepted with a special covenant 'not to take down the outward walls and foundations of the Great Room and stone building and pillars there, but to continue & preserve the same'. That summer Boone spent £550 'in rebuilding & bettering the same', that is, on internal alterations, and then asked that the lease be made out in the name of his son-in-law, Christopher Terne, doctor in physic. Dr Terne (1620-73), one of the original Fellows of the Royal Society, had taken his M.D. at Leyden and was assistant physician at St Bartholomew's Hospital and lecturer on anatomy to the Barber-Surgeons' Company, where Pepys heard him in 1663. Terne's daughter married Sir Thomas Browne's son. Surely there were learned flights of discourse in the garden then. In 1673 Terne died at his house there in Lime Street and was buried at the parish church of St Andrew Undershaft.[6]

A peculiar circumstance is that the company's private planbook, completed in 1686 (Fig. II) and always kept at the Hall, labels the great garden room 'Chappel' although it was never so called in the minutebooks. Possibly election services were being held there, by arrangement with Terne's widow, there being no company chapel at the parish church and services with a strong flavour of dissent were not to be flaunted then. This private place kept its secrets, if any. In 1735 there were bitter complaints from one of the Lime Street tenants when the rear wall of his house collapsed with the pulling down of the old garden house and gallery. In contrast to the Fishmongers' status symbol on the Thames, the essentially private nature and situation of the garden seem to have ensured that no one drew a view of it. Yet it must have been known to members of other City livery companies. Although the Carpenters' 'Great Room' of 1664 was a more elaborate structure and a substantial part of their hall (since rebuilt), it may have owed something to the Fishmongers' great room.

CHAPTER 5

River, Wharf, and Drains

THE WHARF was a vital limb of Fishmongers' Hall and the Thames its most troublesome neighbour. Keeping Thames wharves river-worthy, doctored by dynasties of water-carpenters, was a process infinitely old and recurrent as the tides. In 1603 Thomas Swete carpenter reported on the 'waterworks' of old Stockfishmongers' Hall, that 'the Thames water doth gull in' at the brewer's wharf downstream of it 'and eateth and wasteth' under the building itself 'and cometh out againe here' at the dyer's next door, beside Fishmongers' Wharf. Forty years later John Swett, 'a water carpenter', perhaps Thomas' son, was making a new starling for the company before the dyer's house, promising 'to fill up the same with Chawlke' – a most permeable stone, one would think. In 1646, having got £70 for new starling and stairs here, he undertook to keep said starling 'filled up with chalk for the term of four years' because he had been caught filling 'upp the same att first partly with small rubbish'. In 1645 Stockfishmongers' Hall itself (still so called but let to tenants for more than a century past, rebuilt 1617-18) was 'in danger of rending asunder & falling, & the Campshire next the Thames . . . not yet mended', to which the tenant responsible replied that a workman had the campshed in hand, and matters were left at that as the lease was running out. In 1649 workmen inspecting the house were divided in their views, one that it would go on 'swerving into the Thames', another that it would stay put, but all thought a sure remedy would be '8 or 10 piles driven in the starling close to the stone [wharf] wall & a piece of stone set thereupon to the jutty'. The next year Swett was mending the campshed in front of Fishmongers' Wharf and promising to 'fill it up with such stuff as will not ouse out as that did wherewith he last filled the same'. It was all very empirical.[1]

Campshed is a word little known away from the water (also spelt campshot, campsheeting, camp-sheathing, that is, land-protecting) and here appears to be used interchangeably with starling for a chalk-stuffed double row of timber piling as a facing protecting a wharf. The great starlings like islands protecting the Bridge piers nearby worked, or failed, on the same principle. Today at low tide before Fishmongers' Wharf one can see the type of campshed where an outer row of piling props up a barge-bed like an artificially raised beach, but the works of the Swett family sound more (temporarily) compact.

The notes for Chapter 5 are on pp. 188-9.

Masons dealt with the wharf-structure itself. Accumulated experience passed from master to apprentice, as from John Somner, freeman of the Fishmongers' Company and probably a bridge-mason, to Alexander Meriam (free 1616), who seems to have come from Maidstone near the chief quarries for Kentish ragstone (another Meriam from there being apprenticed to him in 1630). In 1626 Meriam was appointed company mason, the first such appointment in the records that survive, and probably the mason who had just raised the level of the Hall wharf to keep the cellars from flooding. The year after that he took an apprentice Thomas Bedford, son of a yeoman of Headington in Oxfordshire (London masons often came from neighbourhoods of quarries), and Bedford claimed his freedom of the company in 1635. In 1647 he was admitted company mason in place of his deceased master, having worked under Meriam 'for fifteen years past for the Bridgehouse, this Company, and other places'. Bedford was to work on the post-Fire Hall, until his death c. 1673, in partnership with a much more sophisticated mason, not a riverside man, Edward Peirce. A young Bedford made free by patrimony in 1662 may have been the Thomas Bedford who was then Clerk to Morrice's waterworks at London Bridge. The human waterside network was as widespread as the campsheds.[2]

One matter for waterside masonry then and later was the drain-mouth. An abnormally high tide's most tiresome habit was to rush up the mouth of the 'common sewer' fitted into the wharf-structure and on up the drain, flooding any floor or yard with a 'sink-hole' in it. A Hall committee was appointed in January 1641 (that being the worst month then for high tides) to deal with flooding that had ruined the kitchen floors, and Alderman Gayer was pleased to promise assistance 'if his leisure permits'. But action was only taken a year later in January 1642 when Gayer arrived with Meriam the mason in tow 'to view the passage through which the water cometh', that is, the sewer or 'Sluce', presumably at dead low tide : 'and conceiving that if the mouth of that passage be stopped at times of high waters with some Plugge or other device it would keep the water from coming into the said rooms without any prejudice, did therefore direct Mr Meriam to consider how this might be done.' (A drawing was made in 1833 in Henry Roberts' office for just such a drain-mouth valve in the wharf rebuilt for the present Hall.)[3] In central London still, when heavy rain pours down the gutters and a strong east wind reinforces a seasonal high tide at the right phase of the moon, the Thames is as ready as ever to rush up a few drains, although the Hall itself has no drains into the river now.

Each of the long narrow original sites between Thames Street and the river seems to have had its own arm of the common sewer : in 1395 one was mentioned under the premises later called the Pepper Querne, and subsequently at least part of the Hall kitchen drained into that. The path of the Hall's own drain is implied in an order which also tells us that the company's coal cellar lay partly under the streetside tenant's yard and partly under the long entry, convenient to the great kitchen and probably a very old cellar indeed : 'The pitt in this Company's coal cellar for receiving the water running from Mr Manby's house & yards through

the same cellar & cross the Company's entry & under the east side of the same
entry & this Hall into the Thames be stopped up & the watercourse to run continually away, & a close grate be made next Mr Manby's house.' (Manby being
Clerk to the Leathersellers probably had a subtenant there.) Ever since an act of
Common Council passed in 1538 to protect the river from pollution, 'strong iron
grates' had been installed 'at riverside and streetside' wherever a watercourse ran
down, the grates made 'as of old accustomed' at least two feet high with the
gratings an inch apart to stop dung and bones and dead cats that belonged on the
common laystalls from which 'common rakers' removed them in dung-boats.[4]
These grates did not, however, protect one part of a shared site from another and
perhaps Manby's tenant's slops were surfacing at the sink-hole in the long entry,
one more reason for not wanting a tavern in that house by the Hall gate. Also over
this drain sat the company's 'stool for easement in the entry'. The drain's route
under the parlour block is suggested by concern for the foundations of its east wall
in 1660, though workmen found the sewer near it to be 'strong & substantial'. The
'house of office' off the great chamber two storeys above, as well as a stool in the
Clerk's fuel and beer cellar, will have drained into it. Gravity and the next
rainstorm may have operated well enough, except during drought or when
unusual tides reversed the flow, because it is only with the next Hall that the hire
of men to empty a 'necessary vault' or cesspit enters the minutebooks, very irritably. Although it has seemed clearer to postpone explaining that first drain until
now, after describing the rest of the premises, the drain was at the bottom of it
all. The wharf structure, protective though it had to be, accommodated this
highly vulnerable outlet.

Wharf construction, as discussed during repairs in 1639, was an old affair too.
At the meeting in the garden in August, after mended hammerbeams and window-
grilles were settled, 'it being conceived that Portland Stone being harder than
Ketten will be better for the wall next the Thameside', Thomas Baldwin thought
he could get some from the royal quarries by jogging Inigo Jones's elbow. But of
course this hard white stone was no gift, and so much money had already been
spent on the Hall we note that the next decision on the subject of the wharf wall
was only 'to cope it with Portland stone', and thereafter it was not mentioned
again – even though the Surveyor General did procure some for the Goldsmiths'
Company in 1635. (It is only fair to note that accounts for the early 1640s are so
faded that a payment for it could be overlooked.) A 'wharf wall' was the wharf's
whole face to the river, down to the muddy bottom, and the battlemented portion
above the paved surface of the wharf was the parapet of this wall. A few weeks
after the above meeting, Meriam told the wardens 'that if it were his own [that old
craftsman's phrase] he would take down 20 foot thereof in length & 3 foot in
breadth & new make it' at 3s 4d. per foot, and was told to go ahead. The 'breadth'
will have been the depth of it, backed up by rubble; the height from the bottom
they took for granted. A fourteenth-century limestone wharf wall was unearthed
just upstream by archaeologists in 1974. At the end of September 1639, it was
agreed that the new river wall of Fishmongers' Wharf should be of ashlar (evenly

cut stone) inside and out, 'viz. the outside with Kentish stone & the inside with
Ketton stone, and that a band [bonding] stone be therein laid every five foot' (the
kind of thing that had been going on at, for example, Tower Wharf in 1389, for
which the contract survives: facing of Kentish ashlar and a long end-stone every
ten feet). The Fishmongers' parapet – so distinctive in early views of this shoreline
of skew-built jetties – was to be restored: 'And the wall to be raised [above wharf-
level] in height three foot & ten inches with the crest, which crest shall be new
made to the gate and the crest stones cramped with iron.' A later item in the
accounts for painting 'the ffeince, railes & gates at the waterside' may refer to
protective railings down the steps to the water below the watergate. During the
weeks 'when the wharf was down', one of the almsmen from St Peter's Hospital
acted as night watchman (paid 25s.3d. including cost of candles).[5]

The Hall water-stairs seem to have been used a good deal then (although early in
the next century the tide was thought too dangerous for embarking or disembark-
ing so near the Bridge). The guests who came with Lord Arundel to dinner the
day after Christmas in 1633 arrived by water. But when the water-stairs were out
of repair in 1645, and also in view of wartime disturbances in the City, it was
thought best to order 'no goods to be landed thereat to pass through this Hall'.

Water-supply for the kitchen came mostly from the river, though conduits in
Old and New Fish Streets with inland sources were maintained by the company
for the trade ('the cornetts [spouts] of this Company's conduits in Old Fish Street
to be covered with lead'). In 1605 the tenant of the Pepper Querne premises
was sharing with the company the costs of a pump at the waterside, and in the
1640s we hear of a cistern kept in the warehouse on his little wharf 'pumping
water to serve this Company's great kitchen', also called 'the pump at the waterside
next to Mr Trattle's back door . . . that brings water . . . into the Company's great
kitchen' – pump and cistern standing beside or on the site of Walworth's water-
tower. The incoming Clerk in 1639 installed a new pump in his own kitchen,
where his predecessor had already 'a pipe of lead in the ground', probably from
the river. Separating the waters drawn up these inlets from the drainage washed
down the sewer outlets was left to the flux of the tides. In 1660–1, as part of the
brave new world of the Restoration, arrangements were made for supply from the
'waterhouse' at the Bridge, an enterprise harnessing the power generated by the
tidal rush through the north arch of the Bridge, founded by a Dutchman, Peter
Morrice, in 1582: for a £5 fine and 26s.8d. yearly, a sixty-one year lease from
Michaelmas 1660 was sealed between Thomas Morris, gentleman, and the
wardens of the company 'of a watercourse to this Hall from the engine or water-
work', route unspecified.[6]

For fire prevention, 'twoe new long Ladders and Hookes' were hung in the
entry off the wharf in 1643, and probably another pair were already slung on the
wall of the long entry, like those hanging still today, trophies from the past, in the
entry to No. 20 Swithin Lane off Cannon Street. The company's hand-operated
pump must have been heavier than some of the little squirts then available: it
was thought wise to lend it to fires at company-owned houses with 'wheels to be

made to carry the engine'; a more liberal attitude being taken after a while, that 'the Company's engine against fire may be delivered out of this Hall, to be used in any place within the Lines of Communication'. In 1662 a founder was paid the large sum of £10.18.0 for mending the fire-engine '& making a new tub thereunto', so it carried a water-supply.[7] And that is the very last we hear of it.

CHAPTER 6

Neighbours, Plague, and Fire

THE FABRIC of the old Thames Street mansions, parcelled into smaller tenements, lay like kindling beside the Hall. East of them, in Hollar's long view, real firewood was stacked on a wood-merchant's wharf. Thames Street was famed for its warehouses loaded with pitch, oil, flax, wines and brandies; Pepys walked down here to price tar when he thought the Navy was being cheated. In the years before the Great Fire, Fishmongers' Hall had dyehouses on either side of it. During 1642–55 the upstream premises, including the stone building beyond Trattle's 'little wharf' and wooden warehouses behind it, were in the hands of a dyer whose chimney 'much annoyeth this Hall by the lownes thereof' and the danger of fire 'by any spark or candle' where he 'layeth his dying weed, being a very Combustible stuffe, in a room with Timber walls' between the chimney and the Hall parlour block's 'stairs leading unto the Leads'. The neighbours on that side were a particular nuisance because they were not company tenants (until the nineteenth century) and so were less controllable.[1] In 1610 the court had suddenly become aware of the danger in 'an old forest chimney' there and requested its immediate replacement in brick. In 1612 when the neighbour, then a mercer, was building a wooden warehouse that promised to be as high as the west windows of the company's great hall, it took more diplomacy to invoke the ancient-lights principle – one of the oldest in town-planning – and stop him from going higher than the former building there or making dormers toward the Hall. That this building was very close to the great hall is shown by the same neighbour's complaint in 1635 that the hall buttresses were 'fastened to his tenements or doe rest upon the same and soe doe beare the same backwards'; the company craftsmen's report, that the buttresses 'were beneath the same' and doing 'no wrong', suggests that the neighbour had a series of cantilevered upper storeys jutting out farther and farther as the buttresses sloped back – an encroachment that was allowed to pass without comment.

On the downstream side, adjoining the other side of the parlour block, was a dyehouse rebuilt in the 1590s by a company tenant at the river end of the Nun's Head premises (Fig. Iy). Fixtures and fittings listed in 1663 have a certain interest : two coppers each over seven feet across and four feet deep, three circular vats each over five feet across and five feet deep, two leaden cisterns, one near

The notes for Chapter 6 are on p. 189.

the vats and the other next to a pump and the river, one large lead pipe with brass stopcocks for conveying water from pump to coppers, and the floor paved with stone. The customary drying-poles for hanging out great lengths of cloth from the upper storeys (Hollar shows some farther upstream) were forbidden by the court. In 1616 when old Stockfishmongers' Hall next door to it, also occupied by dyers, was falling down this was blamed partly on 'the hanging of clothes upon poles out of the top of the house' and not on defective 'water-workes', the clinching argument given being that 'the house sinketh not to waterward but to landward'. But that argument, which crops up elsewhere, probably meant that the landward foundation piles dried out sometimes whereas the waterward piling never did. The tenant was also warned that digging and breaking the ground for the 'setting in of dying pannes' was a chief cause of decay. Hence the later stone floor next door.[2]

The rebuilding of old Stockfishmongers' Hall (Fig. Iz) in 1616–18 had shown how strong the timber building-tradition still was then. Robert Ross, carpenter, agreed in August 1616 to take down the old timber frame for £10, 'without spoiling or breaking any tenaunt ([tenon] or mortise thereof but what needs must' and to 'lay the same into lighters & take it up to his own wharf at Whitefriars' (summoning up a picture of prefabricated house-frames floating up and down the river). The new building was delayed by the remaking of the wharf in 1617 by Edward Kynsman (later Inigo Jones's principal mason on St Paul's cathedral). Finally in December 1618, when Ross had made a new building with new timber – the court planning to use the old timber somewhere else – a committee reported on his work as 'sufficiently built but somewhat awry or askew which they consider he might have altered during the building', doubtless one reason why it was 'swerving into the Thames' thirty years later, but Ross was paid. Perhaps it was he in 1618 who gave the new house the pair of pedimented 'artisan mannerist' gables faintly visible in Hollar's long view (Pl. 3b), crudely classical gables of a type known to architectural historians as Holborn gables, a mannerism that seems to have been introduced to London artisans by Inigo Jones himself on house-fronts in Holborn and the Strand soon after his return from the Continent in 1615. If Hollar is to be trusted in this matter, Ross must have been one of the more up-to-date master carpenters. Again the use of drying-poles 'out of the top of the house towards the Thames' was refused, 'the house being high & standing upon the Thames as it does'.[3]

It is often noted by writers on pre-Fire London that houses were much intermingled with one another. Dwellings and warehouses overran and interpenetrated other dwellings and warehouses in a higgledy-piggledy, hugger-mugger fashion that greatly complicated ownership of the underlying ground. One of the main reasons for this is not always appreciated. It happened especially where big medieval mansions and their appendages were split up in an *ad hoc* way into small tenements, particularly in the sixteenth century when grander households moved westward. The Fishmongers' Company owned some classical examples of intermixing, all tinder for the Great Fire. For instance, in St Magnus' parish near the Bridge and the Gully Hole there was the White Lyon, an ancient 'great messuage' irregularly divided among six tenancies by 1655.[4] Premises between the White Lyon and the Hall included the old Nun's Head and the old Flower de Luce, both parcelled out among tenants of the company : as these two sites were to be merged in the Hall site after the Fire, the impedimenta that filled them until September 1666 were part of the past of the present site.

The Nun's Head, apart from the dyehouse at the waterside, was principally divided between two tenants in the years before the Fire, a broderer and a grocer, their shops side by side on Thames Street with their dwellings on three floors above, probably each under his own gable (there being a total frontage of about 36 feet here), and behind there was a chaos of rooms, yards, sheds and cellars as far as the edge of the dyer's domain. That point was marked by 'the great Beame', apparently supporting a pair of scales for weighing goods brought to the water-steps, and upstairs near the great beam were three lodgers. The broderer in 1654 had a typical shopkeeper's house : shopfront less than 15 feet wide and shop 36 feet deep, first floor with hall, parlour, kitchen and buttery, second floor with two chambers, a 'studdy' or office for the master of the house, a 'house of office' or privy, and garrets above. When shared use of the passage alongside his shop leading to the wharf became too great a source of friction, the broderer was assigned the strip of passage nearest the street to add to his shop. For the rear tenants a cartway to the street was then taken through a warehouse behind the Flower de Luce into its existing passage, thereafter called Flower de Luce Alley but still private, with a gate to the street. A schedule of fixtures attached to a lease of 1650 for the front part of that tenement mentions a latticed gallery 'in the hall behind the shop', another room 'crested about with crests of wood', and a room 'glazed to the streetward with ten casements of iron in it & the same also glazed backward with six wooden casements in it'. Some of this might date from redecoration done at the time of sealing an earlier lease in 1605.[5]

Some fixtures in these Thames Street houses were doubtless older than the surviving schedules that list them, as would be the case with possibly Tudor or Jacobean panelling in the Bishop's Head, nearly opposite the Hall, for which a schedule of 1656 listed 'wainscot with turned pillars roundabout the room half the height of the room', a buttery with 'carved pillars' in it, and a little parlour wainscotted 'with benches & turned pillars'. Although the Bishop's Head came into company possession only in 1620, as part of an endowment for St. Peter's Hospital, the house was not then new. A jolting footnote to art history is that James Wood, the tenant who signed the deed of 1656, 'was hanged for unsealing his effects when a Bankrupt' according to a clerical note on the deed; Jerman measured the site (Fig. III) for Wood's widow after the Fire.[6]

Behind the main house of the Flower de Luce there emerges in the lease of 1650 another mysterious private chapel, or 'room called the Chappell'. Originally apparently part of the medieval mansion's domestic entourage strung out down the long site, it may have been used by the court of the Stockfishmongers when their Hall was at the waterside there. Oral tradition was strong if this did hark back to a pre-Reformation domestic chapel.

Fumes from a brewery east of the Flower de Luce caused a tenant to complain

in 1611 that he could get no subtenant, the steam and smoke were so bad, to which
the brewer's reply was that it had been so for twenty years. When in 1657 Trattle
talked of subletting his house by the Hall gate to a soap-boiler, a committee
obligingly went to visit premises where soap-boiling and tallow-melting took place,
and that was the end of that idea. By this time the coal-fire on every domestic
hearth compounded the commercial vapours, the 'Clowds of Smoake and
Sulphur, so full of Stink and Darknesse' that John Evelyn indignantly deplored in
his tract of 1661, *Fumifugium or the Inconvenience of the Aer and Smoak of
London Dissipated*. Evelyn deplored too 'the Deformity of so frequent Wharfes
and Magazines of Wood, Coal, Boards, and other course Materials, most of them
imploying the Place of the Noblest aspect for the situation of Palaces towards the
goodly river'. At least Fishmongers' Hall was keeping the neighbourhood tone up.
Evelyn's recommendation of 'a Key . . . so contrived on London-side, as might
render it lesse sensible of the Reciprocation of the Waters', prophesied the post-Fire
Thames Quay idea. Meanwhile, said Evelyn, there was 'that Hellish and dismal
Cloud of SEA-COAL . . . so that Catharrs, Phthisicks, Coughs and Consumptions
rage more in this one City than in the whole Earth besides'. Between the lines of
the Company minutebooks one senses a similar disgust with the 'brewers, dyers . . .
and soap-boilers' Evelyn wished to see moved down-river. He thought 'the City of
London resembles the face rather of Mount Aetna' or 'the Suburbs of Hell, than
an Assembly of Rational Creatures', almost in the words of Herman Melville on
London Bridge in 1849.[7]

One of Evelyn's complaints, of narrow incommodious streets in the 'busiest
places of Intercourse', rendering London 'a Labyrinth in its principal passages',
began to be remedied a little even before the Fire, with two Acts of 1662 'for the
enlarging of several strait and inconvenient Streets' and 'Common High wayes'.
An effort by the court of this company to preserve pedestrian rights in Thames
Street – for themselves proceeding to and from the Hall, for instance – failed in
1663 after a warden was delegated to ask Peter Mills, City Surveyor, 'that upon
the next review of posts & stalls in the streets of the City . . . they do consider of
the posts standing before this Company's Hall gate especially for the preservation
of horse & foot passing near thereunto against carts & coaches', which Mills
promised 'to procure' his commissioners to consider, but soon their order came
that the posts 'shall be taken down & set close to the wall of the same gate'; carts
and coaches had won.[8]

No court minutes survive from the period July 1664 – August 1666; there may
have been no meetings during the summer and autumn of the Plague year 1665,
and such minutes as lay in the Clerk's office in rough form for the elective period
1664–6 will have been passed over during the heavy rescue work from the treasury
during the Fire. Such financial accounts as survived from the Plague year mention
payments to the poor that were kept up 'in the tyme of the Visitacon'. The Clerk of
the Vintners' Company died at their hall not far away. When the Carpenters'
Company beadle died, fires were lighted at that hall to fumigate. People afterward
remembered the unblinking sunshine and the stench of the streets, the piles of

refuse and the unflushed drains after months without rain. There was so little traffic, in the quiet men heard the rapids at the Bridge, and trade was dead on the river. The death toll was not at its worst in the City, but in the burial register of St Michael's Crooked Lane it was bad enough: 132 in this small parish during the four worst months, August to November. The 'visitation' came first in the parish at the end of May and early in June to two families, both of fishmongers, freemen but not tenants of this company, the Hayes household losing four in two weeks, the Timms household losing four in just over three weeks; they may have been neighbours, and were followed early in July by the sexton who had buried them and his two sons, with few other deaths in the parish before the second week in August.[9]

In the summer of 1666 as usual, an election of new wardens was held in the parlour by the Thames and an election sermon presumably preached in the old parish church – gowned procession up Miles Lane beforehand and down again, beadles parting the rude traffic of Thames Street – and an election dinner served in the great hall, as in June of every even-numbered year. About two in the morning of Sunday, September 2, a fire at a bakery in Pudding Lane, igniting hay and other combustible stuff in the stableyard of the Star Inn lying between Pudding Lane and Fish Street Hill, sent flames racing downhill – there had been fires like that before. But in Thames Street, with a strong east wind behind it, the Great Fire of London was really born. Once it caught warehouses and wharves piled with inflammables, there was no holding it. St Magnus' church was burnt out, and the first houses on the Bridge, and Morris' waterworks. Then on it roared through the tarred boarded jutting disorderly labyrinth of old Stockfishmongers' Row – White Lyon, Bishop's Head, Flower de Luce, Nun's Head, Fishmongers' Hall – the first of forty-four livery halls to go. Warned by the noise of the flames, like 'a thousand iron chariots beating together upon the stones', and the fiery beacon of St Magnus' tower while the night was still dark, John Lee had to get the valuables and his family out. We know the names of some who helped him. Thomas Tanner, who was soon to succeed Lee as Clerk and who lived 'above 15 years' at the Hall as 'the Clarke's man', was granted £30 extra gratuity in 1668 'for his service in the tyme of the late dreadfull fire', which means he was chief rescuer of valuables, dragging the iron money chest downstairs and saving the most important documents. John Jekyll, a member of the court, either rushed down from his house near St Stephen's Walbrook or helped Tanner at some water-stairs upstream, and took charge of the company silver, later claiming 28 shillings he had 'expended in the carriage of this Company's plate . . . and for watching the same', apparently being able to shut it up in some warehouse he had outside the line of fire. The chief carrier of everything Tanner was able to bring out of the treasury and down to the wharf was a lighterman, William Dawkes, who came in November humbly petitioning 'for some allowance for his labor & attendance with his Lighter at Fishmongers Hall to preserve their goods in the time of the late fire' and was granted twenty shillings, more graciously increased soon to forty.[10]

Few City institutions with valuable records had a direct private exit to the

Thames. While the 'most horrid malicious bloody flame' raged out of control for four days, the river became gorged with boats and every other highway with carts laden with goods and terrified people. We owe to Thomas Tanner and William Dawkes, and the river Thames, the vellum deeds and charters and the fine paper pages of minutes and accounts that tell this half-unravelled story.

PART THREE

THE RED BRICK HALL
1667–1827

'Fishmongers' Hall . . . a curious and capacious Building of Brick and Stone. By the Street you enter thro' a handsome Passage paved with Free-stone, which leads into a large, square Court, paved in the same Manner, encompassed by the great Hall, the Court-Room for the Assistants, and other grand Apartments. . . . But the Front next the Thames, which has been lately repaired and beautified, at a very extraordinary Expence, exceeds every Thing of its Kind in this City, and yields a most graceful and pleasant Prospect; with a magnificent Flight of Stone Stairs on the Wharf.'

William Maitland, *History of London and Westminster*, 1739, II. 833–4.

In 'a continued range of wharves, yards and warehouses for the . . . immense trade which supplies the Metropolis . . . one edifice only, for shew and pleasure, Fishmongers' Hall . . . relieves the eye and imagination.'

John Middelton, *View of Agriculture in Middlesex*, 1807.

CHAPTER 7

The Circumstances, 1666–8

BY THURSDAY 6 SEPTEMBER the worst of the Great Fire was over and nearly four-fifths of the City of London lay 'buried in its own ruins'. A week later, 'A Meeting intended for a Court of Assistants [was] holden at the late Garden of the Company of Fishmongers in Lyme Streete on Thursday the thirteenth day of September Anno Dm 1666', with half the members able to be present 'to consider of the Affaires of the Company'. About them where they sat deliberating in the garden they had leased to Dr Terne were still grass and trees, probably powdered with ashes – as Hyde Park was to be during the Blitz of 1940. The flames had passed by this open space, though Fenchurch Street a few yards southward was 'all in dust' (Pepys on the 5th). But for the smoke rising from cellars that continued to burn for months, one could have seen from the south end of Lime Street the glint of the river across open ruins that were 'now no longer a city' (Evelyn on the 10th). Every occupier of a family house, counting-house, warehouse, shop, wharf, or combination thereof in the destroyed area was a refugee, though some had friends or relations or other property beyond the City walls to go to. If the seventeen men in the garden that day individually saw ruin staring them in the face, they met as an ancient body, trustees of property that concerned hundreds of people, tenants and pensioners. Each City livery hall destroyed in 1666 was the centre of such a web of dependencies. The fabric of the Hall was the main concern of the first meeting:

> And Mr Edward Jerman being here present was desired to goe & view their late Hall in Thamestreete & to consider what is there that may be preserved & what Chimneyes & walls are fitt to be pulled downe to prevent danger And hee returning testifyed here That there were five Chimneys & parte of the wall next the waterside are fitt to be taken downe And that the East north and west partes thereof may be bounded [bonded] & secured with old brickes without Mortar And Mr Tanner the Bricklayer here likewise present was wished to cause the same to be done And alsoe the said Chimneyes & walls to be pulled downe as Mr Jerman shall direct.

This was the first decision to take when a whole network of civic life had been disrupted: secure the safe remains and get rid of the unsafe ones. For full-scale

The notes for Chapter 7 are on pp. 189–90.

rebuilding – supposing those who had fled came back – there were bound to be shortages of labour and materials, and high prices. Outside London, for more than a year after the 'great plague', deaths from plague continued. The nation was at war with the Dutch at sea, and alarms of arson by foreign spies were raised in London. That was the climate in which decisions had to be taken.

Few of them in the garden that day, or at better-attended subsequent meetings, were natives of London. Ralph Trattle, Prime Warden, had been born the son of a yeoman in the moorland village of Rosedale, North Riding. John Jekyll, second warden, was the son of Thomas Jekyll, gentleman of Bocking, Essex, probably the antiquary of Bocking and Clifford's Inn; and John Jekyll's son was to be Sir Joseph Jekyll, Master of the Rolls in the next century. The fourth warden John Greene's father had been a currier in Oxford, the father of the fifth warden Thomas Pearle, a yeoman of Glastonbury in Somerset. Few on this court were in the fish trade. Jekyll was a haberdasher, John Bathurst a wealthy linen draper, John Hayne a scrivener. John Owen, who was to become prime warden in 1668, was a stationer and bookseller, Nathaniel Hawes a cheese-merchant with many warehouses in Thames Street, and James Bartrum a vintner. Many were religious dissenters, though some were not. According to the political labelling of the 1680s many were Whigs, a few were Tories. Yet this far from homogeneous lot were all Londoners.[1]

Before the court met again, arrangements were made for a temporary meeting-place at the old Bethlehem Hospital for the insane, or Bedlam, just outside Bishopsgate where Liverpool Street Station now stands (northeast of the Moor-fields hospital site built upon in 1675). Civil War wounded had been cared for there, and it not clear whether the fifty-nine inmates recorded in 1667 were lunatics or not. At any rate, the Fishmongers' Company rented space there in which court meetings could be held and documents stored from Michaelmas 1666 to Christmas 1669, paying certain bills during that time 'for firing Tobaccoe pipes & Candles' and for use of rooms, attendance and cleaning. Similarly, with Guild-hall and the Royal Exchange in ruins, both City Corporation and City merchants removed to Gresham's great house, where the Royal Society had been meeting, in the unburnt area between Broad Street and Bishopsgate Street. And so every necessary organization calmly made its arrangements for survival. Parishes of ruined churches continued to elect churchwardens. Burials continued in the ruins of St Michael's Crooked Lane : death brought some parishioners home again.[2]

Rent-producing property being the basis of a livery company's charity, support-ing almspeople far beyond the City's walls from the proceeds of London leases, the Fire struck at the lives of many besides occupiers of burnt houses. Rather than suspend pensions at Newington and Harrietsham and Bray, or out-pensions in London, until leases were productive again, the court decided on September 27 to sell all but a few reserved pieces of the company's plate, which had greatly in-creased since the last century. That this was punctiliously not impulsively done is shown by a sheet of committee minutes for September 21 : legal advice was first to be taken 'whether the Company is liable to pay charitable uses from houses burned

& consumed or not'; and dinners were to be forsworn.³ In November the sum of
£433.8.9 was realized 'for the present occasions of the Company' from plate
turned over to the banker Sir Robert Vyner. And the Prime Warden paid £47
from his own pocket for several pieces, including 'a fair gilt salt', presumably to
return them to company possession; for in August 1669 he delivered to Mr Owen
his successor 'a greate silver Salt wth Scollops of the guift of Mr Rushout . . . to
be kept for the use of the Company'; so the company owes its continued possession
of that handsome Dutch silver-gilt piece of 1654 to Ralph Trattle, who had done
well since coming down from Yorkshire in 1624: before and after the Fire he
held company leases not only for houses west of the Hall but for unburnt property
at Cripplegate; he had loaned the company over half its share in the cost of the
ship *Loyal London* levied on the City that summer, and he now bought fifty
barge-loads of timber, the company's third source of revenue, from its woodlands
at Bray.⁴

Good native timber was already scarce before the Fire. Much had to be imported for shipbuilding as can be observed in Pepys' diary. Even for new brick-
faced houses, the frames were still of wood; the whole City was to need timber.
The Fishmongers' Company had already begun dealing in it in 1663: Alderman
Edward Backwell the celebrated goldsmith – later called principal founder of the
English banking system – paid the company £285 in October 'for timber sold to
him that was felled on this Company's lands at Bray', presumably for building-
work at his Lombard Street shop which was being enlarged in that year. A tanner
bought bark, a cooper bought hoops 'sold to him by Mr Jerman out of the wood
felled at Bray', a 'Mr Henry Johnson & partners', probably carpenters, bought
timber, someone else paid 'for elms', and so on. For supervising these operations
and paying 'charges of felling cutting pilling [peeling] barking & selling of timber
at Bray', Jerman was paid £254 before the plague came.⁵ Immediately after the
Fire, all timber sales at Bray were stopped and Jerman was told to view the cop-
pices, decide which trees were ready for felling, and send all felled timber from the
wharf at Water Oakley to Fishmongers' Wharf to be laid up for future use.
Here began six years of confusingly recorded and unrecorded transactions involv-
ing barge-load after barge-load from Bray to London. Some of this wood ended
up in the new Royal Exchange building; the clerk and beadle of the Mercers'
Company were gratefully paid twenty shillings each in 1671 for tracing that
transaction.⁶ The gradually emerging tangles of the company's timber-supply seem
mostly the result of the carelessness of young Thomas Lock the master carpenter,
who in May 1668 was told to keep track of it, in a generally chaotic situation.

During the second of the two desperately busy years left in Jerman's life after
the Fire, he became more deeply concerned at Bray. (One suspects some other
compelling reason for his going there; errands for the Goldsmiths' Company, who
were also getting wood from Berkshire, perhaps some building work at Windsor;
possibly members of his family were there since the plague.)⁷ From December or
earlier in 1667, he was being asked to pay the almspeople in Jesus Hospital their
pensions and to dole out firewood for their fuel; in January 1668 he had 'to ride

to Bray with money to pay the poor . . . & to find out how things stand there' for the company, and in May also to find out what tenants on the company's other lands there owed in rent; in July he reminded the court that the almsfolk's pay-day was due and that he was riding to Windsor, and so again on October 8, in the last weeks of his life. The payments made to him by the company now included pension money as well as timber money, although no payments since the Fire for surveying; perhaps he simply let surveying charges accumulate : the brief report signed by him on the Bishop's Head site (Fig. III) opposite the Hall shows that some of the company's surveying work was indeed done by him. At the time, he was heavily engaged in supervising the building of the Royal Exchange, as well as being one of the City Surveyors under the Rebuilding Act, and concerned in the rebuilding of several livery company halls besides the Fishmongers' and the repairs to Goldsmiths' Hall. In some cases of livery halls for which he provided drawings, their execution must have been left entirely in the hands of the crafts-men concerned, but the companies for whom he acted as company surveyor (including also the Drapers and Apothecaries) expected more than that. When building was finally under way at Fishmongers' Hall in July 1668, it was decreed that the building committee should meet at the site every Thursday afternoon at two o'clock, 'at which time Mr Jerman promises to attend them there & to consider how things go on'; and he was then expected to proceed with them to the meeting-room at Bedlam 'to treat with tenants & give such further direccon concerning the Company's affairs as shall be requisite'. By October 29, a plaintive note crept into the minutes of a Fishmongers' court meeting held at the new Pope's Head tavern : 'Ordered that Mr Edward Jerman do forthwith make up an account of all this Company's timber felled at Bray & what has become of it & how much brought to London & where & to whom delivered And that Mr Locke the Carpenter do likewise give an account of all such timber as has been brought from Bray to Fishmongers Hall or any other place . . . And what has become of the same'; and Jerman's presence at the next committee meeting was demanded. That meeting, not recorded, he probably could not attend.

On November 9 Jerman made his will, and he died a fortnight later of 'con-sumption' – consumed by overwork. He was buried on 26 November 1668 in the church of St Giles Cripplegate, recorded in the register as 'City Surveighor'. In his lifetime only one payment relating to a new Fishmongers' Hall was recom-mended for him, by a committee in August 1668, approved by the court in October ('£50 at present in part in respect of his [other work for the company] and about their building at Fishmongers Hall'), and in the leisurely processes of such things, finally awarded to his widow Rose Jerman in 1672.[8] The story of Jerman's initial design for this Hall must be seen in the context of his overworked life at the time. The Royal Exchange committee thought him 'the most able knowne artist' (besides Peter Mills) that the City had; although he is not known to have designed any building outside the City, there can have been little he did not know about the art of building in the City. Incidentally, after the Great Fire, when his experience and judgment – first called upon by this company in 1639 –

were in sudden demand, Jerman was never again referred to by this company as a 'workman'.

The Hall ruins that Jerman inspected on 13 September 1666 were of course those of the Tudor great hall and parlour blocks. The riverside 'great vault' of the latter, that is, the stone-vaulted cellar, was still partly intact, and Lock made new doors for it as a storage place. Eventually a shed was made there for the company beadle Thomas Atkins (whose house in Black Raven Alley was burnt), for him to lodge in and keep watch over the remains. Many little decisions then simply related to picking up the pieces and guarding them. Pewter and lead found in the rubble were melted into 300-pound 'piggs' and kept 'in the greate vault fast locked upp' until disposed of; for some of it a founder gave £20, but old armour 'taken out of the rubbish' brought only ten shillings. On one of Jerman's trips to Bray he was asked to consider the question of sending stone from the wreck of the Hall upriver (as return ballast in the timber-barges) for any repairs to Jesus Hospital, so some early-sixteenth-century stonework in perhaps quite menial forms may lie at Bray still. After it became clear that rebuilding of the Hall could not start in 1667, the company blacksmith Henry Brookes – who was later to work on five Wren churches[9] – was allowed to set up his bellows and forge in the ruins of 'the new kitchen' (of either 1605 or 1660) subject to removal at three months' notice.

Rebuilding was at first intended to start as soon as possible. By February 1667, sixty-two barge-loads of timber had come to the wharf and, doubtless after seeing how much space that took up, the court let the Prime Warden have it for his own rebuilding, reserving only enough to make a crane on the wharf; though that first requirement for building was apparently not made until a year later, and the timber landed with some temporary hoist. Hawes the cheese merchant on the court, who had thirty-two loads delivered there for himself, was asked in March 1667 to remove them so that the company's building might not be hindered, but a year later he was still being allowed to have wood delivered there. When in April 1667 Jerman warned them that a large amount of timber he had had piled at Bray was becoming sap-rotten and would decay if not moved, he was instructed to dispose of it, though little building was going on in the City as yet and demand cannot have been great; with so many ruins uncleared, there was little space for it to 'season'. But suddenly in June a new spirit of resolution (or source of cash) inspired the company's wardens. With two hundred loads waiting at Bray, Jerman was ordered 'to cause as much as the water would bear' to be brought speedily to London. Such speed was impossible that week, the court order being given on June 6, and Pepys recording on the 8th, when the Dutch fleet was off Harwich, that 'all the Westerne Barges' – those plying between upstream ports such as Windsor or Maidenhead and London – 'are taken up to make a bridge over river about the Hope [near Tilbury] for horse to cross', as had been done in 1588. Yet the wardens had decisive plans in mind, seemingly oblivious of national danger. The wood when it finally arrived was to be stacked on the dyehouse site next door if the tenant there would 'give way'. And in the same breath, at this meeting of

6 June 1667, 'Mr Jerman was desired to consider of a modell for rebuilding this Companyes hall'.

The suggestion that the dyer east of the old Hall might surrender his lease intimated that the new Hall site was to be extended that way. By taking the new site to the parish boundary along the east edge of the old Flower de Luce, while still letting off six houses along the street to tenants, the area for the Hall could be increased from about 9000 to about 13,000 square feet. If the early plan we have (Pl. 5a) was Jerman's 'modell' ordered in June 1667, it is proof that the court then felt sure of the willingness of tenants at the riverside end of the old Nun's Head and Flower de Luce ground to give up their leases, but at least two of them only accepted compensation in the following year, and a third was still arguing over the amount in 1670. All had subtenants to consult, a network no mere fire could invalidate. In August 1667 there was a grand meeting of interested parties among the dust heaps by the river with Jerman 'bringing here a mapp or plott of the ground whereon the Companyes Hall did stand & of all the ground of this Company between the Old Swan & the waterhouse for the better disposing & leasing thereof' – a plan that has not survived.

There was not only the problem of inducing the riverside tenants east of the former Hall to leave, but the more intractable one of urging certain streetside tenants to rebuild more rationally. Isaac Foster the grocer (Master of the Grocers' Company 1657, died 1670), whose premises at the Nun's Head had been so inter-mixed with those of Henshawe the broderer, stubbornly liked what he had had and discussion with him involved more than one appointment with the wardens, standing about in the ruins. Henshawe soon decided to surrender, 'to avoid differences'. In December 1667, 'Mr Foster's late house ... having lain intermixed with other rooms of the houses adjoining', he was offered one or two parcels of ground 'to build upon upright' which he refused to take, 'or anything but the same proportion & quantity of ground he had before'. (There had been Fosters on that ground for a long time; one, according to a deed of 1474, Dame Agnes Foster, may have been the widow of a Fishmonger Lord Mayor; and Isaac's first wife had the same surname as the fourteenth-century builder of the original great house there, Simon (de) Morden.) So the case went before one of the Fire Courts set up to settle such differences: this one, doubtless complicated by Foster's having lent the company £500 just after the Fire, was eventually settled in the company's favour and at the end of 1668 Foster took his compensation for the unexpired lease and went elsewhere.[10] His case perfectly illustrates two forces with which the Fire Courts had to deal: on the one hand, medieval contentment with a form of high-density interpenetrating urban sprawl; on the other a preference more characteristic of the Renaissance, for 'building upright' in self-contained blocks. The legal tissue that sustained the old irrational intermixed buildings was not wiped out. However, while the symmetrical avenue-plans devised by Wren and others were too unnatural to impose on a community unable to function at all until its houses and work-places were rebuilt, the more enlightened owners of interlocking leaseholds who were able to control the intermixed parties saw to it that a certain amount of disentangling was done.

If the old Pepper Querne ground had not been under lease to the Fishmongers'
Prime Warden in 1666, and if a more difficult tenant had flounced off, probably
the old strip tunnelling down through the cellar ruins to the little wharf at the
upstream end of the company's wharf would simply have been absorbed into the
Hall site and all signs of its previous existence erased, with due regard for neighbourly rights to light. Instead there was a compromise, allowing Trattle to build
three houses, the Rose, the Crown, and the Star (later Nos 110, 111 and 112
Upper Thames Street) west of the new Hall gate, a further lease giving him the
old riverward strip behind the westernmost house, over and along which the new
Hall structure was about to be fitted. East of the new Hall gate, two new houses
(later Nos 113–14 Upper Thames Street) were built approximately on the ground
Henshawe and Foster had had – one built partly over the Hall gate – and a third,
easternmost house (later No. 115 Upper Thames Street) was built at the street
end of the old Flower de Luce site, with its alley moved to become a stableyard
entry. Leases for these three new houses were granted to John Warren, carpenter,
in 1670.[11] With the monetary payments made or promised on the signing of these
brave new building agreements there remained a medieval stipulation : the lessee
to deliver 'a good fatt bucke in the season thereof uppon eight dayes notice', or £6
in lieu. The 1668 election dinner consisted largely of venison provided by Trattle,
'promised on taking his lease'. The Fire that destroyed the medieval City left
some medieval habits behind.

The neighbour west of the Hall and Trattle's houses, not a company tenant,
was from about 1655 Samuel Lamott, a merchant and friend of Robert Hooke
the architect and scientist who was one of the City Surveyors under the Rebuilding
Act. At first Lamott was in no hurry to rebuild there, and asked only to remove his
own bricks that had fallen on the Hall ground during and after the Fire, which
he was allowed to do in the presence of the Prime Warden. Subsequently
there were to be party-wall and ancient-lights arrangements with him when his
buildings were keyed into Trattle's and the Hall's interlocking back premises. (On
his ground, acquired by the company some two centuries later, were to stand the
Victorian premises of the Old Shades and No. 109 Upper Thames Street.)[12]

At the Hall site in 1667, the intransigence of tenants was only one reason for
delay. In April a committee of wardens had hopefully laid all the groundwork
for the court orders required to start things rolling that summer, but while the
court of June 6 was asking Jerman to 'consider of a modell for rebuilding', the
City began to realize that Dutch warships were indeed heading for the Thames.
On the 11th Pepys heard 'the beating-up of drums this night for the train-bands,
upon pain of death to appear in arms tomorrow morning'. The trained bands were
the City militia, in which some members of this company's court acted as part-
time officers. On the 12th came news of the Dutch raid on Chatham Navy Yard,
on the 13th Pepys sent his gold to be buried in the country and made his will.
The Dutch ships retired but London remained conscious of them, both for their
threat of invasion and for their actual interference with coastal and foreign trade
in, for instance, coal, cheese, wine, and fish. And so in 1667 the ruins of the City,
where only a few tenants had dusted off their old cellar walls to be measured for

new leases, lay mostly open still. In late March a few main streets were already 'marked out with piles drove into the ground', but lesser streets took much longer to be set out, with arbitration of privately surrendered strips to widen them. In July the company ordered Jerman to value any company ground so staked; but he was still being implored to do it in December with the company beadle to help him; a surviving plan of Porter's Quay (perhaps one he had drawn before the Fire) is marked for additions to Thames Street.[13]

Meanwhile, no building was done at the Hall in 1667 and only scatteringly elsewhere in the City. There did come up quickly, like brave mushrooms here and there, houses 'let out to Alehouse-keepers and Victuallers to entertain workmen imployed about the city' – that is, builders' workmen (just as, during the great Victorian-suburb goldrush, the first structure in each grassy staked-out hopeful development was apt to be a public-house, to feed and hearten the builders and give them an address, where they could be found and dealt with). One of these prompt rebuilders in Thames Street (north side, west of the Hall, opposite the lanes to Old Swan Stairs, in St Martin Orgar parish) was a company tenant, Pepys' young friend Miles Michell, or Michael Mitchell, keeper of a 'strong-water house' whose wife Pepy admired (20 Jan. 1667, 'and they showed me their house which, poor people, they have built'), a house probably only partly finished in January since Mitchell's new lease from the Fishmongers' Company was dated from September.[14] And John Sawyer, keeper of the Pope's Head tavern off Cornhill before the Fire, who sat on the court of the Fishmongers' Company from early 1667, immediately after the Fire set up another Pope's Head in St Helen's off Bishopsgate Street, where the court held its election dinner in June 1668, going in gowned procession from Bedlam. By October of that year, they met on Lord Mayor's Day at the rebuilt tavern on his old site and held a court there.

The ruins were lonely. Pepys went home with his sword drawn, when he could find a hackney coachman willing to go that way. And after their coach backed into an open cellar the Navy Board preferred to go 'round by London Wall for fear of cellars' after dark. In daytime the ill-defined dusty track that remained of Thames Street made 'a most dirty walk to Old Swan', where the public landing-stairs, not yet repaired, were still in use. Bridge Ward was less lonesome than most, with its traffic from the Bridge, its taverns, its stream of walkers to and from the boats at Old Swan, and its principal ruin inhabited by that hardy character the company beadle in his shed guarding the 'great vault', supervising the landing of timber, and busily weeding out lead and iron from the rubble. Payments to ward constables by the company were only begun in the following year.

Towards the end of 1667, probably well aware of the impending scarcity of building craftsmen, and looking ahead to the spring, the court ordered 'that Mr Edward Jerman do make an agreement with the Bricklayer & Carpenter for their workmanship in building or as much as the Company shall appoint to be built at Fishmongers Hall', the company finding materials and scaffolding, 'and that hee drawe up Articles for the same' and agree also with 'the Lyme man to deliver in Lyme' for mortar – arrangements implying that a design had been made.[15] Until the spring of 1668 the new building remained a project on parchment and in the wardens' minds, along with considerable doubt as to how much of it could be built.

CHAPTER 8

Rebuilding, 1668-9, 1669-71

THE NEW HALL was to bear no outer resemblance whatever to the old Hall, and not only because the site was bigger. The seventeenth century was a period of change. The company's riverside block of Henry VIII's time could have been built in Henry VI's time so far as its outward appearance went, so far as we know it. But something happened to the Englishman's idea of architecture during the time of James I, so that a wholesale rebuilding of London in his grandson's time could not possibly be the same as a rebuilding of London after a great fire in, say, 1566. The generation of Londoners that grew up before the Fire knew Inigo Jones's buildings in Whitehall and at Greenwich, his new 'piazza' houses for Covent Garden, and his plainer terrace houses for Lord Maltravers' Lothbury development. Some men in the city were aware of the courtly country houses of Roger Pratt and more were aware of the clever country houses of Peter Mills. The Fire of London was no Hadrian's Wall between an old medievalism and a new classicism. The flames cleared ground that was ready for clearance.

The new Fishmongers' Hall was to have two main storeys, with garrets and basements, on four sides of a courtyard approached by a long passage from Thames Street and separated from the street by six tenants' houses. At the entrance to the courtyard, an open portico was to penetrate the ground floor of the north range and link the courtroom on the east with the Clerk's office on the west. The east range with parlour and chamber was to link the courtroom with the head-table end of the great hall; the west range behind the Clerk's parlour was to contain kitchens linked to the service end of the great hall; and the south side of the courtyard was to consist mainly of the great hall itself, facing the river – the 'back front', it was often called. The north, east, and west ranges were begun first.

Early in March 1668, with 'a draught here produced by Mr Jerman of a parlour & some roomes' in hand, the building committee met at the site to oversee the staking-out of the ground. All we have now is an unsigned plan (Pl. 5a) drawn on vellum in black ink with slight tinting – a plan that includes a great hall 60 by 30 feet or thereabouts. This seems to be the hopeful 'modell' ordered in June 1667. It may be the only drawing left in London that can be firmly attributed to Jerman.[1] Some of its measurements are fairly inexact, being taken before the

The notes for Chapter 8 are on pp. 190-1.

rubble was cleared away (five feet too many drawn for the waterside frontage, hardly cleared at all before 1669): staking-out must have become progressively more exact as ruins were removed. A 'parlour & some roomes' sounds as if expectations had become more modest by March 1668, but a decision in July to have a larger hall seems to refer back to an earlier plan with a great hall. Certain arrangements drawn on the plan will have been altered on the ground: the drawing shows wings projecting toward the river, one containing a courtroom to preserve the court's old view of the Thames, the other labelled 'tenement to the Thames', or rentable space perpetuating the old Pepper Querne's wharfside sheds. The riverside ground labelled 'garden to the key' was drawn firmly enclosed at both ends, ignoring any notion of a public Thames Quay; though not made law until 1670, a public quay was forecast in the King's first proclamation after the Fire, and the first Rebuilding Act forbade building within forty feet of the water between February 1667 and March 1669.[2] But the Fishmongers' Company was used to its old river frontage near the water and protected at both ends: before the Fire, common resort along Fishmongers' Wharf was unthinkable. Yet the Fire will have shaken this resolve, in that fire prevention was one argument for an open quay. Jerman was certainly aware of the forty-foot clause of 1667 and so, presumably, were his employers. But all along, while he was surveyor to both City and company, he was apparently leaving room here for a river frontage with its east end less than fifteen feet from the water. (The irregular shoreline inherited from the ancient wharves behind Stockfishmongers Row meant that only part of the new Hall front would break the forty-foot rule.) In proceeding with their plan, from which the siting of the riverside block had to follow, the wardens must have counted on mitigating circumstances or changing official views, so that the company could resume its ancient relationship with the Thames, if not its exclusive right to the wharf. The special dispensation they were to receive in the matter bore them out.

Between March and July 1668, while clearing of ruins began, it was apparently realized that the original plan for a courtroom on the river-front, too far from the Clerk's office, would not suit. Levels were worked out and lettable space relegated to the basement at riverside ground level. The principal rooms were to be a few steps above Thames Street ground level, which became a first floor at the riverside. A planned long gallery flanking the parlour on that floor was omitted and subsequently provided upstairs, over courtroom and portico in the north range. (The placing of upper rooms has to be inferred from references in minutebooks, as no plan survives for them.) In July it was decided to increase dimensions for a future great hall from the 60×30 feet of the first plan to 66×33 feet. By then the idea of wings projecting at right angles from the south front will have been given up (Tyttenhanger in Hertfordshire – of 1654, apparently by Peter Mills – shows what such a front might have looked like). The south range facing the river – its dimensions conditioned by the kitchen and parlour ranges flanking the courtyard behind it – was to be a showpiece block, resembling a quite separate building externally. It was the last part to be built; the ground for it was not even all cleared until three months after Jerman was dead. Housing the Clerk and the court's deliberations, nearer the street entrance, had priority.

The basic layout was settled in the drawing of 1667 (Pl. 5a). The route via long entry, portico, and courtyard to the great hall entered a screens passage leading to the main door on to the river, providing a long view and furious draughts if all gates and doors were open at once. The added ground from the Nun's Head and Flower de Luce sites meant that the great hall could lie alongside the river, with the dais for the head table on the site of Stockfishmongers' Hall. Yet this new position for the great hall, parallel to the street and lying at the rear of the courtyard, was a quite conventional one, often found in the City where there was space for it, and the position of parlour and kitchens followed from it, even though they were built first. The triple-arched 'porticoe', later also called piazza or loggia, had an arcade on Ionic columns, reminiscent of the Royal Exchange walks Jerman was rebuilding, although an arcaded loggia on the opposite side of a courtyard from the hall was a familiar feature of large Jacobean houses. We can suppose it was an arcade, only from a much later remark by the company surveyor in 1820,[3] rather than the straight lintel on columns of the portico (now filled in) at Apothecaries' Hall.

Later side views give an idea of the dual character of the post-Fire Hall. Reading one of these (Fig. VI) from the right at Thames Street to the left at the river, first there was the tenant's house and shop with the Hall's stableyard behind, then the courtroom and parlour range with multiple gables, then the riverside block with hipped roof. In those two rooflines, actually formed within a year or so of one another, the early seventeenth century and the late seventeenth century collide. Yet the window-system of the two main floors throughout was decided, within a few inches, from the start. How much the character of the riverside block was settled in the spring of 1668 with Edward Jerman, how much in the spring of 1669 with Thomas Lock, advised by some more qualified person, and what Edward Peirce contributed in 1670, remain to be seen.

In the spring of 1668 the crane was made on the wharf: small payments to Bedford the mason probably for the base, £75 to Lock the carpenter for the rest of it, and £20 to a ropeseller for ropes for it – doubtless a cumbersome affair in its timber housing, like those in Hollar's long view on Three Cranes Wharf upstream. In June a William Coles was paid £20 on account for clearing rubbish and digging foundations, and eventually there was a final undated payment to him of £65 more 'in full for pulling down walls, screening rubbish & digging the foundations'. Coles was still busy on part of the site in January 1669 when the court urged him to 'go on with his work as speedily as he can', that is, on the remains of the old riverside block 'with the Arches [cellar vaults] to be forthwith pulled down'. And the beadle's shed was to be removed by the end of February. These brief references are all we hear about foundations for these buildings, until discoveries of uneven layers of rubble in 1752. Those discoveries were to reveal that the foundations of 1668–9 under the cellar pavement consisted of a three-foot layer of 'made Ground partly of Rubbish [debris from the Fire] & partly of

Rubble and Chalkstones', apparently packed down over existing timber piles (mentioned in 1642). No payments were made after the Fire for pulling old piles or driving new ones except for the wharf. When Thames Street was raised three feet after the Fire, to lessen the incline for carthorses struggling up to Eastcheap with heavy loads, the wharves were raised too; eighteenth-century views suggest that Fishmongers' Wharf was by then higher than the cellar floors behind it (Pl. 6 at left). Payments to masons and bricklayers in 1668 were not itemized. After Coles dug down to the piles, Thomas Bedford with his bridge-mason's training probably stuffed the chalkstones in, as was done over the centuries to the starlings at the Bridge, and everyone hoped for the best.[4] A reference in 1752 to 'the brickwork of the foundation' meant the footings, or widened brick courses at the base of each wall resting on the made ground. That the walls resting on these footings contained structural timber as well as brickwork was to cause all kinds of trouble.

A hopeful order was given on 20 July 1668 that the first range should be roofed in 'before October 20 next' – not far off if 'next year' were meant. The carcase, or roofed but unfinished shell, of the building on three sides of the courtyard was erected between July 1668 and November 1669; to contain, clockwise from west to east, kitchens with beadles' quarters above, Clerk's house and office, portico and courtroom with long gallery above, and great parlour with great chamber above. The carcase of the riverside block, closing the courtyard south of these, was erected between June 1669 and late 1670.[5] Throughout there were the two main storeys, except for the single great storey of the dining hall, and under all were cellars, the northernmost ones entirely underground, for there was still a marked slope from street to river. The principal building-period here, 1668–71 including interior work, coincided with the first wave of building in the City after the Fire, that of the more indomitable businesses and private houses, and certain determined institutions. The first snapping-up of craftsmen and materials came then, the rebuilding of churches later: 'I hope a few years will rid away much of the private worke of the town, and then handes and materials will be cheaper', said Wren in 1668 to the Dean of St Paul's (begun 1675).

Work on the Hall got under way with the purchase of 200,000 bricks and an agreement with Abraham Holmes to serve lime for mortar. Scaffolding was bought (apparently of lesser woods not grown at Bray) and carefully itemized in the court minutes as 2000 deals (planks), 20 standards (poles), 100 putlogs (short supports for the planks), 60 ledgers (supports for the putlogs), with a payment for basseropes (ropes of bast fibre) for lashing them together – all pre-Fire terms. Scaffolding, except for some interior work such as plastering, was the master carpenter's responsibility. The earliest stages of the work in 1668 seem to have been the joint responsibility of Lock and of Thomas Jones the master bricklayer, successor to John Tanner who as City Bricklayer was busy elsewhere. No early agreement with the mason seems to have been thought necessary and the first masons' bill mentioned in November may have been small, whereas the bricklayer was being paid money on account in July. The basement 'arched vaults', a series

of tunnel vaults, will have been of brick; there was also a 'great cellar', divided in
1719 into two more 'arched vaults'. The basement was about eleven feet high
inside from pavement to crown of vault, though some cellar pavements were raised
periodically after serious flooding when, in the old immemorial way, the tide
backed up the drains. The great cellar and five vaults, from 1719 seven vaults,
were for letting. An eighteenth-century plan of the cellars[6] shows a series of smaller
cellars or sheds along the west side, outside the main west wall supporting the
kitchens, and representing the Pepper Querne strip running down to a quayside
warehouse under the main riverside building, later let as a coachhouse, the series
of sheds sloping uphill behind it as stables, overlooked by the Hall kitchen's and
Clerk's windows.

Externally, the entire Hall appeared to be a brick building. Bills paid for brickwork from 1668 to 1672, including the workmanship of Thomas Jones and his
men, bricks bought separately and bricks provided by him (some from Rainham
in Kent), with lime and sand for mortar, came to about £2655. Thomas Lock,
for carpentry work and materials during 1668-71 (after deducting £333 he later
paid the company for timber from Bray) was paid about £3260. That sum was
for more than roofs, floors, partitions, and staircases: there was more timberwork
than met the eye. In 1751, a settlement of the wall between courtroom and parlour revealed 'the ground plate, a large piece of timber, decayed and rotten . . .
not sufficient to bear the weight depending upon it' – the ground plate being the
sill or lowest horizontal member of a timber frame. In 1753, the north wall of
the great hall (riverside range) adjoining the staircase compartment (eastern
range) was found to stand upon 'lintels & posts of timber' unable to support it.
In 1762, 'the upright post . . . intended to support the north-west corner of the
roof' of the riverside range 'had sunk near 6 inches & the brace framed into the
post [was] in immediate danger of falling'.[7] That is, the brickwork was the fireproof fashionable skin for a traditional timber skeleton. Now, the Act of 1667
for rebuilding the City of London provided that the *outside* of every building
was to be of brick or stone, excepting only doorcases, window-frames, and certain
parts of shopfronts. While laying down the thickness of outer walls and other
matters, the Act of 1667 did not forbid structural timberwork behind the brick
face. A generation later, the dangers of decay in some situations were realized
and the Building Act of 1707 provided, among other things, that no brickwork
in any new front, party or partition wall was to rest on timberwork, but that did
not affect existing buildings.[8] And there had been little time for the timber brought
from Bray to be properly seasoned before use.

Masons were still necessary. From the payment of £20 on account to them in
January 1669 we learn that Thomas Bedford had taken a younger man as partner
for this job, Edward Peirce, who was to become well known as a sculptor in both
wood and stone.[9] From what we know of the ranges begun in 1668, the masons'
work probably included the columns of the portico, some window-dressings, and
paving, with a more elaborate set of stone dressings to come on the final range
begun in 1669. During 1668–72 the partners Bedford and Peirce were paid about

£1345, an unspecified part of which included materials, and £594 worth of stone was also bought, with £192 more to Peirce alone for carving, indoors and out (some of this in wood) during 1670–2, or a total of about £2131 for masonry and carving. More can be said about individual craftsmen and women, but first to continue summarizing the expenditure (in sums given to the nearest pound).

The next most expensive item was a total of about £1163 for joinery, the wainscotting or panelling of interior walls. The joiner at first was John Greenough alone, afterward in partnership with John Syms or Symmes, and after that the latter alone, supplying their own inch-thick oak. A total of about £976 was paid for leadwork (£277 for labour, £699 for material), much of it covering the hip roof of the riverside block; the master plumber in charge was Elizabeth Heard, widow of the plumber who had melted down the old lead in 1666. The chief supplier of lead (paid £574 in c.1671) was Sir Thomas Bludworth, now remembered as the shilly-shallying Lord Mayor at the time of the Fire.[10] Cheaper materials roofed the rear ranges, £59 worth of tiles covering part of these. For roofs visible from the courtyard, slates were apparently preferred to harmonize with the leaden hue of the great hall's hipped roof: John Jay, slater, charging 36s. per 100 square foot for slates and workmanship, was paid £66. Plastering, mainly of ceilings, by John Grove (whether senior or junior not said) came to about £666. Ironwork by Henry Brookes and ironmongery supplied by Henry Maynard totalled about £389. Glazing work and materials from John Runwell and then Emanuell Runwell, came to about £148, also £25 for painted-glass coats of arms by a Mr Dutton for the east windows of the great hall (behind the head table) and £10 for 'cases of French glass' for the parlour's five windows (on the courtyard) and the courtroom's three (two on the alley to the east and one on the stableyard to the north). And Margaret Peirce 'widow, the painter' received about £146 for unspecified painting work, which may have included much of the wainscot inside as well as the wooden eaves cornice outside on three sides of the riverside block, though no decorative painting by her, or anyone else, is mentioned. In addition to the above payments, almost £600 was disbursed for a series of small bills by John Golding, who from October 1669 for about two years acted as a sort of clerk of the works on the building site; he was paid £40 in 1670 and £50 in 1671 for his services. In sum, over the six years 1666–72 (including delayed settlements with Lock and Grove, but excluding furnishings and other embellishments) the new Hall cost just under £13,000 (or about £130,000 in terms of, say, 1972).

After Jerman died in November 1668, no one person kept track of the works at the Hall at first, although the building committee promised to go down there periodically to see how the workmen got on 'and to quicken them therein'. Thomas Lock as the most deeply involved master craftsman – though not the most senior in years, still with something of the carpenter's old ascendancy – was busy elsewhere as well, being probably the 'Mr Locke' appointed in Jerman's place at Apothecaries' Hall. Until the autumn of 1669 the Fishmongers were tentatively disposed, *faute de mieux*, to regard Lock as Jerman's successor for them

too. Although a generation younger than Jerman, Lock's recent working experience on Horseheath Hall, in Cambridgeshire near the Suffolk-Essex borders,
must have enhanced his reputation since his first small carpentry jobs for the
company as its cornkeeper's son in the decade before the Great Fire. In fact, a
certain William Allington, who from about 1666 sat on the court of the Fishmongers' Company and who had been listed in its apprenticeship records as son
of a Giles Allington of Bury St Edmunds, gent., may have been some relation to
William Lord Allington who built Horseheath, a few miles from Bury, for the
names William and Giles seem to have predominated in both families. The
company's William Allington, however, seldom attended court meetings (until
becoming Prime Warden in 1674). The recent presence in the City of Sir Roger
Pratt the architect of Horseheath (as a Royal Commissioner for rebuilding the
City until 1668) could have set up some esteem for Lock's work on the City grapevine, except that the only references to Lock in Pratt's notebooks concern his
mistakes and his overcharging.[11] Lock probably lacked that bone-deep sense of his
craft that Jerman inherited. (For what it may be worth, compare the reports from
Jerman and Lock, Fig. III and IV between pp. viii–ix.)

In 1669 both site and design for the Fishmongers' showpiece block were officially settled and its walls rose partway. Until October, Lock was referred to in
the minutebooks as 'the Surveyor'. Although he continued thereafter in charge
of carpentry on the Hall for the time being – the company could hardly help this
with the prevailing scarcity of craftsmen – his diligence seems to have worn off
after October, when an agreement was made for a 71-year company lease to be
granted to him, for two house-sites on the old White Lyon site so advanta-
geously placed near the Bridge. Fifty years later the neighbours were still re-
peating that he built his two houses there 'with the Chips that he pickt up at the
Hall'.[12] The period of Lock's most respectful attention to the Hall, in the spring
of 1669, will have included the 'surveying & drawing draughts for the same
building' later mentioned in his list of charges.[13] A crucial drawing must have
been prepared in April/May 1669. In April arrangements for the riverside block
began with an order 'that the Bricklayer & Carpenter & Mason do forthwith bring
proposals of the prices for their several works at Fishmongers Hall to Mr. Warden
Owen & to treat & agree with the Committee for the same', an order that assumes
some specific design on which treaty could be based, but no such meeting took
place until June. And 'the measure of the foundations' was to be 'forthwith
entered at Guildhall', which led to an entry in the City Chamberlain's posting-
book for receipts of moneys paid for staking out foundations in the ruins of the
City: '1669 May 11 Fishmongers, there Hall' [sic].[14] Either Peter Mills or John
Oliver, the City Surveyors who dealt with the measuring of sites, will then have
pointed out that part of its frontage would contravene the still-pending Thames
Quay legislation. On May 25 Lock informed the company's court that permission
for the Hall to 'remain on the same ground whereon it is now situate' would be
forthcoming if the wardens attended on Dr Christopher Wren, newly appointed
Surveyor General of the King's Works, from whom 'the King's pleasure [was] to

be had in writing'; in other words, Lock had already shown a drawing to someone – or had a drawing improved by someone – and obtained an unofficial verbal promise, possibly from Wren himself, more likely from Robert Hooke, who came to be regarded as Wren's deputy. The company's counterpart (Fig. V) of Wren's 'Certificate to the Lord Maior concerning this Companyes building of their Hall' – for which the Prime Warden paid 'to Doctor Wren . . . tenne pieces of Gold' – reads as follows :

> Whereas the Company of Fishmongers were represented to have built their Hall Irregularly and within the prescribed distance of the River of Thames contrary to his Maties late letter to the Citty in that behalfe These are therefore to Certify the Right Honoble Sir William Turner Knt Lord Maior of the Citty of London That a Draught of the said Buildings and the wharffe adioyning haveing beene represented to his Matye by mee his Matyes Surveyor Generall of his Matyes workes according to his Matyes direction in his said Letter His Matye was Graciously pleased to be satisfied with the Necessity of Building the said Hall in such manner & forme as was represented to his Matye in the said Draught By reason of the unequall Lyne of the Wharffe or Key in that place and the necessity of bringing the Water to the Mills. Given under my hand & Seale this 27th day of May 1669
>
> Chr Wren[15]

In other words, for the east half of the frontage at least, a Thames Quay full forty feet wide would be impracticable anyway, so close to London Bridge and the waterworks at the northernmost bridge-arch. The bay receding from Hall to Bridge (in contrast to the shore wharfed-out by medieval merchants at and upstream from the Hall) could accommodate a quay only of irregular width though still to be a public way. The completed Hall, it was appreciated, was to stand on a uniquely prominent spot, even more so than the old Hall had done on its smaller site. It is unlikely that any actual walls had then arisen for the riverside block, only that the east and west ranges were ready to be keyed into it.

We gather from this certificate that the drawing 'represented' (presented and reported on) by Wren to the King included not only a site-plan but an elevation for the intended river-front. Most unfortunately 'the said Draught' does not exist in the Public Record Office or Corporation of London Record Office today – though it might lie unrecognized somewhere – but the intention it conveyed was of sufficient quality for Charles II and his Surveyor-General to allow the requested exemption : it suited their idea of a new City of London. Of any other drawings by Lock for comparison, we have only certain elementary house-plans that might be from his hand,[16] and the supposition that he completed Jerman's design for Apothecaries' Hall. For the Fishmongers, what did he have to go on, besides Jerman's 'modell' of 1667?

Jerman left no surviving known buildings designed and completed wholly under his supervision. A fragmentary frontispiece from Mercers' Hall, now incorporated in Swanage Town Hall, if part of his original design, suggests a taste for

congested detail in the City artisan-classical tradition. Engravings of the completed Royal Exchange, if they represent Jerman's intentions, suggest ability to
master a large work with plenty of precedent to go by. A new form of free-
standing hip-roofed house or group of houses had begun to enter the City landscape when Jerman and the wardens were young, not only in Inigo Jones's designs
for the rebuilding of Lothbury and other sites, but in Nicholas Stone's rebuilding
of Goldsmiths' Hall in 1635–8 on which Jones was consulted.[17] Jerman will also
have been aware of country houses designed by his City contemporary and
colleague Peter Mills during and after the Commonwealth.[18] But the nearer and
more familiar building both to Jerman and to his clients Trattle, Jekyll, Owen and
the rest, was indeed Goldsmiths' Hall which all of them could remember being
built as something rather modern. Edward Jerman's father Anthony and brother
Hugh had worked on it and Edward in 1668 was supervising its repair, for it
survived the Fire. There had been an old friendship between the two companies.
Some adaptation of the Goldsmiths' 110-foot Foster Lane front, or else the simpler
north front, to the Fishmongers' 123-foot river front may well have been agreed
among the latter's wardens before Jerman died. Certain features of the Goldsmiths' conventional plan were adopted, principally the entrance/courtyard/great
hall relationship, and the first idea may have been to surround the Fishmongers'
open quadrangle with hipped roofs as at Foster Lane. Stone's building probably
was the Fishmongers' original model. Therefore, the existence of that standing
example nearby, with the company surveyor specifying vertical dimensions and
staking out horizontal dimensions on the site, provided enough basis for treaty
with master craftsmen without further ado about drawings, beyond those working
details they would draw out for themselves.

   When Lock was called upon to produce a drawing for the King's approval, we
don't know who encouraged him to adapt the above conception to a modernity
he had closely observed at Horseheath. Whether Wren or his deputy Hooke, or
one of the older City men, Mills or Oliver, in unrecorded informal conference
with Lock as the company's representative between the 11th and 25th of May,
indicated by a few lines with a drawing pen what would 'go down' well, we can
only guess. Wren must have been intensely busy in the spring of 1669. Mills
was experienced in town and country, and Oliver was a seasoned surveyor responsible for rebuilding Skinners' Hall and for completing Jerman's design for
Mercer's Hall. But the advisory hand it is tempting to see at Fishmongers' Hall in
May 1669 is that of Robert Hooke, also one of the Surveyors for the rebuilding of
the City, a considerable scientist and soon to be an architect, never of the first
rank but working closely with Wren and as aware of both English and Continental
precedent as Pratt. Hooke's journal, surviving only from 1672 on, seems to mention Lock occasionally in a well-acquainted way (if one could disentangle the
various Locks Hooke knew).[19] That Hooke's hand may have guided Lock's in
redesigning the riverside front remains entirely in the realm of guesswork. No
money was paid to Hooke or anyone else by the company for it. (The ten gold-
pieces paid to Wren were for the official licence.) But Lock didn't care much, and
Hooke was a secretive man.

At any rate, the model Lock knew and was encouraged to adapt was that of Pratt's three great houses of the 1660s: Horseheath in Cambridgeshire, Kingston Lacy in Dorset, and the Lord Chancellor's or Clarendon House in Piccadilly (of which only Kingston Lacy, much altered, survives today).[20] These houses set the pattern of the miscalled 'Wren' or even more miscalled 'Queen Anne' house in England. Such a pattern could be easily grafted on to the concept adapted from the Goldsmiths that Jerman left behind him, because the one was simply a further stage of evolution on from the other. Two main floors of nearly equal height were already prepared for on the other three sides of the quadrangle. The river-front, in red brick like the rest, was now to be nine windows wide in three groups of three, the centre breaking forward and crowned by a pediment, ends and centre emphasised by stone angle quoins, and the central doorway by a carved-stone doorcase (Pl. 6, 7). The great hipped roof, underlined by a carved-wood modillion cornice, was to rise to a large flat on which it was intended to place the balustrade and central lantern so typical of Pratt's houses. But early in 1671, when roof and platform were almost covered with lead, there was concern over the weight of the lead and 'the great height of the building next the Thames, which standeth directly to the south west windes'; and in the interest of safety it was decided that no 'cupolo or lanthorne' or 'parapet of bannisters' should be placed there. (Concern over 'the great occasions for money to carry on the several works' at the Hall probably had something to do with it.) There was indeed more height here proportionately than in Pratt's houses on their semi-basements, for the river-front basement had to be a full ground floor.

Therefore a greater rise of steps to the main south door from the wharf was needed. Here another concession to urban space limitation produced twin lateral flights of steps, since a frontal flight would extend partway across the public wharf. (Morgan's view of 1681 shows that these steps were not added later.)[21] Although a protective wall with a gate to each flight and iron railings beside the steps were soon added, this grand staircase was until 1788 quite visible from the highway of the river. Contemporary Thames views show a certain grandeur in it, and eighteenth-century London historians singled it out for praise.[22] Inigo Jones's curved double staircase-frontispiece to the Queen's House at Greenwich, and other Palladian sets of steps by Jones that no longer exist, provided more elaborate examples of this sort of thing. Before them was that much-engraved subject, the Capitol at Rome, with Michelangelo's great twin set of lateral steps in front of the Senators' Palace. Even to the arched niche in front – though without the complexity of Michelangelo's compound flights or Jones's curving flights – the Fishmongers' stone staircase seems to have had some such baroque source, perhaps via Serlio's engraving of the Capitol or from engravings of Dutch buildings derived from it. The Capitoline and Greenwich designs were sculptural in conception and so, on a much less grand and subtle scale, it was here, linked as the Fishmongers' steps were to the whole centrepiece behind: twin balustraded 'Belconyes' flanking the top landing before the door, doorcase of engaged Ionic columns supporting a broken pediment containing a heraldic cartouche, and more heraldic carving in the main pediment (Pl. 6, 7). The sculptural character here may have accrued in 1670–1 in discussion between wardens and masons, especially Edward Peirce, whose visual inheritance from his painter-father was to continue in his own collecting of books, drawings, and prints. Young Peirce had also been working at Horseheath Hall. Everything we know of his subsequent career as a sculptor implies greater sophistication than we can attribute either to Bedford, his partner on the Hall masonry contract, or to Lock. The type of doorcase, probably adapted from Stone's entrance to Goldsmiths' Hall, was part of the Jones repertoire that carvers went on using. The armorial carving in the main pediment was characteristic of Pratt's houses, for example the six-foot shield at Horeseath, carved by Peirce. The alternating curved and angular window-pediments, ever since the great impression made by the Banqueting House in Whitehall, had become a common 'artisan-mannerist' device in London, though not used by Pratt. The stone aprons under the windows could have come from Horseheath or from Mills's Thorpe Hall, while the vertical overlapping of these window-dressings linking upper to lower windows was a French device that Mills had used, instead of the horizontal emphasis of storey-courses that helped to give Pratt's houses their landed look. Although the Fishmongers' front had no artisan-mannerist scrolls or circular windows, it was 'busier' than a Pratt front, reflecting a City taste that had, however, matured since the Goldsmiths' Hall of a generation before (and not all City taste had so matured). The professional finish of this front may be partly due to Peirce. Façade-analysis is rewarding in the case of a building that represented more than itself : the civic character of the Capitoline reference suited a livery hall on the City's front doorstep.

Inside, medievalism lingered. More than half of this apparently two-storey block consisted of the single-storey great hall, containing five out of nine double tiers of windows, including the entrance bay, on the south front and the three double tiers on the east, plus some windows on the courtyard. It was a medievalism tempered with modernism : how this block did straddle a watershed between two ages. Entirely surrounding the interior of the great hall at upper-floor level was a gallery supported on brackets or cantilevers, the music gallery at the west end extended all round, more than necessary for upstairs circulation between great chamber wing and upper service wing : 'the gallery round this hall.' (Written evidence, descriptions and accounts, are all we have for it). We know from Pratt's notebooks that there was such a cantilevered gallery all round the hall at Horseheath : 'ye Pergolo rownde ye Hall', 'ye Modiglions [cantilevers] for ye Pergolo in ye Hall', 'Balusters &c for ye Pergolo of ye Hall', and strongly supported girders (beams) 'espetially when ye greate modiglions of ye hall are boorne up.'[23] And of course what Pratt had had in mind were Inigo Jones's two-storey, galleried halls for Whitehall and Greenwich. Lock was applying something he had done before. But the Fishmongers' great hall was a great mixture. For some sort of screen under the music gallery did exist : in June 1671 the passage 'behind the skrene' was to be coved and plastered as quickly as possible. Hatton's *New View of London* (1708) describing the Hall mentions 'a Screen of the Composit Order with a Golden Busto under the Pediment'. Probably it was a fairly open

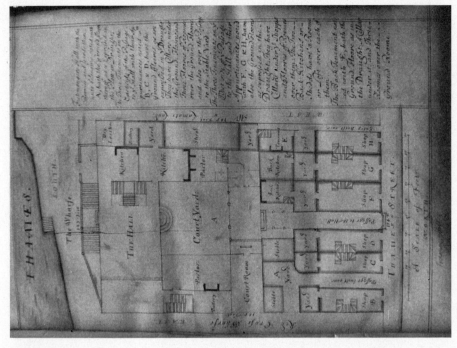

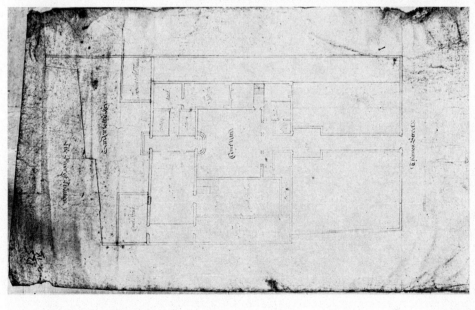

Pl. 5 The post-Fire Hall. South (river) at top. (*a*) Early plan probably by Edward Jerman 1667, not as built (pp. 61,65). Pen and wash on vellum, *c.* 27″ × 15½″. Fishmongers' Company collection, Guildhall Library. (*b*) Plan-of-record by William Leybourne, 1686 (pl 87)' Pen and wash on vellum, 18½″ × 13½″. Planbook at Fishmongers' Hall.

FISHMONGERS HALL
near
London Bridge.

Pl. 6 Hall river-front as built 1669–71, engraved view *c.* 1700, this state unsigned, 'sold by John Bowles opposite to Stocks Market & at Mercers' Hall in Cheapside' (first state probably one dedicated to the Fishmongers' Company by 'B. Lens', probably in honour of Sir Thomas Abney, Lord Mayor 1700–1, some states signed by Sutton Nichols), original view datable by women's headdress and also by young trees planted 1698–1700; water-stairs possibly imaginary (pp. 91, 97). Fishmongers' Company collection.

Pl. 7 Hall river-front as built 1669–71, engraved view of *c.* 1753 or a good deal earlier, this state signed by Sutton Nichols, *delin & sculp.* (a similar state published in 1754 edition of Strype's revised Stow, *Survey of London*), showing tavern entrance at lower right (p. 97). Fishmongers' Company collection.

Pl. 8 William Daniell, view of the City and London Bridge: aquatint engraving, 1804, Guildhall Library (an original sketch, is in Fishmongers' Hall collection). This view shows the old Bridge divested of houses, and the City churches still dominant, including St Michael Crooked Lane just up right from the Hall (p. 123). E. W. Cooke's set of drawings of the rebuilding of the Bridge (Guildhall Art Gallery) show the Hall in more detail than this, but without Daniell's sweeping range of view.

screen (like the four columns at Skinners' Hall): a partition had to be installed before the kitchen door later 'to prevent the stench of the kitchens'. How the colonnade-screen was married to the cantilevered gallery, one cannot be sure. As the plan of 1686 (Pl. 5b) shows no screen at all, it may have been a movable piece of joinery.

Another question is how the great hall was heated at first, having neither open roof nor chimneypiece apparently – probably by a stove in the middle, although an ironmonger was paid twenty shillings in 1673 'for his loss in respect of the great iron grate made to stand in the great hall which was returned to him again'. No outlet from a stove was mentioned. In the end, a register stove, with three fire-screens, was auctioned in 1827. With two tiers of windows on three sides and strong gusts off the river, it must have taken a deal of good drink, soup, beef, gowns and propinquity to withstand winter in that great double cube of a room, 66 by 33 feet and apparently about 33 feet high. With a loft over it, there was no open timber roof as before, but a coved ceiling plastered by John Grove in 1671. The only painting known to have been hung in the great hall, Beechey's portrait of the Earl of St Vincent (during 1806-25), was said to have suffered temporarily from 'its exposure there to the Effects of the damp and the Heat of the Sun' and, doubtless, reflections off the water. As seen from the river after dark on a dinner-night, that great hall must have seemed the heart of warmth.

The hall gallery connected two staircases, one off the east or head-table end of the great hall serving the parlour-chamber wing and one rising from the screens passage to the music gallery at the west end of the great hall. 'The Staircase', Sir John Soane was to tell young architects of his day, 'has justly been considered as the most embarrassing circumstance in the arrangement of the Plan of a building.'[24] Thomas Lock's handling of that essential element early in 1671 was the last straw so far as his employment with this company was concerned: 'setting upp of a stacke of ovall staires from the cellar unto the top of the house . . . contrary to directions & one pair of narrow stairs at the west end of the Hall . . . both which by reason of their unfitness for these places & insufficiency were pulled down again & others more fitt convenient & substantiall built in the room of them.' By then the company had given up expecting any general surveying work on their property from Lock. In May 1670 there had already been 'doubts questions & differences' over his Hall charges after his work there had been 'viewed measured & valued' by an outside man. When trouble arose over the staircases in the spring of 1671, Lock utterly refusing to alter them in any way or even to come and discuss them, the building committee brought in two carpenters to rebuild them, one being William Pope, a warden of the Carpenters' Company at the time.[25] The poor quality of the Clerk's ink in the years just after the Fire has allowed some of the indignation generated by Lock to fade from the minute-books, but enough remains to show how the Fishmongers bore with him until the roof was safely on and most of the floors boarded. At a grand settlement of his accounts in September 1672, justice was tempered with mercy: a substantial sum was deducted from his last bill, but he was allowed to postpone paying his rent arrears as company tenant until his carpentry and surveying bills were actually paid. Finally in 1674 the court ordered 'that Thomas Locke Carpenter by reason of his very ill management of this Companyes affairs in the building of their Hall shall henceforth never be any more employed to do any manner of Carpenters worke for this Company.' The interesting thing about the last row with Lock is the 'ovall' staircase he made for them.

'Ovall' may have been a clerical error for 'circular', though Pratt used the word for a staircase in a circular space.[26] But a carpenter's circular staircase here cannot have been an imitation in wood of any cantilevered stone staircase around the walls of a cylindrical compartment, such as Jones's circular stair adjoining the galleried hall at Greenwich. Assuming that the eastern staircase of the Hall was the one in question, the compartment was rectangular, with two banks of large windows in one wall and doors in the other three walls upstairs and down. So, a free-standing corkscrew staircase twisted round a central newel and touching neither walls nor windows may have been what Lock imposed on them : there is a spectacular example[27] at the top of the house in Peter Mills's Thorpe Hall – quite unsuited for dignified corporate ascent. The staircase as rebuilt between the two main floors apparently rose in two opposing flights, with a 'house of office' off the landing. The east side of these stairs, overlooking a timber yard next door, was wainscotted with deal against the windows as high as 'the rayle & bannister', that is, modifying both east winds and curious glances from outside. The rebuilt staircase was entirely replaced in 1788 and no further description survives; it was probably not unlike but plainer than those still standing in the Skinners', Apothecaries', and Vintners' Halls.

The staircase replacing Lock's at the west end of the great hall seems to have risen centrally between two butteries to a landing from which twin upper flights proceeded at right angles, a T-shaped staircase; the only existing plan, that of 1686, is somewhat offhand about stairs, but this seems to have risen between walls. 'Mr Aggas, Lymner' was paid forty shillings late in 1671 or early in 1672 'for making the prospect on the Staires att the west end of the hall' : perhaps a mythical landscape, or a view of the pre-Fire Hall, or a schematic 'perspective' of the new Hall, presumably painted on the wall of the landing visible from the floor of the dining hall. Robert Aggas (fl. 1656–79) was a theatrical scenery painter at Covent Garden and a landscape painter.[28] His 'prospect' probably disappeared long before the Hall did.

There was a bit of trouble with the plasterer too. Here the company had a craftsman of quality, whether he was John Grove senior (d. 1676) or John Grove junior (d. 1708) who was to succeed his father as Master Plasterer to the King's Works. It was probably the younger man, because at one stage he brought in a fellow-plasterer 'Mr. Toogood' to value his work, Henry Doogood being his partner on many buildings by Wren, at Pembroke and Trinity Colleges in Cambridge before the Fire and in City churches after.[29] During 1670–1, Lipscombe a carpenter who had originally been brought in to value Lock's work and with Pope to rebuild Lock's stairs, was employed as measurer and valuer on the company's behalf of 'divers works' of other crafts at the Hall. Each master artisan brought in outside members of his own craft to measure and value on his own behalf, the company's man submitted his survey, and the building committee awarded the lowest sum the craftsman would take. Lipscombe may have seemed too little the impartial valuer for a young but already eminent plasterer to stomach as company's representative, and Grove's work was subsequently valued by plasterers for both parties. In eventual argument over the bill for his work on the long gallery, Grove took a difference of £50 to law, but the King's Bench awarded him only £4 over the company's offer. Grove's work at the Hall consisted mainly of ceilings, beginning with the Clerk's quarters in December 1669/January 1670. (John Lee himself 'being aged dare not come to dwell therein, the walls & buildings being too lately made', that is, damp from new plaster, and permission was given for Thomas Tanner, who was soon to succeed him as Clerk, to live there instead.) Next the courtoom and parlour were to be 'wainscotted from the topp to the bottome and to have frett worke ceelings'. Grove showed the building committee a 'platt or form' (drawing) of ceiling, frieze and cornice : for these two rooms (measuring about 33 by 19 feet and 47 by 23 feet respectively) his price was £100, over which there was no argument. These were the principal 'status' rooms in the first stage of building. 'Fretwork' has an angular old-fashioned sound, unlike Grove's ovals and circles in Cambridge, yet Pratt, on whose houses Grove worked, used the term and these two ceilings at the Hall were probably as up to date as Grove's other work. For other rooms here he proposed prices by the yard for plain work, rendering work, floating work, whitening and colouring work, and scaffolding; it was over the valuing by the yard that disagreement arose.

The courtroom wainscot will have included more joinery than the parlour, in the seats attached to the panelling and the dwarf partition usual in such seventeenth-century courtrooms. These seats being unupholstered benches with hard backs, there were to be periodic orders for cushions – court meetings could go on for several hours – and in 1720 'pinns for hanging hatts on' were required. The 'sweeping woman' was cleaning courtroom and parlour regularly – that is, they were in use – from August 1670; presumably courts and committees had met in the Clerk's office from January to July, and presumably the entire premises continued to be dusty and noisy until the summer of 1671.

For the great chamber and long gallery upstairs, Lock's men early in 1671 did the 'firring and brackitting' – prepared wooden linings to the brick walls for the joiners to work on. The long gallery was then left unfinished for a year and a half. Oddly enough, the great chamber was given the only separately mentioned chimneypiece in the Hall at this stage, and the only piece of stone-carving Peirce did for them that was separately itemized in the accounts, perhaps because it was an afterthought : for 'the Marble Chymney peece in the great Chamber' he was paid £35.[30] At that price it was no plain bolection-moulded piece, though there is no clue to its appearance, for it was removed either in 1789 or in 1827. It may well have been carved with festoons of seashells, in the manner of the great stone vase Peirce made for Hampton Court (now at Windsor), and as the Fishmongers' parlour chimneypiece of 1741 was to be and still is : to a City stone-carver of 1741 the exuberance of 1671 remained in fashion. Other carvings by Peirce included the royal arms in the main south pediment, placed there to acknowledge the royal permission to build the Hall where it was, and sold off in the auction of building-materials in 1827 as 'ornamental antique shield & arms in front of pediment' in one lot with the south and east fronts' modillioned eaves-cornice (the lot making £6.15.0) : one suspects that the royal shield, like the eaves-cornice, was of painted wood. The company arms in carved stone at the Thames Street entrance, with lively merman and mermaid, and presumably by Peirce or his men, does survive – just – on the, as it were, blind side of today's Hall, to which the Grecian taste of 1833 consigned it. In its day, 1671–1831, this approximately five by six-foot piece in high relief, brightly painted and gilded, surmounted gate-piers ornamented with acanthus leaves. Now cemented and out of reach of all but telescopic cameras, it may deserve a better fate. When the courtyard paving leaked in 1674, Peirce was called in to take care of it, Bedford his partner on that contract being recently dead. By then Peirce had begun work on various City churches, carved his marvellous bust of Wren, and been painted himself by Isaac Fuller. The partnership with Bedford was his first (known) bread-and-butter masonry work after the Fire. Margaret Peirce the painter was apparently his sister-in-law. She subsequently executed or contracted for the execution of decorative painting in a number of City churches. No doubt she or one of her men painted the lively heraldic carving from her brother-in-law's yard for the Thames Street entrance.

The presence of women on the working scene was not then surprising.[31] The widowed Mrs Peirce and Mrs Heard, who held the leadwork contract at the Hall, will have been their husbands' partners all along. This was usual when the firm's countinghouse and the couple's dwelling-house were one and the same; when a craftsman died, his widow could carry on because her name had already appeared on contracts with his – as all during the middle ages wives' and husbands' names appeared together on leases – and already she knew the business and was respected by the journeymen working for them and now for her. During the Hall's large repairs of 1639, the master plumber for work on pipes and roofs had been Anne Barsey (or Bardsey), widow, and during the redecoration of 1660 Isabell King, widow, had looked after the carrying away of rubbish. Even in the next century, out of nine master craftsmen in charge of their own trades for building a beadle's house at the Hall in 1721–2, no fewer than five were widows : plasterer, painter, smith, paviour, and glazier. In the year of 'the '45' Jane Hall, gunsmith, cleaned the company firearms – though there was now no separate room for an 'armoury' as before the Fire. During the large repairs of 1788–91 no women's names appear in the accounts, although Thomas Piper the mason's wife was to carry on for him a few years later. Further up the social scale in the seventeenth century there had been the enforced idleness of Mrs Pepys. By the early nineteenth century, with the drift to the suburbs, family industry as a City way of life was finished. So far as City social life went, the customary presence of wives at this company's biennial election dinners seems to have lapsed during the enforced frugality of the Commonwealth. By 1735, court members were inviting their ladies to a 'diversion on the river' in the company barge, followed by a supper at the Hall, and in the 1740s the upstairs rooms there were called 'the dancing rooms'.

In the summer of 1671, three years after it was begun, the building work at the Hall – though not the paying for it – drew to a close, save for some interior finishing. In August there were thanks to the renter warden, appropriately sur- named Husbands, for his care, pains and attention to expediting matters for divers months past. In October the first dinner was held in the great hall on Lord Mayor's Day, for eighty members of court and livery, and part of the ceremonies included welcoming guests 'to survey the Hall', no doubt to a fanfare from the new music gallery by the usual 'six able Trumpeters' who had just performed in the barge on its way to and from Westminster.[32] The first Lord Mayor's show since the Fire had been celebrated in the City that day with the old pomp. Many derelict spaces still lay about, but beyond the Bridge the Custom House was finished that year and a new church of St Magnus was begun at the Bridgefoot. St Michael's in the company's own parish had to wait another thirteen years, its Fishmongers' Chapel beside Crooked Lane indistinguishable from other rubble. Between Pudding Lane and Fish Street Hill in 1671, on the former St. Margaret's churchyard adjoining the company's Star Inn property and the site of the bakery that sparked the Great Fire, the commemorative Monument was begun. Bridge Ward, like the rest of the City, was partly still a neighbourhood of aspiring foundations.

CHAPTER 9

From Lodgers to Affluence

BEFORE THE Mansion House was built in the middle of the eighteenth century, a Lord Mayor had to do his entertaining at home, or else move into some available livery hall. Sheriffs still borrow livery companies' state rooms for certain functions today. During the half-century after Fishmongers' Hall was finished, it was either let or lent partly furnished for a private residence almost annually and all year long in this way, the lending without charge being only to members of this company. Many halls were not rebuilt so promptly or so spaciously. The possibilities of revenue in this situation may have been one reason for making a larger Hall; certainly no resident guests could have been accommodated in the old Hall. The advantages – both to the company's own mayors or sheriffs who could count on a fine place in which to shine, and the company's coffers in taking rent from the others – at first seemed to outweigh the disadvantages (dislocation of the company's own affairs, repairs and nuisance in the annual changeover of lodgers attended by trains of servants). Besides the reception rooms, there was a set of smaller rooms for family life – originally intended for the two company beadles and their families – over the kitchens in the west end of the riverside block and the wing behind it. But it was soon realized that the beadles' children would either be running through the main courtyard or leaving the cellar door to the public quay unlocked, and that in any case each beadle's family was too large for the space. On the other hand, for an elderly couple with grown children living elsewhere, and whose servants could also inhabit garrets in the parlour wing, the rooms beyond the music gallery formed a suitable apartment. One of the larger rooms overlooking the courtyard became a private dining room and a smaller one overlooking the river a lady's chamber. Apparently these were unfurnished and at first not even wainscotted, so that tenants had to bring their own wall-hangings, against the cold.[1]

It all began pleasantly enough in the autumn of 1671 when the Prime Warden, Alderman Jonathan Dawes (knighted in October), was granted the use of the new Hall for 'keeping his Shrievalty', for which he said his gratitude was 'as greate as if they had given him the whole building'. Of Dawes it was said at the time that he had 'a great share of love and esteeme from people of all sorts', and with him there was no need for demarcation lines to preserve some use of the building

The notes for Chapter 9 are on pp. 191–3.

to the company. He died the following April, and when Lady Dawes moved away she left behind her for the company's use three dozen chairs and twelve gilded 'branches', or sconces, for candles in the great parlour, ten tin-plated branches in the great chamber, and two iron firebacks: one advantage in lodgers was that they sometimes left useful things behind. The company had bought very little furniture since the Fire: boards and trestles may have been used for dinner tables, as the accounts only mention green baize bought for 'carpets' to cover them when not in use. Except for painted tiles set into the principal fireplaces, including two 'chimneys' in the long gallery by 1674, little was spent on interior decoration or furnishing until the 1680s.

Revenue being the great need as the last tradesmen's bills for the building were paid, it then seemed wise to seek a lodger not a mayor or sheriff-elect, who would settle down for several years and also take the cellar and 'arched vaults' for goods storage. In September 1672 Nathaniel Herne, merchant, agreed to a lease for five years at £300 a year. Careful covenants were drawn up. He was to have the Hall as a private dwelling only 'and not to suffer the same rooms to be used in any public way for selling wine, coffee or any manner of liquor therein' – that included the basement vaults. The company was to hold four feasts a year as usual, the courtroom and Clerk's office were out of bounds for the tenant at all times, and the long gallery was not to be partitioned off without consent. To all of this Herne willingly 'condiscended' but pointed out that the long gallery was neither ceiled nor wainscotted yet. It was agreed to have this done immediately and forego the fifth year's rent, if he would pay his first year's rent right away. Other 'conveniencyes' requested by Herne and paid for by the company during the next six months included a wainscot partition in the long gallery, a horse trough in the stableyard north of the courtroom, and water pipes to the brewhouse in the basement. But a year after the agreement Herne had still not signed the lease, and his announcement in September 1673 that he was moving out forthwith was followed by months of polite but obstinate argument, in which Herne was backed up by his father-in-law Sir John Frederick, a former Lord Mayor, before the arrangement was terminated. Their objections are not recorded, but the new building must have been cold and damp in winter there by the river, as the old Clerk John Lee had feared, and Herne's wife may have refused to spend another winter there.

When efforts were made to let the western rooms and the storage vaults without the state rooms 'to any able person', none materialized. A new sheriff then asked to take the Hall for the year 1675–6 and this was agreed for a rent of £150 with use of the company's pewter, parlour chairs and sconces, and with covenants as before, but without use of the basement. Separate lettings for main floors and basement, it was now clear, were best. The busy merchant wanting extra riverside warehouse space was not necessarily that man wanting extra entertainment space upstairs, and by 1675 would already have built himself a new house to live in. Even Herne and Frederick found it useful to rent the Fishmongers' cellars for eleven weeks during the summer of 1675 – perhaps to clear a particular shipload – and they inaugurated the long series of warehouse tenants there. At first a succession of short-term occupiers passed through the basement; from one of them two butts of oil were distrained for non-payment of rent. A satisfactory tenant seemed hard to find. Upstairs there began an annually changing series of resident sheriffs (most of them knighted soon after election): John Shorter, John Peake, Thomas Beckford, Richard Howe, Simon Lewis, Henry Cornish, Samuel Shute, Peter Rich, Peter Daniell, vacant year, Benjamin Thorowgood, Thomas Fowle, Basil Firebrace, four vacant years, Thomas Abney, William Coles, Edward Wills, John Wolfe, Bartholomew Gracedieu, Joseph Smart, Jeffery Jeffries, which brings us up to 1700 and Abney again as the Hall's first Lord Mayor-lodger. An eventful, even dangerous, period is implied in that rollcall of names during the 1680s when the royal power deprived the City of its charter and the livery companies were forced to reveal the political sympathies of their members. Henry Cornish, who in 1680 was elected sheriff, alderman, and master of his company (Haberdashers) and inhabited Fishmongers' Hall during 1680–1, held to be 'a plain, warm, honest man and lived very nobly all his year', was hanged at the corner of King Street and Cheapside in 1685 for suspected conspiracy in aid of the Duke of Monmouth. If Shepherd the City vintner who was said to have conspired with Cornish was the same as, or father of, Samuel Shepherd, vintner (1648–1718), later a director of the East India and South Sea companies, briefly an M.P., and contractor to the Navy for oil and wine, Cornish may have brought the Fishmongers one of their most long-standing tenants.[2] For in May 1681, while Cornish was still resident upstairs, Shepherd agreed for a lease of the great cellar and arched vaults from Michaelmas, at a yearly rent of £45 (later increased with much grumbling) and covenanted not to make any fires therein. He was still storing pipes of wine there in the last months of his life in 1718, and vintner tenants continued to store casks there for over a century thereafter.

The sheriffs of the mid-eighties were appointed by the King, and sundry repairs were made for them at Fishmongers' Hall that had not been done for their predecessors, it being politic, however hateful to the Whigs on the company's court, to 'pleasure' a King's man. In 1685 the lodger's dining-room, apparently for the first time, was wainscotted and shuttered at Thorowgood's request; both Rich and Daniell had been allowed a certain abatement of rent toward the cost of providing hangings of 'greene Stuffe', also called 'printed Stuffe' (and so perhaps imported Indian), for the lady's chamber. For Fowler in 1686 it was apparently enough to whiten the parlour ceiling and stop 'the stench from the house of easement near thereto' (on the stair-landing) and to allow him the use of 'three standing cupps and three beere bowles'. (It became usual to weigh the silver before and after lending). But Firebrace in 1687, a more awkward person to deal with and no freeman of any company, was more demanding and required the use of 'the outer parte' of the courtroom itself, for setting up tables with 'Scrutores' (portable desks) for his own business purposes. This was uncomfortably close to the company's own treasury, which lay off the courtroom, an area always previously reserved to the company's own use. Yet in the political climate of the time it was thought fit 'to pleasure the said Sir Basil' and his use of the courtroom was authorized 'during the pleasure of the court.' At his request, moreover, two 'lodging chambers' received fireplaces they had not had before, presumably being warmed by stoves or braziers until connections were then opened to existing chimneystacks 'for safety from fire'.

London was still fire-conscious. During 1680–1, several schemes for insurance against fire were hatched in the City, including Nicholas Barbon's. And the Fishmongers' Clerk recorded in October 1681 :[3]

> Also this day came here Doctor Barbone and desired leave to set a Chest of the principal deeds & writings of his & other persons effects settled on Trustees and offered for security to persons in case their houses within this City should happen to be burned in some convenient room within this hall That recourse may be had thereunto as occasion should require And he would give 40s a year for such conveniency And further satisfy the Clerk for his trouble & attendance therein Which being taken into consideration, it is ordered that he have Liberty to bring & place the same in the Little room within the Company's Court room for the use & purposes aforesaid during the pleasure of this Court.

No more was heard of that proposal, nor any such rent noted as received for it, but it shows that the foxy Barbon knew a good strong new building well away from his own premises when he saw one; yet the Hall itself was not insured against fire until 1687, with the Friendly Society (for £4000, less than a third of the cost of building). Fire-buckets and sacks, 'large Baggs for the more convenient Removing' of records and plate in case of fire, were kept on hand and a 'hand Water Engine with a hose thereto' was 'laid up in the Arched hole' under the stone steps. Later on, in 1737, a fire-pump on wheels with a copper-lined oak cistern and two forty-foot 'sinks' was bought, and a man hired to keep 'the leathers' and wheels oiled for an annual fee – one more member of the dense network of part-time retainers ministering to the smooth operation of the City companies.

Water was still piped from the waterworks at the Bridge through a series of hollowed tree-trunks laid in Thames Street and along the quay, to which the company connected its own lead pipes. But in 1680 'the frequent want of water . . . by reason of the often defects that happen in the pipes belonging to the waterhouse' led the company to employ a smith to set up a pump in 'the oven room' to draw water from the Thames into 'the great cistern' in the scullery yard. This auxiliary source cannot have been wholly successful, for in 1685 a well was sunk – the fact that it was called a 'new well' implies there had been one before the Fire, as on so many premises in the City – presumably somewhere in the basement, with a pump for it, and made by an entirely different set of craftsmen from men of the same trades (bricklayer, carpenter, plumber and smith) then engaged on building-repairs for the company : wells and pumps were a speciality. 'Mr. Aldersey' who got £10 for supervising the operation was probably Robert Aldersey, engine-maker, also employed at Hampton Court and Chelsea Hospital.[4] In 1709 the proprietors of the Bridge waterworks were 'acquainted' that their

pipes along the wharf, so near to the Hall front, were defective, in 1718 there was
more complaint of 'great detriment', and in 1720 they were implored to lay iron
pipes 'instead of the trees now laid there which are continually breaking . . . and
may prove dangerous to the Fondation of the Hall'. By 1736 we hear no more of
the well, and the 'engine' of 1680 had been useless for years, whereas the main
pipes from the Bridge were in good form. It was even perfectly easy to pipe water
up to the garrets in 1729, under pressure from the water-tower at the Bridge.
'Fire cocks' were fixed to the mains in the street – a crude plan of about 1760 in
the company collection[5] shows where these then were in the neighbourhood – so
that supply could be concentrated in one part of the system when necessary. No
running water flushed the 'house of easement' or privy yet, though in many a City
dwelling it might be on an upper floor, with a vertical pipe to the necessary vault
in the basement. (As when in 1748 the closet of a neighbour on the uphill side of
a company tenant in Pudding Lane projected over the latter's top-floor closet, and
upon discovery that the former's father years before had attached his downpipe
to that of the company tenant, a committee of wardens arrived with company
carpenter and constable to stop this inconvenience, but as the neighbour protested
that the want of it, with a large family and only one necessary, was very great,
and as his own lease was running out, he was allowed to pay two shillings for the
liberty.) On an eighteenth-century plan of the Hall basement,[6] an unexplained
twelve-foot-square mass of brickwork under the eastern range, dividing one of
the wine vaults almost in two, presumably represents the Hall's principal necessary
vault – apparently emptied not from the alley outside but from inside, because
the wine merchant had to be consulted.

That alley along the Hall's east side was known variously as Red Cross Alley,
or Graves's Wharf or Thompson's Gateway after the timber merchant on the
other side of the alley. He was given to piling faggots along the Hall side, sometimes endangering the Hall windows, and his carts rounding the corner from the
wharf sometimes endangered the Hall's brickwork and were thought to use the
quay in front of the Hall far too often : 'for the preserving his Own Gateway to
his Wharffe causes all the Loaden Carts that brings goods to his Warehouse to
pass over this Company's Wharffe whereby the pavement is continually tore up
and the Hall much Shaken by the continual passing of the Carts.' (That refrain
was to recur in 'the jarring of the building arising from the heavy loads constantly
passing' to and from the wharf of the next Hall, for example in 1885.) The concept
of a public quay was a relative one in 1718 : much tried by these wood-carts, the
wardens had the passage at both ends of the company's wharf barred forthwith
to all but horse and foot passengers. But when in 1755 the landlord of the Swan
alehouse put in similar posts near Old Swan stairs, those were seen as a detriment
to the company's tenants and other 'Gentlemen Inhabitants' anxious to test the
right of way. Late in the century certain coal merchants questioned the company's
right to 'moorage in Fishmongers Hole', or, to charge rent for offshore mooring
of lighters there, which involved discussion with the City's Thames Navigation
Committee as to wharf-owners' rights of driving offshore piles – the complexities

of riparian rights continuing to make the administration of the Hall site more complicated than that of any inland site. The peculiar shoreline inherited from the
four medieval wharves still helped to define these moorings, as when, in 1801,
'as far as the bending in the Wall' referred to the point where the medieval Fishmongers' Wharf had extended beyond that of the old Nun's Head premises.[7]

Maps and plans, after the Fire, came to be regarded as indispensable to large
property-owners. In January 1669 it was 'ordered that plotts be taken & made
of all the ground & houses belonging to this Company in London And the just &
true measure thereof be set down upon the same plotts And kept in the fashion of
a book'. Such a 'book', doubtless quite blank, was got back from Lock in 1672
and may have formed the planbook eventually made. For in March 1676 William
Leybourne the versatile surveyor and mathematician was commissioned to 'plott
in Vellumbe' every one of the company's houses at four shillings per house and
'particularly describe the same in writing', doubtless basing the plans on a survey
he had just made of the whole City.[8] During the latter 1670s and early 1680s Leybourne was busy making extensive surveys for the City Lands Committee and for
the Bridge House Estates. Not until nine and a half years after his agreement with
the Fishmongers was some enquiry made, and 'then came Mr Liborne & promised
to perfect the plotts' which he duly did by Octobeer 1686, for which in the end
he received £34. This planbook is a manuscript folio volume of twenty-four
vellum leaves (about $18\frac{1}{2}$ by $13\frac{1}{2}$ inches) with a contents page and an illuminated
title page gorgeously embellished with the company arms in red, blue and gold
('Thomas Penson Pinxit') and entitled *A Book of Planographies or Ground Plots
. . . Surveyed and Ploted by William Leybourn Anno 1686*. The plans show no
consistent relation to points of the compass. Every ground-plan, starting with that
of the Hall (Pl. 5*b*), is shown as a person approaching the street entrance would
conceive it. The wardens on their annual spring tour of company property,
accompanied by craftsmen and planbook, wished to know where they were, and so
their point of entry to a building was generally placed at the foot of a page. *They*
were the centre of this little universe.

By then, however, there was a modern map of the City to go by, generally
known as 'Ogilby & Morgan 1677', a detailed street plan showing buildings, to a
scale of 100 feet to the inch.[9] Leybourne apparently did the actual surveying and
Hollar some of the drawing (delectable little sketches of river-craft nuzzling the
public water-stairs or bringing loads of hay or daring the rapids) for the enter-
prising publishers John Ogilby (died 1676) and his wife's grandson William
Morgan. In December 1679 the Fishmongers' court asked Morgan 'to take down
the great map of London by him hanged up in the Hall . . . considering that at
present they have no use thereof nor any convenient place' for it (the twenty
sheets mounted together would measure over eight feet wide by almost five feet
high), but in October 1681 Morgan came again, probably with his new map
covering a wider area, Limehouse to Westminster, to a smaller scale in twelve
sheets but similar in overall size, and this time he got £3 for it: encouragement
by the City companies, listed in the margin of the map with the names of bishops

and nobility, apparently preceded the placing of this map on public sale in 1682. But 'Mr Morgan's Mapp' of 1677 is our earliest visual evidence for the situation of the Hall finished six years before, though the map has three shortcomings in this area: the shoreline is smoothed down for a superimposed Thames Quay (added as an ideal to be hoped for), omitting the jutting line of river-bank remaining until 1828 from the pre-Fire wharves; Lamott's property to the left is shaded as part of the Hall,·which it was not; and the mainly open back area between the Hall kitchen wing and Lamott's premises could not be shown because the ground was occupied by Trattle's low shed over his right of way.

In February 1673 when Robert Hooke as City Surveyor went to 'Lamot's with Lock about fishmongers', amicable party-wall and rear window-light arrangements were concluded. The Hall's riverside block shared a party wall with Lamott's new riverside house and warehouse, although Lamott's projecting frontage – shown in 1677 as thirty feet in advance of the Hall – having been inherited from the fourteenth century or earlier (as we know from the company's deed of 1395), called for no compensation. In the northwest corner of the company's riverside block was the company's scullery yard, at kitchen-floor level, resting on part of the party wall on the west and almost entirely open on the north side, with Trattle's warehouse/coach-house underneath and one of the Hall's private apartments overhead. This yard, more like a room lacking one wall, apparently with the same high ceiling as the kitchen and very much the 'Mary Ann behind' of the elegant great-hall block, was to figure periodically in the records of that building. One way of preventing leakage from such a raised yard to a cellar below was to 'lay the yard in lead', that is a lead flat; in 1736 when this yard was 'ruinous', its floor-joists sunk and rotten with water dripping from the 'great cistern' into the vault below, repairs included new-casting of the lead, though by 1759 a 'tobacconist' using the warehouse next door was complaining of leaks. The copper in which water was heated for boiling tablecloths, napkins, curtains etc. stood in this yard, set in brickwork with a hole under it for a coal fire. The yard was protected only a little from the north winds by 'pallisadoes' on the open side, for the effects of steam upon structure were thought – as still in this century in this country – curable by fresh air. A kindly committee, meeting in the winter of 1762, directed that this fence or palisade be 'enclosed with glass lights to restrain the excessive draught of air' – remembering, perhaps, the deceased 'scowering woman' who three years before had left much uncleaned pewter behind her. The great corner-post found, later in 1762, to have sunk six inches and about to drag down part of the supports of the great hipped roof, stood on one side of that Achilles-heel of a scullery yard.[10]

Partly perhaps because of the political tensions of the 1680s, there came to the surface in 1682–4 a certain anxiety over visual proof of the company's historical identity. One might have supposed that the company's regard for its past ran low in 1678, when two members of the court were desired to speak to some goldsmith in Cheapside 'about this Company's old rich burying cloth for making the best advantage thereof to this Company', or, to ask what melting down the gold thread in this relic of the old religion might yield in practical business terms; nothing more was heard about that, and the Elizabethan embroidered pall still survives. In 1682 the churchwardens of the parish of St Michael Crooked Lane came to discuss with the company's court the rebuilding of the parish church which, it soon became clear, was not automatically to include a new Fishmongers' Chapel. That is, the coal tax from which by Act of Parliament the rebuilding of the City churches was being subsidized would not cover private chapels, and the company felt unable at this stage to foot the bill. Since not only the chapel, but the entire fabric of the early-medieval church had come out of the pockets of eminent fishmongers, it must have seemed to their successors most unfeeling of the church authorities not to replace the company's historic shrine out of the sea-coal fund. Protests to the Lord Mayor, the Bishop of London, the Archbishop of Canterbury, and Sir Christopher Wren proved useless. When Lovekyn had stepped forward to rebuild the whole church, Walworth to erect a college of priests there, Brampton to add a south aisle for a company chapel and Knesworth's successors to rebuild it, they had been able to pay for it. Finally, in January 1684 the company accepted the inevitable and agreed that the chapel site should be 'appropriated to this Company's use for a burial place', that is, an outdoor burial ground, with use of the church for election services when desired (but presumably without any control over its decoration, although £30 was given towards wainscotting it). And so, out of piety thereafter, that plot of earth between the church and Crooked Lane, where Thomas Tanner the Clerk was buried in 1710, and his son and successor Matthew Tanner in 1740, was known as 'Fishmongers Isle' or aisle.[11]

In the same breath in January 1684, the court directed that an effigy of Sir William Walworth – whose tomb had been destroyed with the chapel – should be made and set up in the Hall, certain members to enquire after a sculptor and treat with him for an (imaginary) portrait figure. The conscious attitude towards the new Hall as ancestral shrine began then. By 18 February 1684 'Mr Peirce the Carver' had agreed to carve the figure in wood for £30. As half the sum was paid him on account before mid-June, the statue was designed in the spring of 1684. By the following February it was in place.[12] From various later records it can be deduced that the over-lifesize figure now dominating the main staircase of the present Hall, stood in a recess behind the prime warden's chair in the great hall, presumably centred at the east end. The three east windows behind the head table were listed in lot 71 of the demolition sale of 1827 as two plus '1 ditto at the back of recess', and lot 75 included 'nich & dressings round ditto at east end', a niche perhaps in the central window recess with the inside shutters permanently closed; or so it may have been after a plasterer charged for 'Niche in Hall' in 1789, with some similar arrangement during the century before, the taste for precedent being what it was.[13] Hogarth's version of the Fishmongers' dining hall in his Industrious Apprentice series of engravings can probably be discounted, because he left out the upper gallery that surrounded the room, not so much depending on second-hand information as simply not caring to produce a completely faithful view of any particular livery hall: expecting topographical accuracy from Hogarth is like expecting it from Dickens. At any rate, Walworth was a splendid figure in robes painted red and blue and gold, like a Jacobean tomb effigy, colouring that was removed only in the twentieth century. Peirce, working here in the baroque vein of Quellin and Bushnell, chose to portray a moment of arrested action, just after the Lord Mayor stabbed Wat Tyler in 1381 (did men think in terms of tercentenaries in the 1680s?). The moment of recoil, interpreted by some critics as unseemly shrinking, could be contained within the borderlines of an indoor niche, as the moment of attack, more suited to an outdoor monument with space around it, could not. We shall see how the generations of the 1830s and 1920s sought to deal with the figure's theatrical character; in the great hall of the 1680s–1780s it must have looked at home, especially when other gilded ornaments accrued.

In the last years of the seventeenth century, as prosperity began to return a little after the Revolution of 1688, a few furnishings could be acquired : an oval table for the great parlour, a 'wallnut tree couch', numerous cane chairs with later payments for mending them, a dozen 'Rushia Leather chairs' bought from a Josia Casimire for six guineas, looking glasses and stands and walnut tables for the great chamber.[14] A determined effort was made to plant trees by the waterside, between the public quay and the stone staircase, during the 1680s and 90s (Pl. 6), perhaps partly for privacy, partly to temper the wind off the river, partly to soften an outlook of sky, buildings and water; and not to be confused with the wooden water-pipes also called 'trees'. Canaletto drew trees there in the mid-eighteenth century.[15]

A new company barge was the prime source of expense in the 1690s. It was the third barge commissioned by the company; these decorative vessels usually lasted thirty to forty years each.[16] An old barge they had owned in 1632 was probably bought secondhand, but in 1634 Richard Mitchell, shipwright, made the company a new one for £78, and a bargemaster recommended by the Earl of Arundel was hired. In 1642 a new bargehouse at Vauxhall (just downstream from the site of the present bridge) was arranged, together with the Mercers' and Clothworkers' Companies, on copyhold ground of Vauxhall Manor, of which they were able to buy the freehold during the Commonwealth. In 1662 Henry Forty, bargemaker, built the Fishmongers a new barge for £110 plus £28 for extras and £50 to two painters for painting and gilding. And in 1691 a Mr Loftus, bargemaker, was paid £110, plus £9 for special joinery, £6 for new oars, painting by 'Mr Bird' for £38, and carving by 'Mr Mayne' for £27. The painter was probably Edward Bird who was doing painting work at the Hall from 1682 : Edward Bird (fl. 1678–93) did much work for Chelsea Hospital and City churches including several altarpieces. The carver was probably Jonathan Maine, carver in wood and stone for a number of Wren's City churches – for instance, in St Clement Eastcheap near the Hall – and at St. Paul's. We have no descriptions of the carvings on the barge of 1691, but very likely Maine's work provided (or passed on) patterns for the traditional figures in gilded wood that were to decorate the company's barges of 1734 and 1773. In fact, the figure of St Peter from the last barge, now standing in the present Hall (and, as is fairly clear from the records, originally made for the barge of 1734 described below), could in his rather baroque attitude have been modelled by company request on a predecessor carved by Maine in 1691. It was agreed with Loftus in 1691 that overall dimensions, unspecified, should be those of the Clothworkers' barge, that 'the house' should be 31 feet long 'with twisted banisters' eighteen a side, and curtain rods to the windows: for in late October, even with warm gowns and a supply of cakes and sack, it could be a cold rough voyage to Westminster on Lord Mayor's Day. In 1705 and 1715 this barge was lent to carry Middlesex voters to Brentford.

After the tiresome tenancy of Firebrace (who, having enjoyed the place so much that he asked to keep it as his private house, was instantly refused) the Hall took no tenants, except Shepherd in the basement, for four years after the Glorious Revolution of 1688. But there were large repairs at the waterside to pay for, where water-stairs crumbled and campshed timbers sheathing the wharf rotted in the old way. Country carpenters who brought sixteen loads of timber down the Thames from Bray were enabled, by special City permit, to work on the wharf because they had worked on the rebuilding of the City 'by the space of seven years' after the Great Fire. One barge was used 'for five weeks for the workmen to stand in to drive in the piles' with the aid of the carpenters' 'Ginne' or pile-driving engine, hoisting and dropping a heavy ram in the old way. It was decided in 1701 after five years of debate not to renew the 'Stairs into the Thames . . . the same being judged both dangerous & useless', and the next year when those who still thought the company should embark from its own wharf brought the matter up again, they were voted down 'by reason of the inconveniency that attends the same' – probably from untrustworthy currents so near the Bridge. Water-stairs were to be made there and used, later in the century, but those shown in Pl. 6 may be imaginary.[17]

In 1700, when Sir Thomas Abney moved into the Hall as its first Lord Mayor guest, according to custom 'a Triumph or Show [was] made on the Land at this Companyes charge' – that is, a street procession, not a water pageant – on October 29 on his return from Westminster. 'Mr Settle the Poet' was given £10 'for composing the Show' (this is Elkanah Settle, ridiculed by Dryden for his poetical bombast), and George Holmes, pageant maker,[18] was paid £195 'for the several pageants by him made for the publicke Show . . . Hee bringing the Merman & Mermaid' to the Hall, where their gilded bombast will have enlivened the great hall thereafter, as Peirce's heraldic stone creatures enlivened the Thames Street entrance. Between 1700 and 1735, the Hall was occupied by two sheriffs and ten Lord Mayors during their terms of office; and for seven of the latter as company members this company staged their triumphs (after Abney, for Sir John Parsons – who paid for most of it, having been translated from a lesser company – Sir William Withers, Sir James Bateman, Sir John Fryer – similarly translated – Sir Peter Delmé, and Sir Edward Bellamy, the last tenant, although processions at company expense continued occasionally thereafter). In 1720 the court thought over the whole matter of taking in lodgers, 'and the great inconveniences and Straits this Company are put to', and decided to take only members of the company. By 1744, to a further request for tenancy of the Hall, refusal was absolute, duly weighing 'the irreparable damages' that might be sustained from fire by negligence of the Lord Mayor's servants or from 'the dishonesty of ill-designing persons to whom the Company's Treasury & Clerk's Office . . . will unavoidably be exposed'.[19]

The membership became decidedly grander after 1700, with more aldermen and knights, than in the years just after the Fire. With the death of William III it was felt that a Whig-inclined company's debt to him should be acknowledged. In 1702 portraits of William and Mary were hung in the great parlour, his painted by a 'Mr Payne' and hers by James Baker (probably John Jacob Bakker, one of Kneller's assistants, a painter of feeble copies of royal portraits); these seem to have been quietly replaced in 1779 by the present pair, painted by Kneller's more skilful contemporary Thomas Murray.[20] And in 1701 it was ordered that 'the Eschutcheons of the arms of several members of this Company be set up about this Hall', though nothing was done about it for some years, the cost of 'triumphs' being what it was. Before the Fire, probably ever since the Elizabethan romantic-medieval revival, shields were carried with hired javelins by hired men in mayors' shows. Finally, during 1727–31, shields with 'the several arms of the principal benefactors & prime wardens of the Company (& whose arms are not painted in the Hall windows)' were carved and 'painted in proper colours . . . beginning at the Revolution by the late glorious King William & his Queen Mary', and hung 'under the gallery which is round this Company's publick Hall'.[21] In December 1728 Joseph Wade, King's Carver in the royal shipyards of Deptford and Woolwich (whose own monument hangs in Rotherhithe church), was paid £40 for having carved twenty shields for the great hall. In December 1730 'Mr Brooken Herald Painter' was commissioned to paint them, and as 'Mr Booking' was paid £27 in May 1731 (possibly the father of Charles Brooking the marine painter). Wade got fifteen guineas more in 1733 for a large 'Company's arms' to be set up in the great hall, probably the arms now hanging over the main door to the present banqueting hall. All these shields were presumably of wood, but he also made two of carved leather, in 1740 when he was 76, one of them the company's arms for display 'in the long Passage' from street to courtyard. The most beautifully carved shields now hanging in the banqueting hall are apparently Wade's work. As late as 1815, when Alderman Matthew Wood became Lord Mayor, the shields still had webbing and straps for processional use.[22]

The great hall bore arms in its windows too. At first, all the Hall windows of 1671 will have been casements. Whether the great hall's lower windows were mullioned and transomed, or simply divided into two lights each, depends on which engraving you look at (Pl. 6, 7). 'Mr Price glasspainter' who was paid 55s. in October 1705 for unspecified work at the Hall and 10s. during 1706–8 for mending glass there, was probably William Price the elder, master of the Glaziers' Company in 1699, or his younger brother Joshua.[23] By 1731 or before, certain windows on the south front had as many as six panels of arms each, with room for more. Because of the gales off the river, all had to be 'defended on the outside with wirework', also called 'Skrine work', frames of wire mesh that had to be painted periodically. The Crooked Lane neighbourhood (according to later trade directories) seems to have specialized in 'wirework', conveniently enough : sieves, screens, bird-cages, fishing-rods, and so on. The southwest winds could be such that in December 1681 'the lower lights in the windows of the garrett next the waterside [were] made with deal boards & painted like glass on the outsides by reason of the extremity of the weather that often breaketh the glass formerly set up within'. East winds may have had something to do with the decision in 1701 to install sash windows in the courtroom, the part of the Hall in which the court spent most time, the senior members seated directly in front of the two east windows there; and the sashes were replaced with better ones in 1738 after becoming 'insecure from the cold winds'. When Sir Humprey Parsons was allowed, because of his father's brief connection with the company, to spend his mayoralty at the Hall in 1730–1, he not only agreed to a rent of £300 but that he would at his own cost 'Substantially Sash the Several lights in the Company's long Parlour'. That explains a drawing marked 'Plan of Great Parlour Windows' showing five great sashed windows on the scale of the east side of the courtyard, that is, fitting a space about 45 feet long with a storey-height of about 16 feet.[24] Conversion to sash did not reach the great hall until about sixty years later. Meanwhile, to light that room more splendidly, a great brass chandelier was given in 1717 by Sir James Bateman the South Sea and East India tycoon, in gratitude for his mayoral stay; eventually in 1793 that chandelier was given away for use in the new Surrey Sessions House on Newington Causeway.[25]

There were celebrations at the Hall and on the river in 1734–5 in honour of the last lodger, Sir Edward Bellamy, a member of the company and governor of the Bank of England with several generations of increasingly prosperous merchants of his name behind him. Directions were given in the spring for the painting of much wainscot 'before the damp weather comes in', that of 'the long gallery and state room' (great chamber) to be painted 'a bright Olave Colour', or olive-green, a shade that had become fashionable as a background for gold frames (country-house rooms of the 1720s at Ditchley, Wanstead, Eastbury and Houghton are said to have been painted 'olive' originally).[26] Two large roasting-jacks costing £46 were installed in the kitchen, with screens 'for standing before the fire when the meat is roasting', coppers were 'new set' and drains scoured. A new barge was finished in time for the ritual voyage to Westminster, this time with sash windows all round, hung with new crimson silk curtains, and with new crimson plush caps for the oarsmen, and new gowns for bargemaster and steersman (old ones to be worn if bad weather), accompanied by musicians on four silver trumpets, two french horns and a kettle drum, engaged for £9, if to satisfaction 9 guineas. (In 1795 Mr Sleep and his men were to provide for the court's entertainment to its ladies a gentler consort of instruments for an August day's 'Diversion on the Water' : one trumpet, two french horns, four hautboys (oboes), and a bassoon, to go in the barge and stay afterward in the Hall, all for six guineas.)

The new barge was the handsomest yet.[27] There survives a detailed contract for making her, signed by John Hall of Lambeth, barge-builder, and dated 6 February 1734, for completion by August 1 for a lump sum of £439. Specifications included a length of 74 feet 'aloft exclusive of the Lute' (sternpiece and rudder), beam amidships $11\frac{1}{2}$ feet, minimum draft amidships 2 feet $8\frac{1}{2}$ inches, the 'house' 33 feet long and 6 feet 4 inches high, fluted columns around the house to form 36 'compass-headed' windows, with sashes, six forms in the house to sit on, 18 best ashen oars, and staves for banners. Banners were ordered separately, specifying silver tissue for certain fields instead of 'silver plaistering', the weight of which 'subjects the banner to damage upon every gust of wind' – a serious expertise in stagecraft the Georgian livery companies could afford to cultivate. Two years before, at his yard on the south bank opposite Whitehall, John Hall had built the handsome barge designed by the architect William Kent for Frederick Prince of Wales, now one of the treasures of the National Maritime Museum at Greenwich; it has much carving by James Richards, Master Carver to the Crown. Detailed specifications for carved work in the Fishmongers' agreement with John Hall will have been subcontracted to an unnamed carver paid by him (it is quite possible that the carver was Joseph Wade) for the following work: 'heraldic shield' as sternpiece, 'two figures of fame sounding trumpets butting on the shield', two sea-lions 'for elbows' at the prime warden's seat with the royal arms above and festoons down each side, a merman and mermaid 'fixed before the house', two boys riding dolphins each side of the house abaft, 'the figure of Saint Peter on the fore bulkhead not exceeding four feet and a half in height', sea nymphs, a Triton and seahorses, all gilded with leaf gold and screwed to plank pedestals (from which for land processions[28] they could be unscrewed, under the supervision of the company carpenter's and smith's foremen, and attached to stands borne through the streets, with the foremen walking beside). A table was fixed before the prime warden's seat for the usual refreshments, four gallons of canary, say, drunk from eight dozen 'beechen cups', and fifty pounds-weight of cakes. On a fine day there would be great weight of assembly on the roof of the house (often in need of 'strengthening') while the steersman aft did his best to see ahead, as in 1722 'upon a mischance that hapned to the Barge and the Terror of the Company therein [when] a Hoy in the River . . . bore down' and some banner-staves were broken. The company's next (and last) barge in 1773 was modelled almost exactly on that of 1734 and retained a number of its ornaments, although those near the waterline needed replacement.

Meanwhile, in the latter 1730s there was no great expenditure on the state rooms of the Hall, although the company's affluence grew as post-Fire leases to its City properties were renewed. During the 1740s–60s, however (with pauses for dire repairs to basic structure), the great parlour, which was the court's private dining and state reception room, became the Hall's most elegant modern room, whereas the great hall with its heraldic and ritual ornaments remained the most traditional room. Emphasis on the parlour, as the room the court liked best to beautify, began after the lodgers moved out. The great chamber overhead, once traditionally a more private withdrawing-room, finally lost that character for good in 1749 when leave was magnanimously given to the liverymen to sit in it after dinner, several times a year. Already by the 1740s both state rooms on the upper floor – where the long gallery had never been very useful – were being called 'the dancing rooms', a use that apparently lasted only until the early 1750s, when the structural weaknesses then discovered posed a danger to stout parties.

In August 1741 the parlour chimneypiece, probably partly or wholly of wood, was judged to be a fire risk, and the company mason Charles Easton was asked to 'prepare a Plan of a proper marble chimneypiece', a drawing was approved a week later, and he was told to go ahead. Two months later William Sittwell & Co. were paid £24 for a stove for the parlour, that is, for a grate to fit into the new chimneypiece, though Easton's work still required alterations in January. This handsome piece, standing just over twelve feet high and almost ten feet wide overall, commanded the long wall opposite the windows of the parlour. The lower part, which no longer exists, was apparently of white marble, the opening enclosed by shaped panels and a central keystone-console under a shelf just over six feet from the floor. The surviving upper part consists of a panel of veined bluish-black marble bearing a triton-mask and seashell garlands of white marble in relief, under a broken pediment mounting the company arms, the panel originally flanked by consoles. The overmantel flanked by volutes and crowned with heraldic broken pediment was typical of carved chimneypieces in great Palladian houses of the 1720s and then publicized in widening circles of builders' manuals. The flanking scrolls, and the attributes of the shield's supporters, the merman's weapon and the mermaid's hand-mirror, with the topmost tip of the coronet-crest, are all gone. The only record of the original appearance of Easton's chimneypiece is a scaled pencil sketch made in Henry Roberts' office in 1834 when the question of use in the present Hall was raised. But it was too far out of spirit with the strict Grecian mode of 1834, and only entered the Hall in truncated condition, in this century, after a sojourn in the suburbs (p. 174). Charles Easton, whom we can assume to have been the carver, may have signed the piece on the lower part that is now gone. His father Robert Easton, who in c. 1722–3 carved the figure of James Hulbert for St Peter's Hospital (now at Bray), had been only briefly mason to this company, in succession to Bartholomew Woolfe (company mason c. 1706–c. 1721), and Robert Easton only had time to do a little work for the company before he died in 1723–4. Robert's widow was still taking apprentices in 1727, and Charles did not take his freedom (run his own household) until 1728, but was probably working for his mother by 1726. He set up his yard in Eastcheap, eventually was appointed City Mason, served in 1754 as master of the Masons' Company, and was well known in the City as a deputy alderman, while continuing as mason to the Fishmongers until 1782, when he must have been nearly 80. With two or three church monuments, the chimneypiece panel now handsomely remounted in the present courtroom must be one of his few surviving works.[29]

The next object commissioned for the parlour was a great silver chandelier. The idea for it may have originated in the driving ambition or sense of fitness of Slingsby Bethell, a prominent member of the Fisheries Council who became in

1749 an alderman, a member of Parliament, and renter warden to this company, which he had joined only two years before. In December 1749 the court ordered 'that a Silver Branch be provided in memory of Sir Thomas Knesworth a principal Benefactor to this Company' – a suitable branch to hang the idea on – 'to be hung up in the Great Parlour on publick & other Dinner Days . . . expense not to exceed £200'. A committee in February treated with Joseph Dyer, silversmith of Lombard Street, authorizing him to have it made according to 'the drawing he now shew'd' of a chandelier in two tiers, one of eight and one of six 'Nossells', for not more than £250, for delivery in April. That chandelier was hung in time for the Prince of Wales's visit to accept a charter for the British White Herring Fishery in October 1750, when he was 'attended into the parlour' to listen to speeches. (Subsequently the freedom of the company was presented to him, on Christmas Day at Leicester House, only a few weeks before his death early in 1751.) In January 1752 the court had a double dose of bad news: not only were the foundations of the Hall defective, but the chandelier was a fraud. The discovery was made during repairs in the workshop of William Alexander, founder, plateworker and brazier of Wood Street, who usually supplied the company's brass lanterns, moulds for casting the company mark for its buildings, and kitchenware. One of Alexander's men, mending the silver arms, heated one too hot, causing it to open: it was 'loaded with copper' and so were all the others (made probably by a method called 'close plating', rather than the fusion later known as Sheffield plating). Dyer being an entrepreneur, not a craftsman, had employed William Gould of Foster Lane to make the piece. Two of Gould's workmen concerned in finishing the work having testified that it must have been done 'before they came to work in the morning', Dyer confronted Gould, who confessed and subsequently was prosecuted. In March an assay was made of the entire chandelier, and the Fishmongers' Company asked Dyer to provide them with a new one in consultation with Alexander, 'but he refused to be concerned with any one out of the Trade'. Dyer thereupon returned to the company the difference between the value of the silver melted down at Alexander's and the total amount, £484, that the company had paid him (the initial notion of the price in the autumn of 1749 having inflated somewhat). A committee examining 'several patterns of chandeliers' which Alexander – who had now hired Gould's two workmen – was able to provide, fixed on a pattern called 'Dolphin' with one tier of twelve arms, to be delivered for election day that June, 1752. Alexander's bill for the new chandelier, chain, and case came to £650 which with the value of the silver he held made the total price just over £929.[30] The firm of Alexander & Shrimpton, as it became (probably when Alexander became an alderman in 1753), subsequently appeared in some trade directories as goldsmiths, as well as founders etc. In November 1761 when George III and the whole royal family were entertained at Guildhall, the chandelier was lent and hung 'very near Their Majesties canopies where it was much admired', as also in the 'summer of sovereigns' 1814, and on other royal occasions. It now hangs in the court dining room on special occasions (Pl. 23b).

In the great parlour the twelve candles of the dolphin-branched chandelier will have been supplemented by candles in wall-sconces. The parlour panelling was always painted, and gilding was mentioned in 1731, though not the colour. It must have been a fairly bright room by day, with the long west wall full of windows looking into the quadrangle. In 1765 Robert Phipps, an upholsterer and member of the livery, gave a pair of full-length portraits of George II and Queen Caroline in gilt frames to be 'fixed up in the Court Parlour' opposite those of William and Mary. In 1767 eight paintings of fish by Arnold van Hacken were bought for £50; the fact that their frames were the only ones changed when the present Hall was built suggests that those were too deliciously rococo for the Hellenism of the 1830s.[31] Discussions with a frame-gilder in 1781 mention six pier-glasses in the parlour, probably flanking each of the five damask-curtained windows and reflecting chandelier, chimneypiece, fish, royalties, and Grove's plaster ceiling.

And down below, underneath parlour, courtroom, quadrangle, and great hall, lay the vintner-tenants' wine-casks, under the shadowy curved brickwork of the 'seven arched vaults' or cellars let for wholesale warehousing. All but the southern-most were entered from the stableyard off Thames Street. The southeastern vault, lying under the dais of the great hall, was entered through part of the fenced enclosure that protected the Hall's riverside entrances from the common wharf. A fine engraved view of the Hall, first published around 1700 (according to the women's *fontange* headdress, and probably also the young trees known to have been planted in 1698–9), shows the easternmost entry in the oblique bit of fence at the right as a blind gate (Pl. 6). By 1754 there were signs of some activity other than warehousing there. A different engraved view of the Hall, published in the 1754 edition of Strype's revision of Stow's *Survey of London* (Pl. 7), shows that easternmost gate open and hung with a welcoming lamp, and a little sash-windowed extension from the basement filling the fenced enclosure there – features apparently added at some time to an existing plate.[32] In March 1754 when William Smith, vintner, was renewing his lease of the 'Vault under & at the back of the Hall' he agreed 'after some conversation' that all fixtures should be scheduled as company property 'Except the Sashes & Tables'. Now the sashes might refer to the new window to the wharf, or to an interior sash-windowed bar, of a type developed for serving rather than consuming (as still at the George in Southwark). Behind the bar the wine was drawn directly from the barrel, and before it presumably the seats were fixed and the tables movable. This seems to have been the nucleus of 'The Shades', so called in company records only from 1790 but in a manner denoting familiarity. When this William Smith, who kept the Rummer by the Hall gate from 1740, first took a lease of the southeast vault under the Hall in 1748, he was apparently already occupying it as assignee of a deceased tenant and so, by 1754, tasting among the barrels may have been going on for some time.[33] Any construction extending Smith's space into the fenced enclosure was not even hinted at in the company's minutes – often packed with trivia about the Hall's tenants – yet a good deal of underpinning of south and east fronts went on during 1752–3 that may have included this bit of minor construction. There are plenty of pitfalls and ambiguities in citing either an engraving or a minutebook as evidence for the *earliest* date of something or other, but both in this case offer the *latest* possible date for the beginnings of a tavern in the Hall basement off Fishmongers' Wharf. There seems to have been neither pre-Fire nor post-Fire precedent for it, whatever the mythmongers say. The corporate memory of the court chose to forget earlier refusals 'to suffer [the Hall] to be used in any public way for selling . . . any manner of liquor therein' (1672) or to allow a tavern by the Hall gate (1608). The Dolphin alehouse, subsequently Rummer tavern, in one of Trattle's former houses beside the Thames Street gate by about 1730, was the entering wedge. From at least 1753 until 1827, the modest but civilised arrangements in the riverside basement were fondly regarded in the neighbourhood. But stories of earlier Shades here, based on outsiders' romantic conjectures after 1827 and still repeated a century later, can be discounted.[34]

There were occasionally less peaceable uses upstairs. In December 1745, at the approach of 'the present Unnatural Rebellion' from Scotland, the great hall was briefly occupied by two companies of 'Train Bands, ordered out to preserve the Peace of this City in the Night', and one company by day. In June 1780 the gentlemen of Bridge Ward, assembling for defence against the Gordon rioters, met there 'to learn the military exercise', perhaps in the courtyard, or else in the great hall under Sir William Walworth's astonished gaze.

CHAPTER 10

The Return of the Company Surveyor

DURING 1670–1730 AND 1733–40 the Fishmongers had no company surveyor. At first, with a new Hall and most of the company's property newly built and under long leases, there must have seemed little need for one. In 1715 the houses, warehouses, and cranes at Porter's Quay, a lucrative property ever since Knesworth left it to the company two centuries before, were destroyed in the fire that consumed Wren's Custom House next door. In the rebuilding of Porter's Quay during 1716–17, costs of about £9400 included £40 to 'Mr Gould' as 'Surveyor of the buildings at Porters Kay'. Gould (probably the man who in 1710 got three guineas for a 'new platt' of the Lime Street premises) was paid five months before the roofs were on at Porter's Quay and nine months before final payments to carpenter and bricklayer there: that is, he was not supervising the complete construction, yet was obviously responsible for more than simply drawing the plans. He was probably James Gould, subsequently surveyor to the South Sea Company, related by marriage to the Dance family and thus a link in one of those dynastic artisan-valuer-designer networks from which much of the London architectural profession was to emerge.[1]

The first reference to anyone as 'the company surveyor' since the dismissal of Lock appeared in 1731. This was George Sampson and he lasted about a year, until his design for the Bank of England was chosen and building began there in 1732.[2] Sir Edward Bellamy, as governor of the Bank and prominent Fishmonger, may had something to do with his introduction to the company in the spring of 1731 when Sampson drew up agreements with craftsmen for more work at Porter's Quay. Various other properties came under the eye of 'Mr Sampson the Companyes Surveyor' in that year and still in the spring of 1732 when he prepared estimates for repairs to certain houses coming out of lease in Thames Street, but by August (when building began at the Bank) the company bricklayer was providing such estimates instead. Sampson, on being asked 'what Gratuity would satisfy him' for his services, told the court he expected fifty guineas, a sum they reduced to forty after requiring a written account, the company clerk adding the marginal comment 'Very well paid'. Ten years later Sampson was consulted for an outside estimate on some company work. His only other entry into these records suggests his over-eagerness to please both then and in 1731–2, while his plans for

The notes for Chapter 10 are on pp. 193–5.

the Bank of England were hanging fire, an uneasiness still remembered in 1743 when the company carpenter Samuel Bennet Smith wrote to the court objecting to the valuing of his work by 'Prejudiced' men, 'or anyone that might have a View of receiving future Favours from the Comp^a One of which he had some reason to believe is Mr Sampson from what passed at the doing the Work at Porters Kay sometime past' – an authentic growl among the muted voices of the minutebook.

As leases fell in and the company decided to repair or rebuild the houses on its estates rather than let them on building leases, the lack of a coordinator was increasingly felt. All over the City, as post-Fire sixty-one and seventy-one year leases fell in, that is from 1728 on, misunderstandings were bound to occur in dealings between independent master craftsmen and oligarchic groups of laymen who lived in houses built new for their fathers or grandfathers, not for themselves. Possibly the supervision of building programmes was not eased by the age of the company clerk, Matthew Tanner, whose death in 1740 completed almost a century of service to the company by his father and himself. At any rate, the conduct of building by the company was clarified during the years 1739–43, not without strain, for the court itself was divided as to what sort of 'skilful and faithfull Person' was wanted 'to Oversee the Workmen and to take a Distinct Acc^t of the Materialls used as also to measure the Work so done that the Comp^a may not be imposed on by their Workmen'.

In 1739 a member of the court, Edward Price linen-draper, soon to become a warden, was one of two members of a committee considering craftsmen's drawings and estimates for certain rebuilding in Thames Street who 'Advised with sev^{ll} Persons of known Ability and Skill in the Profession', after which it was ordered that 'Mr. Price, Joyner [presumably an error for Junior] a Person well Recommended' for his knowledge of building, should supervise the work 'from time to time'. This was John Price, apparently the man whose father of the same name (died 1736) had designed the church of St George's Southwark, for which the company bricklayer James Porter had held the principal contract.[3] John the younger had been assisting his father ever since they built St George's Yarmouth in 1714–16, that is, in 1739 he was an experienced man in his later forties. In 1753 he served as Master of the Carpenters' Company. He may or may not have been related to Edward Price the linen draper; one can but note that their ascendancies coincided. John Price's employment by the company seems to have been occasional at first (no money was paid to him until 1742) but by 1741 he was being referred to as 'Mr Price this Company's Surveyor' and he so continued until his death in 1765. In 1740, however, while the situation was still somewhat ill defined, certain members of the court had moved the appointment of an overseer of the company's workmen who would also oversee tenants' repairs and payments of rent – the old call for a 'renter's clerk'. Such a post, it was decided, should have a fixed salary of £70 a year, and Alexander Bower, Turkey merchant and member of the court, proposing himself as a proper person for it was appointed and filled the post, or at any rate drew the salary, with scarcely a visible ripple on the surface of the minutebooks, for twenty-five years, while he continued to sit on the court.[4] So far as supervision of workmen was concerned, as John Price came to be more and more depended upon, there was probably little for Bower to do, except irritate them, and what 'quickening' the tenants amounted to does not appear. During the twenty-five years 1740–65, John Price (who would also have other irons in the fire) earned in fees, for 'surveying estimating measuring & taking schedules etc' and 'drawing plans etc.' for the company, just over £1000; Bower's salary as overseer of workmen during the same period came to £1750. A salaried surveyor was still far in the future.

But John Price's surveyorship was an advantage to the company's master crafts-men who now had a colleague to mediate for them when too much was expected of them in too little time and to certify their rights to payment, as well as an advantage to the company when their estimates were too outrageous. Various half-explained irritations came to a head early in 1743 with moves to get rid of both the company carpenter and the company bricklayer, moves that come to nothing, and then one grand showdown while Bower was Renter Warden, and so perhaps a test case, that demonstrated some of the uncertainties in the building world then.[5] For a major rebuilding on company property at Queenhithe, a tenant's bricklayer had proposed to build for almost £400 less than the estimate Price and the company craftsmen had prepared. Both sides were summoned to the Hall, bringing outside surveyors to back them up, all being ordered to withdraw and find out where their differences lay, and returning after long discussion to say they 'pretty near' agreed on quantities but 'very largely' disagreed on prices – a meeting that would not interest us now (the company's men eventually did the job) but for the identity of the 'surveyors' whom Price was able to summon : 'Mr Gibbs' and 'Mr Fleetcraft' were possibly the architects James Gibbs and Henry Flitcroft, both of whom Price would have known while building on the Harley Estate in the Cavendish Square neighbourhood. These two brought estimates signed by two measurers (quantity surveyors), one an R. Morris, possibly Robert Morris, who though he wrote books about architecture described himself as a surveyor and is known to have been called in as a valuer in the City at this period. The opposing surveyors seem to have been seasoned but lesser men, 'Mr Steers', possibly James Steere, surveyor to Guy's Hospital and the Hand in Hand Fire Office, and 'Mr Hore', either the builder George Hoare or more likely James Horne, surveyor to the Foundling Hospital. (James Gibbs and James Horne had been called in as assessors over a matter referred to arbitration during the building of the Mansion House.)[6] This was a varied crew of consultants to be sent out of the courtroom to haggle over estimates for a dockside house and warehouse. But a livery company of the standing of this one had much prestige in the City as a client. The borderlines between designers, surveyors, valuers, builders, dealers in building materials, and the upper craftsmen were either blurred or non-existent; standards in that respect were fluid. Bennet Smith the company carpenter, who kept a timber merchant's yard at Shad Thames, Bermondsey, was occasionally paid by the company for 'making elevations and plans' (cut and dried as that was on a city street) as well as for building, and some neat drawings that survive may be his.[7] Certain standards of construction fixed by successive Building Acts, and the long craft experience of the various London building trades, still left room for differences in judgment and so for arbitration, especially if a powerful institutional client were not yet persuaded of the good judgment of its own surveyor. At any rate, this (at the time) inconclusive conclave appears to have established John Price's status with the Fishmongers' Company and ended much contention with craftsmen.

During 1751–3 Price had to deal with serious structural failure of the Hall itself, due to defective foundations and timberwork. The first discovery, of the subsiding wall between courtroom and parlour with sinkage of the 'dancing room' floor above, was followed by 'unequal settlement' of the centre of the south front under 'the Great Door' – very ancient inequality of ground on the medieval boundary with the Nun's Head premises. In the eighty-odd years since the rubble of those unequal cellars was packed down in 1669, 'it appeared that the Water from the Thames had found its way thereto', for instance in the Thames floods of 1682, 1703, 1726, 1736, and 1747; and weather historians mention a great tide that flooded Whitehall in March 1753, which preceded more unwelcome discoveries at the Hall in May. Yet the defects of brick piers resting on rotten timberwork had come about not suddenly but gradually, insidiously, over the years. Settlement of structures had become a public topic after subsidence of a bridge pier during construction of Westminster Bridge in 1747, though its Swiss engineer Charles Labelye was vindicated after its completion. The Fishmongers' court decided in 1752 to call Labelye in to survey the Hall and wharf foundations, but finding that he was no longer in England called in Messrs Marquand & Battison. This will have been Charles Marquand, who had contributed to a recent flurry of pamphlets on bridges a discussion of . . . *the different Soiles where they are intended to be Built, which hitherto seems to have been a Thing not sufficiently consider'd*. Marquand's recommendations, prepared in conference with Price and three company craftsmen, for strengthening the stone wharf with new piling and 'Whale pieces' and 'a good bank of chalk' echo centuries of Thames wharf-mending.[8]

Early in the morning of 3 August 1763 a bad fire in one of the houses between Hall and street emphasized the need for a proper strongroom as part of the Clerk's office, to replace the treasury closet off the courtroom, vulnerable both to fire and to window-entry from the alley outside where the wood merchant east of the Hall kept all manner of sheds. The Clerk's quarters had already expanded into the rear premises of the house west of the Hall entry and were now to be extended over the rear premises of another house. Enlarging the little house opposite the Clerk's office – built in 1721 between the long entry and the eastern stableyard for the senior beadle but ill scaled to the size of his family, and occupied at various times by the elderly 'scourer' and her husband the company 'engine-keeper' (pump-minder) and then by an elderly clerical assistant – was also part of this building programme. In October 1765, in the midst of preparing the required drawings, John Price died suddenly, probably in his seventies. He must have lived somewhere nearby if he was the John Price rewarded with half a guinea for aid during the fire in August – still, in that amount, treated more like a workman than a former master of his own livery company (whereas in 1820 Edward I'Anson, occasional assistant to the company surveyor, rushing down from Lawrence Pountney Hill to help in a similar fire, was asked to accept twenty guineas). Price was succeeded as company surveyor by his nephew and assistant George Silverside, who carried out the alterations already intended.[9] As surveyor Silverside lasted five years, falling victim late in 1770 to an illness of which he died early in 1771. His assistant who managed for him in this period was George Gwilt (1746–1807), active as architect and surveyor in Southwark and later master of the Masons' Company.[10] From mid-1771 the new company surveyor, considerably senior to Gwilt, was John Gorham, builder and surveyor, whose father of the same name had been bricklayer to Gray's Inn.

Gorham seems to have been an upright, downright, quintessential London institution's man of building-business: sometime surveyor to Gray's Inn, the Duke of Bedford's London estate, the parish of St James's Piccadilly, the College of Physicians, the Drapers' Company and the Fishmongers' Company.[11] When he retired from the last in 1796 'on Account of his advanced Age' – almost 80, having worked for Gray's Inn since at least 1738 – the court ordered that 'he be invited to dine with this Company' at all its great dinners thereafter, the first of its surveyors to survive into honourable retirement. His prime work for this company was the supervision of large repairs with the design of the ensuing redecoration at the Hall and adjoining houses during 1788–92. This was almost a gutting of the Hall interior, gone timber-rotten and unfashionable at the end of its century or so. Interiors are often more ephemeral than exteriors, yet the drastic nature of the work then undertaken clearly means that dry rot, more than taste, was at the bottom of it.

In May 1788 Gorham inspected 'the state of the Hall' and the resulting work began in July, to last about two and a half years there – during much of which time company business was conducted from Merchant Taylors' Hall – and a year and a half more for work on two adjoining houses. The entire cost came to over £18,000 including a good deal of new furniture, and payments to Gorham relating to this four-year programme came to about five per cent of the total. No fewer than four intermeshing series of office accounts, by turns intricate and vague, and none comprehensive, were kept in the Clerk's office at this period, but detailed bill-books from seven of the nine firms of building craftsmen also survive.[12] The bills of James Gubbins accounted for the largest slice, over £8000 'for Carpenters & Joiners Work in the Several Repairs and Alterations' (and furnishings) during the four years: old demarcation disputes over carpenters doing joiners' work no longer mattered. Gubbins' workshops and timberyard were nearby on the river side of Thames Street near Dowgate Wharf, and in trade directories he appears both as builder and as merchant. He, incidentally, took care of the beer accounts for most of the workmen on the site; one can tell from this item on his bills which trades were at work in any one week: at first, in July-August 1788, beer for carpenters and bricklayers only, from September beer for masons too and for the next year beer for those three trades only, from

September 1789 beer for smiths as well, and in October beer for plasterers and painters too, and so on. In the first week in October a charge for candles would begin, illuminating the long hours then worked. Gubbins' men not only entirely renewed most floors, wainscot, skirting, staircases, window frames and sashes and shutters, doors and architraves and jambs, and parts of the gallery, but joists and storey-posts and other elements of the structural frame. It was an age of mahogany – 'Delivered 1 Log of Honduras Mahogany Sawn into Plank for Sashes, Sash Frames etc', and 'reduced mahogany (dry Jamaica wood)' for stair-rails – but oak was still paramount for structure, as 'in large Scantlings for Storey Posts', and 'Memell timber' (Baltic fir) was used for much flooring and lesser panelling. The bricklayers rebuilt portions of brick walls, at basement level anyway, with the footings, and there was also 'underpinning foundation' work by the masons. Yet the tide lapping nearby and its old vulnerable point of entry remained unaffected by the forest of piles 'they had drove . . . to secure the wharf & keep water from the foundations' in 1752–3, or by the raising of certain cellar floors after 'extra-ordinary high Spring tides' had flowed up 'the great Drein' and into various wine-cellars in 1756 and 1757; the level of the wharf had been raised in 1753, so that by 1816, for example, the southwest basement floor was to be seven steps below the wharf, according to a rough drainage plan drawn then.[13]

The lead-covered roof of the riverside block also needed immediate attention, and the plumbers' men (from Messrs. Poynder of Eastcheap) removed the lead as Gubbins' men began reboarding the frame for replacement by copper. The post-Fire roofing, probably cast in heavy sheets so tending to slip on the slopes and also to decay on the flat where worn by weather or bored through by timber-beetle, had been causing concern for some time. Copper, first systematically mined in England in the latter eighteenth century, was known to be both lighter and stronger than lead. The riverside block at Fishmongers' Hall in 1788 must have been one of the first prominent English buildings to have a copper roof.[14] The firm employed, at a total cost of £594, were John Buhl & Son of St Martin's Lane, 'Ironmongers, Braziers, and Inventors of the Copper-plate covering for Buildings'. A high wind in 1796 carried off a bit of this roof, which was mended by William Pontifex of Shoe Lane (Buhl's entry in the trade directories no longer including his proud announcement). London's smoky atmosphere ensured that the copper never turned bright green, so far as we can tell from watercolour views taken thereafter.[15]

Gorham's new decorative scheme for the state rooms can only be surmised from craftsmen's bills, committee minutes, and three unused drawings that survive. These and drawings he did for redecoration of Drapers' Hall after a fire there in 1772 show that he had assimilated all the more obvious elements of the Adam style and was a designer of some restraint and discrimination. Gorham's generation of builders and decorators was served by the great proliferation of published design-manuals for everything from house-fronts to tea-urns. The elegant neatness of the title page for his little company planbook of 1772, compared with the brash exuberance of the planbook title page of 1686, encapsulates much cultural change. One of the apparently unused drawings attributed to Gorham shows a colonnade dimensioned, it would seem, for a great-hall screen; but more of a barrier to kitchen smells was wanted, for a 'Screen Partition' of some sort was being prepared in Gubbins' shop early in December 1788 and in January fixed in place with 'pilasters etc to passage', that is, the old screens passage, from which entry to the hall was now by two pairs of folding doors, mentioned in the demolition sale catalogue of 1827.[16]

New 'best stairs' off the parlour end of the great hall were begun in the summer of 1789. Described in 1827 as a 'very excellent Dutch wainscot [i.e. oak] staircase and landings in 3 flights, oak turned ballusters, mahogany cross-banded handrail [the mahogany 'cutt Circular for Wreathd Rail' as Gubbins put it], carved brackets, curteel step, and scroll', this staircase made £18 at auction. The ribbon-bound laurel-garland motif had been a Palladian one. The parlour now had a door directly into the great hall where a traditional 'Beaufett' (buffet or display cupboard for silver) apparently had been taken down after the dry-rot discoveries of 1753; either then or in 1788–9 the parlour was given 'handsome entrances to ends of room with 3/4 columns, carved caps, shield for Arms, etc', according to the catalogue of 1827. It is hard to apportion the columnar carvings in Gubbins' accounts, but certainly such tabernacle door-frames echo the Palladian taste of the early eighteenth century, though there is no record that such were installed then. Gorham grew up to that earlier taste, and his clients here did too. The parlour apparently retained its original raised-and-fielded panelling of 1670, 'with carved bolection, mouldings [and] raised pannels', until 1827.[17] Purity of style and consistency of decoration were seldom considerations in the City – until the years when the next Fishmongers' Hall was built.

In 1790 the long gallery upstairs was divided into three rooms, a ladies' tea-room, a coffee room also called the card room, and a drawing room. Four little hall chairs, with a restrained carved fan-shell motif and painted company crest, now standing in the courtroom corridor of the present building, might be survivors from 'the Chairs in the Card room' specifically exempted from the auction of 1827 and probably designed by Gorham for Gubbins' workshop. Colour schemes can only be vaguely apprehended from the billbook of the painter Thomas Jones (not a contemporary easel-painter of that name).[18] The following seem to refer to the walls of the three new rooms upstairs: 'french grey flatted on stucco', 'fine lemon colour flatted on stucco', 'pea green ditto'. But 'ornamented ceiling picked in ornamented dead white, grounds french grey, green, & pink' seem to have been a new dress for John Grove's seventeenth-century parlour ceiling. 'Carved frieze french grey, and 'Ditto swaggs & shells white ground green' may have been for the parlour too. 'Corinthian Caps to Pillars gilt with lapis lazuli' may refer to the new hall screen. In the great hall, the carved shields were retained and accompanied by gilded festoons with mottoes, but no coherent account emerges of this room. How incoherent the materials for history are sometimes.

There were ornamental gates at both ends of the long entry, at the street and at the entrance to the portico, both sets new made by the smiths John Woodall & Son, and apparently painted Prussian blue like the 'lamp irons', the inner 'pair

verry rich Hatch gates' probably gilded too. Woodall also provided 'truss irons'
for the hall gallery (sometimes laden with dinner spectators) and sets of 'wrought
Gilt' door-furniture. And Jones painted nine dozen garden pots green and white,
for long entry and courtyard. Somewhere between the portico and the courtroom,
dominating an anteroom to the fount of the company's charity, there was installed
in 1791 a graceful statuary group representing 'Charity', a womanly figure with
two children and a shield with the company arms, the whole made of the new
composition called Coade stone from a model probably by John Bacon.[19] Jones
painted the 'Figure of Charity twice dead white & Pedestal 4 Oil & flatted Buff
& white', the pedestal having been ornamented, probably with compo-work, by
Gubbins. Other works furnished by Mrs Eleanor Coade included chimneypieces
and two medallions of nereids and dolphins, the latter probably the two circular
medallions which Willats the plasterer set into the wall of the great hall and
Jones painted 'dead white & lilac'. The carver Peter van Gelder (who had made
the monument to Major André in Westminster Abbey to Robert Adam's design)
carved four new Portland stone capitals for the 'colonnade', probably of the
portico, for £60, and other works in wood including 'two boys holding two
dolphins', quite likely the two panels on the present staircase which came back
to the company in 1954.[20] 'New Veind Marble Chimneys' (chimneypieces) were
supplied by Thomas Piper the mason after removing two old ones, probably
Peirce's from the old great chamber and one Easton had made for the courtroom;
but Easton's parlour chimneypiece remained in all its state. Gubbins also supplied
chimneypieces 'neatly Enrich'd', in fact he supplied a good deal of furniture –
mahogany chairs, tables, and sideboards – whether made in his own workshops or
not, as well as 'spring curtains' (window shades) and Venetian blinds, that is, he
was able to operate as an upholsterer too.[21]

An 'Elegant Japan'd Wine Cistern – to Drawing' (probably Gorham's) was
furnished by Gubbins: 'with Carved Goats Heads at Angles Suspending festoons
of Vine Leaves and Grapes on the 4 faces Enriched with Medallions representing
the head of Appolo and Bacchants on the front and a Lyre in Center, the Top
and Bottom edges finish'd with Borders of Roses (Carv'd) and Supported by
Goats Legs £42', according to Gubbins' bill for March 1790. In contrast to the
good living that implied, Gubbins was forced to add an increased charge of two
pence a day per man (probably for eight men) for the year Christmas 1790 –
Christmas 1791 'On Acct of the great advance in Men's Wages'. Gubbins himself
was able to engage in speculative building in Lambeth during 1791–3, possibly on
the proceeds of his work at the Hall.[22] Gorham thought poorly of him for expecting
the company to pay for his foreman's time, 'It being the Masters Business to give
directions and to see them Executed'. Gubbins obviously employed specialists as
well as all-round carpenters still able to cope with 'repairing Trunk [wooden
drainpipe] in the Thames to keep out the tide', that timeless problem. As for the
drains, the privy on the stairs had been operating by more than the power of
gravity ever since Silverside in 1768 pointed out that there would be no stench if a
marble basin were installed 'and plenty of water laid into the same'. By 1775 there

was a 'Reservoir or Cistern over the Water Closet' in the Clerk's house – quite likely Cummings' patent water-closet of 1775, the first one patented in England.[23] Hall installations sold off in 1827 included queensware basins and mahogany seats; and the glazier in 1791 provided ground-glass windows. The Clerk's house as redone in 1791 had a powdering room (for wigs – a bit late in the day elsewhere – and spelt 'Boudering room'), also a circular staircase, down the walls of which a paperhanger applied canvas stained 'to prevent the Vermin coming thro'. On the whole, the group of buildings pulled down here in 1827 and after were inwardly much more of the late eighteenth century than of the seventeenth.

The Shades wine rooms, under the corner of the great hall nearest the river, were being repaired at this period too, and at last mentioned by name (by Piper the mason, 'setting old base in Shades') and also as 'Woodings Rooms' by Gubbins, preparing 'oak truss girders joists etc', both early in 1790. Simon Wooding, wine and brandy merchant, had taken a lease of the Rummer by the Hall gate, 112 Upper Thames Street, in 1774 and with it (though unconnected by any passage) the riverside wine vault under the great hall held by other vintners before him and, as we have seen, quietly run as a tavern from 1753 or before. In 1791 the court decided to take over the whole of No. 112 and add it to the Clerk's office : with the riverside rooms west of the music gallery and over the kitchens being adapted to the Clerk's residential use, and one of the other Thames Street houses leased to the Deputy Clerk, the old days of minding the company's business in cramped quarters were over. Wooding eventually took the easternmost house, No. 115, from which he could reach his wine vaults through the stableyard and an entry under the courtroom. Gubbins' 'fitting up' for Wooding's wine rooms probably included the fittings that Wooding's son was allowed to remove in 1827 : such as the 'Six Boxes Wainscot backs and seats in front room under Terrace'.[24] The terrace appears to have been made in the alterations of 1790, by extending the original landing at the top of the great stone steps eastward along the south front, with the eastern flight of steps removed and the western flight enclosed from the wharf by a wall, as shown in Daniell's view of 1804 (Pl. 8). By the 1790s the company were so ready to accommodate 'The Shades' that 'they removed a great portion of the upper part of the embankment wall and placed up railing so that the Customers at The Shades might view the River', as legal counsel was to put it much later. For all the best-laid brick and stonework carried out at the Shades in 1790, however, the damp continued to rise, and on View Day in 1796 dry rot was observed 'in the new rooms and girder at Mr Wooding's under the Terrace', which according to the terms of the lease Simon Wooding's newly bereaved widow was obliged to deal with. But she and then her son Simon carried on the Shades successfully there for another thirty years before it was removed to a house just upstream and its name also borrowed elsewhere. Here under the Hall until 1827 a man could sit in a 'box' by the window looking out on the moving tide while drinking wine 'drawn reaming from the butt in splendid silver jugs'. In this period Fishmongers' Wharf was a neighbourly promenade for local residents, 'the little 'Change of the oldest & most respectable inhabitants of St

Michael's and the adjoining parishes . . . here accustomed, both at the ebb and flow of the tide, to take their healthful walk', comfortable merchants of coal, cheese, or wine, or practitioners of the law, still enjoying village life in the City. Some members of the company's court still lived in the City in this period; such a man could live, like Elizabeth Bennet's uncle Gardiner 'in Gracechurch Street, within view of his own warehouses'. (As Jane Austen was doubtless unaware, there had been in Gracechurch Street before her day Messrs Goddard & Gardiner, hardwaremen of a previous generation, tenants of this company.) The Hall wharf provided then one of the few riverside walks without dockside clutter, and Old Swan Stairs had not yet pushed out into the stream as a pier for steamboats. The elder neighbours in Waterloo year, say, could remember remnants of medievalism that London had cast off in the 1760s, the houses on London Bridge and the City Gates, and could recall the gradual substitution of house-numbering for the old signs. The younger neighbours gossiping there in, say, 1825, barely old enough to recall Nelson's funeral procession passing by on the river, were, in their middle age, to see the Thames become a hellish stream.[25]

Modernity began to affect official procedures. For the appointment of a new company surveyor in 1796, a more formal process of selection was adopted than ever before, with three nominees chosen from seven candidates – a formality reflecting the higher regard the company now had for the position. The runners-up were Nathaniel Wright, district surveyor for the northern district of the City, and Samuel Saxon, country-house architect and a former pupil of Sir William Chambers. The youngest and, as it turned out, the most eminent of the three was elected: Daniel Asher Alexander, aged 28, and subsequently surveyor to the new London Docks Company and to Trinity House, having already designed warehouses on Bankside. As engineer and architect he invested warehouses, light-houses, and prisons of the new industrial age with a grim grandeur reminiscent of the drawings of Piranesi.[26] Yet, apart from the easy reference to Piranesi which historians always make about Alexander, the spectacular basements of his London Dock buildings with their brickwork vaulting were simply grander and technically more sophisticated versions of the brick-vaulted cellars already lying under many London buildings – made with techniques that someone with vision and expertise could command from the bricklayers (ready to 'turn a vault' since at least the sixteenth century) when the new clients and needs of the Industrial Revolution were ready for them. Such techniques did not spring entire from the brows of the new engineers. This is not to lessen Alexander or the interest taken by his generation in great Roman monuments and new technologies, but to define roots sometimes overlooked in this connection.

A little irony in Alexander's several surveyorships was that the Fishmongers' tenants with riverside warehouses looked upon the new wet-dock plans as a threat to their livelihood, and the company joined them in furious petitions for compensation. An engraved design by him for the London Docks, preserved among the company's drawings, is dated November 1796. But Alexander's practice managed to straddle the two points of view. During the twenty-five most active years of his working life, he continued as this company's surveyor – mainly, it should be said, with the help of assistants, of whom the best known was Edward I'Anson (1775–1853).[27] The assistant who succeeded Alexander as the Fishmongers' company surveyor was to say that 'from 1806 to 1822 (with a brief interval of about a Year) the Office was discharged by Proxy'. From 1804 on, Alexander was the first of this company's surveyors to be paid a regular annual salary (£150) and to be regularly invited to dinner. Most of his company employment concerned properties other than the Hall, where no major reconstruction or redecoration went on during this time.

The great expenditure on the Hall during 1788–92 had ended just as the impoverishments of the Napoleonic wars began. Thereafter the company had its moments of retrenchment. In 1796, when the Fishmongers' Company was able to subscribe £20,000 towards a City loan to the Exchequer, a custom of giving lemons to members of court was discontinued and spermaceti candles were used instead of wax at evening parties. In 1811 no turtle soup was served except on August 1, no early asparagus, green peas or other expensive vegetables whatever, and attention was paid to 'diminution of expence in the deserts'. In 1818, when there was much paring of bills and displeasure with tradesmen, the stationer's bill precipitated an order that in future playing cards were to be bought direct from the cardmakers, sealing wax direct from the wax chandlers, and red tape direct from the haberdashers. More seriously, in this period there again arose severe doubts about the structure of the Hall. In 1811 several roof timbers were found to be 'greatly affected by the dry rot' although 'no immediate danger was to be apprehended', but by 1813 a full-scale survey was made by I'Anson for Alexander – as one would expect, of the south and east fronts nearest the river. The brick walls were found to be considerably 'out of perpendicular', leaning some inward and some outward from the level of the heads of the lower tier of windows, which sounds like trouble for or from the cantilevered first-floor gallery round the great hall, to which Woodall the smith had applied truss irons and clip braces in 1789. Yet on the whole, the building was judged to be in a state of safety, 'even under all its defects' unless those increased rapidly, if kept under proper attention and repair.[28] The dubious impression thus conveyed is reflected in a special condition written into two leases for the adjacent houses Nos. 113 and 114 Upper Thames Street early in 1817, 'a proviso for enabling the Company in case they shall take down or rebuild their Hall to determine & make void said lease . . . on 12 months notice'. Neighbourly awareness of that proviso was going to be awkward when questions of demolition and compensation came up ten years later. Many old dark brick mansions still lying about the City then, like the one near the river in *Little Dorrit*, were beginning to lean a bit, the Hall, incidentally, was part of the waterfront the child Dickens knew on his walks to the Marshalsea in the early 1820s. By 1820, however, the company was ready to spend some money on enclosing the 'Great Loggia' or portico as a draught-proof 'Marble Hall' between Clerk's office and courtroom.

From 1817 Alexander's company surveyorship fell on the shoulders of his former pupil, 'My Clerk Suter who is set apart to your Work'. By 1819 Richard Suter was signing letters to the company from one of Alexander's offices, either from Chatham Place, Blackfriars, or from West Pier Head, London Docks. In 1821, while Alexander went abroad in a 'very ill state of health', there was much surveying business on hand on company properties after two fires and with several leases about to fall in, and I'Anson (by then practising on his own) was called in occasionally to help Suter. In May 1822 Alexander resigned. Besides Suter, other candidates presented themselves: George Basevi, Soane's brilliant pupil, then surveyor to the Guardian Assurance Company and later architect for terraces in Belgrave Square and South Kensington and for the Fitzwilliam Museum; Mr Parkinson, probably Joseph T. Parkinson who had laid out the Portman Estate and was surveyor to the Union Fire Assurance Office and a free-man of the Fishmongers' Company; Mr. Taylor, probably George Ledwell Taylor, who seems to have withdrawn quickly on discovering that Parkinson, to whom he had been articled, was a candidate; and Peter Biggs, one of a long line of small builders of that name.[29] By December, the others having all with-drawn their names, probably on learning that for five years Suter had 'discharged the duties of the situation', he was elected company surveyor. He was to serve until 1867; as he lived until 1883, he may have been 25 at most in 1822.[30] His experience as Alexander's representative (and also at Trinity House, where he succeeded him as surveyor) seems to have given him the poise he would need to deal with officials much senior to himself during the years 1825–31 when the rebuilding of London Bridge affected so much company property. The ease and force with which he was able to express himself in reports to the Clerk did not, however, come through in architectural drawing. When the new Hall for which he had paved every step of the way (metaphorically) was finally to be designed, he was not asked to do so. It would have been more likely for John Gorham to be asked to act as architect for a complete rebuilding if that had been required in 1788. In 1831, not only were the Fishmongers' expectations higher and the site regarded by the City authorities as an important part of the new bridge-approach in a period fascinated by town-planning, but a whole new competing mob of architects and would-be architects had arisen and the architectural expectations of Londoners in general had ex-panded in the 1820s. That was a stirring decade for architects and would-be architects in London.

CHAPTER 11

A Sacrifice to the Bridge

THE KNELL FOR THE HALL was struck, not by the first Act for a new London Bridge passed in 1823, but by an Act of 28 May 1827, specifically empowering the City to take a strip of ground twenty feet wide from Thames Street to the river, part of the site of Fishmongers' Hall, and directing that the amount paid in compensation be applied towards rebuilding the said Hall. Rebuilding could only be done after levels were settled by an Act of 1829 authorizing the carrying of the bridge-approach over Thames Street by viaduct.[1]

The day the first stone was laid for the Bridge, 15 June 1825 (though preliminary works had been going on since the year before), was a brilliantly ceremonious City occasion and a very local celebration by neighbours.[2] Field pieces of the City's own Artillery Company were stationed at Old Swan Wharf to announce the arrival of the Duke of York and the cavalcade from Guildhall. The Lord Mayor was John Garratt, wholesale tea merchant, born in Bridge Ward and owner of much property between the Hall and Old Swan : his forebears a century before had been company tenants in Black Raven Alley. Marshalling the procession on horseback was William Wadham Cope, freeman of this company and former company glazier who, on becoming a City Marshal, had handed over his company appointment to his brother Jacob, with premises beside the Hall. Among members of the Bridge Committee in charge of proceedings with their painted wands was the company carpenter, a builder and surveyor who was a company tenant near the Hall, John Locke. None of these men, incidentally, can have been unaware of earlier apprehensions of instability in the Hall.

Background to its eventual demolition is supplied by Sir John Rennie's autobiography written many years later : although he remembered the essential point in reverse, one can work it out from what he said.[3] It seems that in 1821, when the first property surveys were made for a new bridge west of the existing one, William Mountague the City Surveyor was directed to confine his measurements to an area within 180 feet upstream of the old Bridge. An 180-foot line measured at right angles to the old Bridge took 20 feet from the old Hall, though measuring this distance obliquely along the receding shore between Hall and Bridge would have just spared the Hall. Spared it, however, for a life ignominious, over-shadowed, and short (supposing it weathered the adjacent construction) and a

The notes for Chapter 11 are on pp. 195–6.

Mid-Victorian rebuilding at the very latest – or so it seems in retrospect. The shorn Hall's potential situation mapped in Fig. VII necessarily omits the potential height of the new Bridge. But as late as February 1827 Rennie was still proposing to shore up the existing Hall, for the whole matter of approaches and abutments bordering on the depths and shoals and ancient campsheds of Fishmongers' Hole seems to have proceeded very empirically indeed.

In February 1827 the company's court considered the situation. Already in December declaring themselves ready to facilitate construction of a new bridge by every means consistent with company rights and security, they had felt it would be most imprudent to vacate temporarily while the Hall was shored up, in case of 'inconvenience and damage far beyond what can now be calculated'. In February the Bridge Committee produced proposals to 'take down the Eastern Wall of the Dining Hall, secure the remainder of the Building during the erection of the Abutment, and when the same shall be completed, make good all damage'. This was declined and a resolution passed that 'this Court, in the full expectation of much greater mischief to the Hall than has been anticipated being inevitable, from the erecting of the Bridge, are inclined to receive a proposal from the London Bridge Committee that may induce the Company to take into consideration the pulling down their present Hall entirely and building a new one'. In March the court further stipulated that no building or erection of any kind should be allowed between Hall and Bridge, and that after bridge-construction was over, public right of way across the company's wharf should be stopped up (a chance to finish off the old Thames Quay idea, or so it was thought). Argument over these conditions was to go on for a long time, but the immediate issue was the amount of compensation offered, £10,000, turned down by the company as quite inadequate. The City authorities, after all, were trying to gain possession of ground to which the company's title 'existed prior to the great fire of London in 1666', as the company's Clerk pointed out to the Town Clerk. Two deputations met at Guildhall on March 19. The chairman of the London Bridge select committee, Richard Lambert Jones, unkindly pointed out that 'considering the dilapidated state of their Hall', the company would rebuild it anyway, and therefore the compensation required 'had no reference to *that*, but merely to the value of the 20 feet at the east end'. This the Fishmongers warmly pronounced to be wholly a misconception, 'they did not consider the Hall to be in a state of Dilapidation, and had no reason to believe that it would not answer its purposes extremely well for the next fifty years'. Maybe. However, even the hardest heads at Guildhall will have realized that the loss of title to some of its ancientest ground – most of the original Flower de Luce site, including most of the Stockfishmongers' Hall ground – was a wrench for an ancient body (as if part of Guildhall's site were taken for a motorway). A deed of covenant was drawn up in April, the company to receive £20,000 for the sale of part of the wharf, part of the Hall site, and all of the site of 115 Upper Thames Street, plus £300 for any damage to the rest of the wharf from the making of the coffer dam required for building the northern abutment. The company had already resolved to arrange its own demolition, the empowering Act was passed in May, and events now moved quickly.

In May it was agreed to sell all the furniture with exceptions that included the parlour chimneypiece, paintings, and jars, the figure of Sir William Walworth and all the shields, brass sconces bearing the company arms, and armorial glass from the windows in the great hall, all mahogany doors in the building, the card tables and chairs, all the drawing-room furniture (from the east end of the old long gallery over the courtroom) with Beechey's portrait of the Earl of St Vincent just rehung in that room. The other furniture and materials of the riverside and parlour ranges were sold in two sales in July 1827. The parlour windows, for instance, yielded five pairs of 'mahogany astragal and hollow sashes, double hung with inside shutters, architraves, mouldings and window seats', five sets of 'crimson damask curtains, with gilt cornices, laths, lines, pullies and brass pins', and 'Five canvas roller spring blinds'. Lighting fixtures assembled for sale in the great hall included three 'sexagon hall lamps' and 'Two bronze figures, with 2 branch lamps, globular shades and the scroll brackets to ditto'. Carpets and cornices and coppers, spits and stoves and six-leaved screens, green baize doors, marble chimneypieces, and enriched fanlights were knocked down along with bricks and quoins and slates by T. P. Creaton, auctioneer of Tower Street, City, and New Cut, Lambeth. Some bystanders regretted the 'sorry breaking up', the dismantling and scattering of long tables and 'cosy high-backed stuffed chairs . . . nay, the very soup-kettles and venison dishes'.[4] Yet it is quite likely that stone-carvings from the river-front were pocked and pitted by years of coal-smoke, and the chairs and kettles well worn out. Perhaps at no other time in the company's history were the wardens so ready to rid themselves of so many trappings of the past, to embrace so many new things; and this was very much what John Stuart Mill meant by 'The Spirit of the Age'.

The Clerk had now to find a temporary home for his family, and all objects reserved from auction were then temporarily stored in his remaining rooms at the Hall, while the company plate was stored in the Bank of England. The riverside and parlour ranges (but not the courtroom and office range) were demolished above basement level in July, after the sale of their contents on the 4th and of their materials on the 16th-17th, enough of the courtyard walls being retained to secure the quadrangle and north and west ranges until further demolition in 1830.[5] Until the end of 1829, company business was carried on in the constricted premises, and until 1835 dinners were held in taverns. For the period 1830 to mid-1835, the company took No. 15 Aldermanbury, the old Court of Requests, up a short *cul de sac* opposite Love Lane (nearly on the site of the present Corporation of London Record Office), for offices and furniture-storage.[6] The company carpenter whose men prepared it for occupation and at the Hall performed the last shoring-up of walls first framed by Thomas Lock was John Locke, though there was no obvious family link between them.[7]

The last gala party in the old Hall – whether known to be the last or not – was a ball for 350 people in May 1826. A stage was set up for Mr Weippert's band of musicians at the west end of the great hall (which suggests that the old music gallery had been enclosed as part of the Clerk's house), Mr Glover chalked the floor, Mr Johnson was engaged as master of ceremonies, Mr Collins lighted the place with oil lamps (an experiment with 'portable gas', it was found, 'would not answer'), Mr Elsmore furnished extra tables and benches for supper in the livery room and 'high benches for the ballroom', Mr Waud made the negus and the butler brought out champagne, madeira, sherry, and port, while marshals regulated the carriages and servants waited on benches in the long entry, guests were received in the courtroom, and (final instruction) Romney's portraits of the Margrave and Margravine of Anspach 'which the Court had been requested to accept' in 1798 during a period of friendship in that quarter, were taken down for the occasion – probably because the Dukes of Sussex and Kent, honorary freemen of the company, were invited and the royal family disapproved of the widowed Margravine, formerly Lady Craven.[8]

In July 1827, a few days after the first auction sale of furnishings, fixtures, and fittings, the court and its ladies embarked for a 'diversion on the water', the customary day on the river then undertaken every alternate summer. It was all very debonair, with musicians 'capable of playing quadrilles' accompanying them in another boat all the way to Richmond. (As when Samuel Rogers, the poet and the company's banker, told Tom Moore one May morning in 1819 that he was 'going on the water to follow the Fishmongers' barge and enjoy the music'.) More debonair, no doubt, than the return down-river in 1825, when 'the London Steam Packet' was engaged for the day, picking up butler, waiters, food and drink at the Hall at seven in the morning to take them up to Kew in readiness for the company barge's more dignified arrival and later, after the junketing at Richmond, to take the barge in tow and spare the rowers for the voyage back to the Hall – a modern experiment not repeated: imagine the clouds of coal smoke blown backward from the tall smoke-stack and down upon immaculate neck-cloths and summer dresses in the helpless barge, and splashes from the foaming wake of the larger vessel.[9] Subordinating the low-slung oarless barge, with its gilded St Peter and ritual paintwork, to the monster it was tied to in 1825 was not unlike the overbearing effect the new high bridge would subsequently have had on the seventeenth-century Hall if the Fishmongers had clung to it. The modernizing of the River Thames was a continuous running theme in the background of the Hall's history from 1796 on.

PART FOUR

THE PRESENT HALL AT
LONDON BRIDGE

'The site . . . presents such difficulties as are rarely found in Combination with great Advantages for the display of Architectural taste. The new Bridge . . . forms as it were a gigantic causeway, the Buildings at the terminations of which should be of a corresponding Architectural character, and the same simplicity of style which accords with the Bridge is equally suited to the commercial aspect of this part of the Metropolis.'

Henry Roberts, 'Description of the
Accompanying Design', 1831.

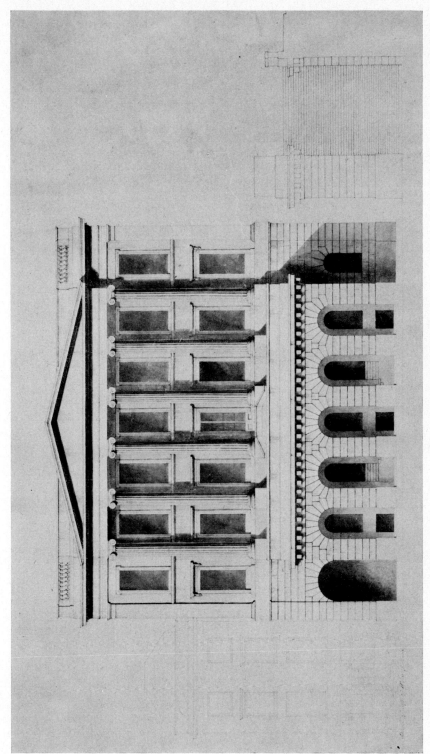

Pl. 9 Henry Roberts, competition drawing 1831 for the present Fishmongers' Hall, south or river-front elevation showing warehouse storeys under the Hall. Length of this front at bridge level 91 feet. Pen and wash on cartridge paper. Fishmongers' Company collection, Guildhall Library.

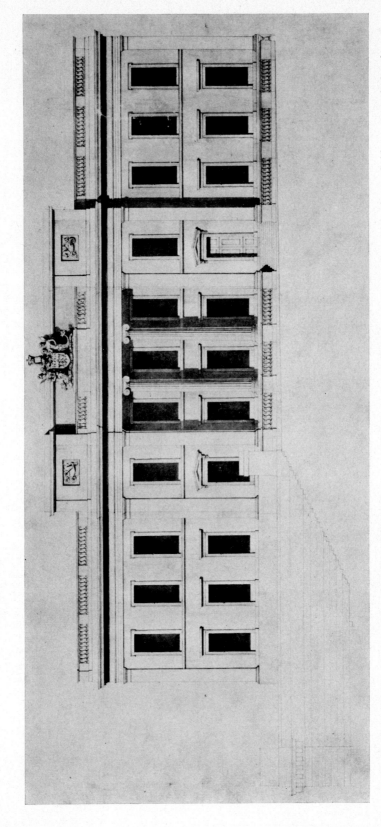

PL. 10 Henry Roberts, competition drawing 1831 for the present Fishmongers' Hall, east or entrance-front elevation on bridge-approach showing main Hall storeys only. Length of this front at bridge level, without terrace, 165 feet. Pen and wash on cartridge paper. Fishmongers' Company collection, Guildhall Library

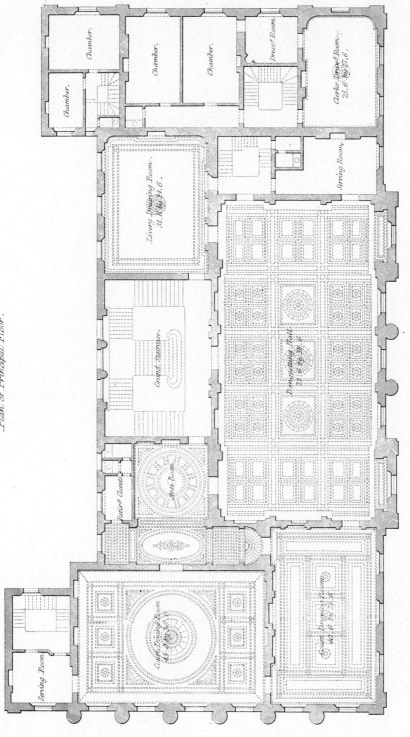

Plan of Principal Floor.

Chamber.

Chamber.

Chamber.

Chamber.

Chamber.

Dress.ᵈ Room.

Clerks Dressg.ᵈ Room.
25.6 × 17.6.

Livery Drawing Room.
31. × 24.6.

Grand Staircase.

Serving Room.

Banquetting Hall.
79.6 × 29.30.

Ante Room.

Petes.ᵈ Closet.

State Dining Room.
44. × 30. × 25.

Grand Drawing Room.
44.6 × 26.6.

Serving Room.

Scale of   100 Feet.

0

Pl. 11 Plan of Hall upper floor, showing ceilings of state rooms, engraving 1836 from *New Practical Builder*, vol. III, 1837, pl. cvi.
Author's collection.

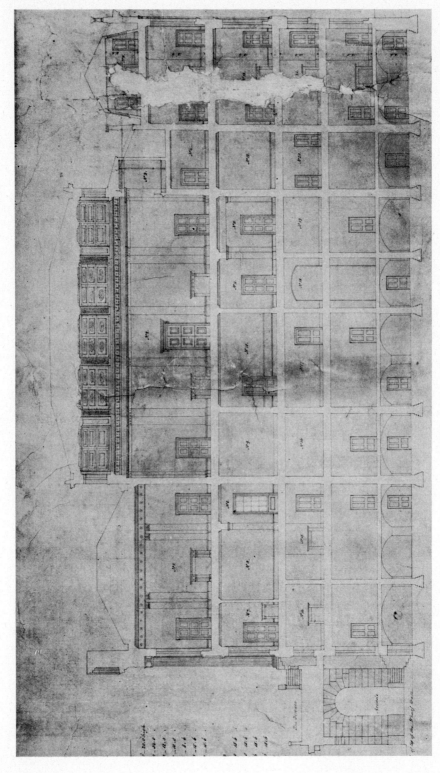

Pl. 12 Henry Roberts, competition drawing 1831, longitudinal (north-south) section showing warehouse storeys, Hall kitchen floor, the Hall's two principal storeys with courtroom and offices at left and Clerk's house at right, not entirely as built. Pen and wash on cartridge paper. Fishmongers' Company collection. Guildhall Library.

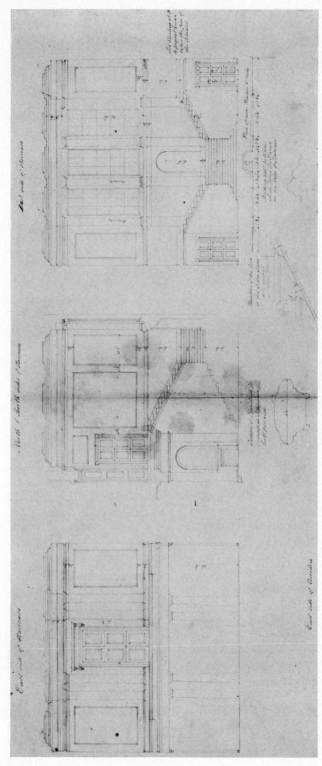

Pl. 13 Henry Roberts' office, details from sheet of drawings for main staircase compartment, 1834, showing granite columns under west wall of great hall, one of the pair of statuary niches with fireplace under, stair-rail section (below), and Walworth niche on the landing. Pen and wash on cartridge paper. Fishmongers' Company collection, Guildhall Library.

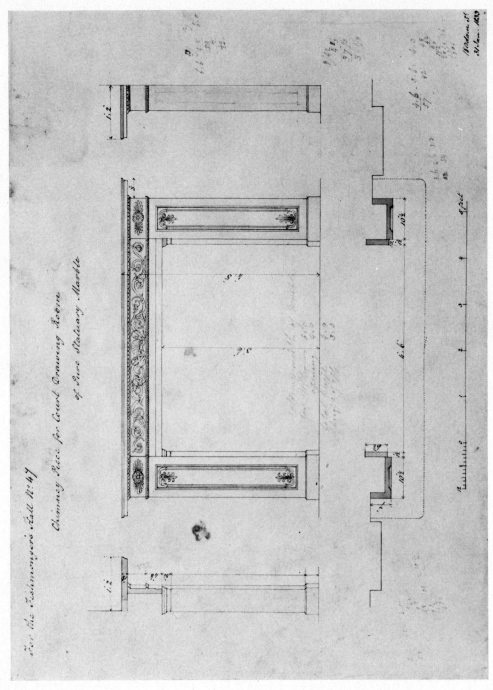

Pl. 14 Henry Roberts' office, drawing for court drawing-room chimneypiece, 1834 (p. 150, Pl. 22). Pen and wash on cartridge paper. Fishmongers' Company collection, Guildhall Library.

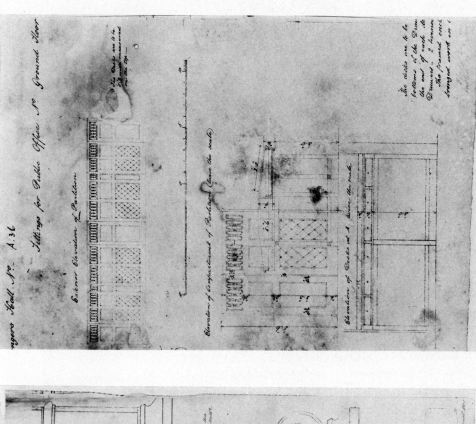

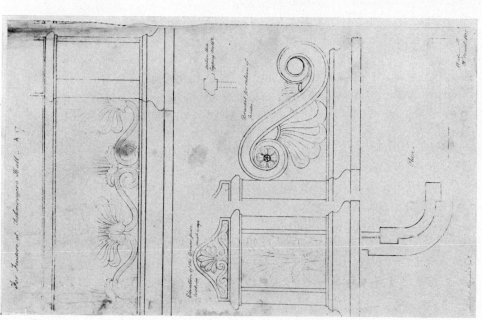

Pl. 15 Henry Roberts' office, details from drawings for fittings, (a) for fenders made by Ashwell & Kennard of Queenhithe, 1835, (b) for office desks and partitions, probably 1835 (pp. 153, 156). Pen and wash on cartridge paper. Fishmongers' Company collection, Guildhall Library.

Pl. 16 The banqueting hall, or great hall, as decorated by Roberts, before the redecoration of 1865, showing brass' gas chandeliers' furnished by Hancock & Rixon of Cockspur Street in 1834 (p. 151). Engraving from *Illustrated London News*, 23 November 1861, of dinner on November 9 attended by two 'Plenipotentiaries of the Confederate States of North America'.

CHAPTER 12

The Circumstances, 1827–31

FIVE YEARS ELAPSED between the decision to demolish the old Hall and selection of the winning design for a new one. During that time great heavings of mud, rock and dust from the new Bridge shook the ground west of the old Bridge. Many London sites were undergoing the turmoil of construction in the latter 1820s, when building-works for Buckingham Palace, Carlton Terrace, the Regent's Park terraces, the Bank of England, University College, St George's Hospital, the General Post Office, the British Museum, King's College, the Athenaeum and United Services clubs, Belgrave Square, and St Katharine's Docks were all going at once. 'Metropolitan improvement' was felt at the time to be 'so rapidly . . . taking place around us that the absence of a few months from London produces revolutions in sites, and alterations in appearances, that are almost miraculous and cause the denizen to feel himself a stranger in his own city', as James Elmes put it in 1827. In that year several City livery company halls were in the builders' hands or soon to be: a new Salters' Hall was being finished. Grocers' Hall was being altered, and the Goldsmiths' Company were preparing to rebuild. Given the changes in local geography being wrought for the Bridge, and given the defects of the existing Fishmongers' Hall, a contagious spirit of improvement in the air must also have influenced this company's decision to rebuild.

In general the urge for metropolitan improvement cannot have been unrelated to the increasingly urgent agitation then going on for political, religious and educational reform. The selection of eminent men for the honorary freedom of the Fishmongers' Company during the decade 1821–31 indicates the cast of its opinions: Henry (later Lord) Brougham, Joseph Hume, Thomas (later Lord) Denman, Viscount Althorp (later Lord Spencer), and Lord John (later Earl) Russell. Three Members of Parliament sat on the company's court: William Smith, until 1830 the well-known Unitarian member for Norwich and champion in the Commons of the rights of dissenters, a collector of pictures who had been a friend of Reynolds, Fox and Wilberforce; Matthew Wood the popular Whig alderman (baronet 1837) of whom we shall hear more; and from 1828 John Easthope, owner of the *Morning Chronicle* 1834–47 (baronet 1841). The Fish-

The notes for Chapter 12 are on pp. 196–7.

mongers' Company was an early shareholder in University College, founded in 1825 as the University of London, free of religious qualifications for entry, offering a wider range of courses than Oxford or Cambridge, and housed in a new 'Greek' building in Gower Street. The architectural revival of ancient Greek style so fashionable in the mid-1820s could have in Gower Street a Radical dissenting no-nonsense businesslike air about it, and at the same time in country houses and clubhouses an air of entrenched privilege, while to all of these, as to public and commercial buildings, it imparted an air of dignified probity. By the 1820s it did not need the philhellene sentiments demonstrated by contributions to Greek independence (as, for example, the Fishmongers' Company's £200 gift to 'the Greek committee' in 1823) to popularize the Greek Revival in architecture.[1]

Presiding over the dissolution and revival of Fishmongers' Hall, as well as the disposal of much other property affected by the new Bridge, was a special committee of wardens, known from August 1832 as the building committee.[2] For ten years its six most devoted members and the company's Clerk acted as corporate client, dealing with the City's Bridge Committee, the Hall architect and various contractors, as the court's representatives and subject to the court's decisions from time to time. Chief among the six was Matthew Wood, alderman 1807–43, M.P. 1817–43, twice Lord Mayor 1815–17, champion of Queen Caroline in 1820–1, later chairman of the House of Commons committee on metropolitan improvements, in whose house a nucleus for the Reform Club was formed in 1834 : he had become a freeman of the Fishmongers' Company by purchase in 1802, when he was a drug merchant of Falcon Square, Noble Street. His handwriting was large and powerful. His descendants were to include a Lord Chancellor (his son Lord Hatherley) and a Field Marshal (his grandson Sir Evelyn Wood), as well as the latter's sister, Parnell's Mrs O'Shea. And there was John Towgood (freedom 1778), brother-in-law to Samuel Rogers the poet and banker, and member of a family network Whig, liberal and Unitarian (and in Rogers' case, at least, outstandingly devoted to literature and art). Another committee member was William Sturch (freedom 1792 as an ironmonger of Stanhope Street, Clare Market), known as a liberal-minded theological writer and from about 1822 one of the original leaseholders in York Terrace, Regent's Park – his daughter was to found Bedford College. The others were Samuel Mills, freeman 1800 as weaver and merchant of Finsbury Place, later resident in Russell Square, apparently in family and/or business connection with certain silk manufacturers sitting on the court; Evan Edwards, freeman 1802 as chemist of Coleman Street, later with patent-medicine warehouse in St Paul's Churchyard beside the Chapter House and suburban residence at Denmark Hill; and Joseph Wilson, silk manufacturer of Milk Street (freedom 1787), apparently brother to Thomas Wilson, one of the founders of University College. The Clerk of the company since 1809 was John David Towse (born 1760, and an assistant in the Clerk's office since 1775), son of a former deputy clerk whose service in the company's office had begun about 1758 – a succession that was to last with two generations more until 1921. Succeeding in 1809 a Clerk whose period in office had been one of administrative disarray, Towse seems to have brought powers of calm organization to the difficult period, late in his life, that began in 1827.

The wine merchants in the basement, invited in May to leave in June, were not at all ready to move out in a hurry. Finding other premises and removing pipes of port were matters for deliberation, as well as subject to the, by then, usual proviso in these leases renewed since 1817, for twelve months' notice in case the Hall were to be rebuilt. During and after the demolition upstairs in July 1827, the Shades tavern and other cellar vaults were shored up and covered with temporary pantile roofs (cheaper than tarpaulin, Suter said) until the vintners' departure the following March, although the Bridge Committee at first objected to the presence of struts and braces on their new ground. Simon Wooding, proprietor of the Shades, having died during or soon after the demolition overhead, his executors refused the insertion of internal shoring in the bar during the ensuing interim period, 'as it would alarm the Customers' and 'the danger is not so eminent'. But after much talking to and fro between City and company, the imprudence of excavation immediately outside the Shades while so much valuable property remained within was recognized, although by November 'considerable effect had take place in the front parts of the Company's premises', that is, subsidence attributable to excavations for bridge-foundations a few yards away, of which the Shades customers cannot have been unaware. In the summer of 1827 Wooding had almost completed purchase of premises belonging to Alderman Garratt just upstream of Fishmongers' Wharf, both as new accommodation for the Shades and as an investment, being of the opinion that it was 'a highly improving property' – an opinion shared by the Fishmongers' Company, then enquiring about all ground west of the Hall not yet in its possession (in case of need to move farther from the Bridge), but Wooding 'was not disposed to entertain an overture'. The Shades tavern was installed there in 1828 by others, the freehold remaining for a while in Garratt's hands.

The riverbank east of the Hall that was to carry the northern abutment of the new Bridge had to be strengthened and extended into the river behind the shelter of a crescent-shaped coffer dam constructed to keep out the water while work was going on. In 1827 it was recognized that the embanking had better be continued westward in front of Fishmongers' Wharf while the bridge-contractors were about it, the company to bear the cost. The company's views on embanking had changed somewhat since 1820 when its court regarded Alderman Garratt's plans for renewal of his embankment next door as 'objectionable'. Complaints from Garratt's solicitors in 1828, blaming cracks in his property on pile-driving for the Fishmongers' embankment, were refuted by the engineers concerned – who had already underpinned Garratt's buildings 'which would have gone into the River two years ago if . . . not prevented' – in words reminiscent of the old water-carpenters. For there continued the same state of watchful touchiness between these two sites as had existed between the Hall and the 'stone building next door' before the Great Fire. The firm of engineers concerned were the great public-works contractors Messrs Jolliffe & Banks of Beaufort Wharf, Strand, who were

constructing the Bridge to the Rennie design. Sir Edward Banks in partnership
with the Rev. William John Jolliffe had already built Waterloo Bridge and Southwark Bridge, the wharf (but not the building) at the Custom House, and much
else.[3]

At this time the Fishmongers' committee and the Bridge Committee were in
a constant state of negotiation. Relations broke down entirely at one point over
the placing of a 'pilaster'. The 'pilaster', actually a tall pedestal-like pier designed
to terminate the spur-wall enclosing the public water-stairs from the Hall site
and to correspond in design to the bridge buttresses, was to rise from wharf level
to a height well above the bridge-parapet; that is, the Bridge was to have two pairs
of outlying pylons, a pair on each shore flanking the approaches by land and
water, and expressing the bridgehead in architectural terms. The northwest 'pilaster' (as engineers and laymen continued to call it although about twelve-foot
square at bottom and resembling an empty pedestal on top) was to stand on ground
required from the company in addition to the ground already ceded. As a bone
of contention between committees this was settled by a quiet interview between
Towse and Jolliffe, while reopening such intermingled questions as planning permission for the Hall's future south frontage, the precise relation between 'pilaster'
and new embankment wall, the stopping-up of the public way along Fishmongers'
Wharf, and the altering of the design of the public water-stairs so as to segre-
gate them even more firmly from the company's newly private wharf. A frontage line for the Hall's future terrace, so that it would not interfere with views
of the Bridge, was laid down by Rennie who explained that both embankment
and terrace could be well forward of what they might have been 'in consequence
of the difficulty of removing the property beyond . . . and which projects so far into the River beyond what it ought to do' (that is, Garratt's property to which the
Shades was to move, wharfed out in the middle ages farther than the premises
just downstream). It was typical of City of London life that an obstacle to the
surroundings of the new Bridge should belong to the former Lord Mayor who
had laid the first stone for the Bridge. Rennie recognized also that it was important
to the company 'to have a good wharf', so that embanking farther inland was
altogether not feasible. The Hall having had an open raised terrace at or near
main-floor level since the alterations of 1790, it was taken for granted that the
next Hall would have one as part of the new setting for the Bridge. In London
the terrace at Somerset House provided a well-known pattern for a projecting
'water-storey'. No obstructions were to be erected on terrace or wharf (no crane
nearer than 28 feet to the bridge-stairs): the terrace was the first part of the next
Hall to be conditioned by planning permission. The question of the future design
of the Hall itself was soon raised when Rennie stipulated in answer to questioning
by the company surveyor early in 1828: 'The Pilaster need not be more than
three feet above the Coping of the [bridge] Ballustrade provided that a proper
Hall be erected adjoining the New Bridge' (and somebody underlined the words
'a proper').

While drawings defining the new frontage were prepared in Rennie's office, drawings and specifications for the new embankment wall at Fishmongers' Wharf were prepared by Suter in December 1827 in consultation with Jolliffe & Banks.[4] It was made of granite, ragstone, brickwork, planking and piling – ancient Thames wharf materials. In the spring of 1828, while that embankment was in progress, Jolliffe and Banks after conference with Suter suggested that they should also lay a foundation for the new terrace, since its position was fixed, before coffer dam and ramming engine were removed. It was agreed that they should take down the remains of the old terrace (the cellars just behind it having now come down) and suitable old materials could be re-used as filling. They were then to excavate the ground, 'strutting and pumping', and make good with a mixture of gravel and stone well-grouted (bound with liquid cement) as specified, or, as seems to have happened, with the above mentioned old brickwork available on the site, packed down with a top-dressing of cement; in short, an only slightly more sophisticated version of the process used by William Coles there in 1668-9. Soon after Jolliffe & Banks' men began this work in June, they found the ground below the old terrace filled with old piles (probably those of 1753) driven lower than the new piling just driven for the embankment. Jolliffe and Banks therefore concluded, with a wealth of soothing detail, that it would not only be detrimental to the new work to draw the old piles, but perfectly safe to leave them there. Suter now showed independence of mind – at half the age of either eminent contractor but with some experience of docks and lighthouses – and begged respectfully to state that it would be safer to remove the old piles than to build upon them. The shameful subsidence three years before at the new Custom House nearby, less than ten years after it was built and thought to be due to decayed piling, will have been in the forefront of his mind. But Jolliffe and Banks, both impressively sitting with the building committee, declared that their method would be secure and the committee was 'of opinion that they have hitherto had reason to place great confidence in the judgment of Messrs Jolliffe & Banks'. Four years later, both confidence and terrace-bottom appeared to have been ill founded.

In the summer of 1828 Suter looked ahead and prepared some drawings on his own, to help the company decide how much of the Hall site to let out to tenants. Nothing could be finally decided about a future Hall until the bridge-abutment was done and the exact level of the approach fixed, but already, as we have seen, questions about the future Hall's design were in the air: probably every architect and surveyor Suter met asked him about it, for already, as one of them said later, 'many young aspirants . . . were on the lookout for an opportunity of showing what the Fishmongers' Company ought to have'. So Suter laid before the committee two designs he had made – although, as they made clear, not by invitation   one with the Thames Street houses and one without, the latter with the Hall occupying the whole site remaining after loss of the eastern strip conveyed to the City. The former plan allowed only for a livery hall without living accommodation for clerk or beadle, and the cellarage for letting 'would be much deteriorated'. The only comment the committee allowed themselves on the architectural quality of the designs (which don't survive) was to note down

Suter's statement that the 'regular form adopted in both designs is rendered necessary in consequence of the height to which the new Hall has to be carried up whereby it will be seen more or less on all sides'. It was noted that the Hall's new height required by the height of the Bridge would darken any tenants' houses, that the houses would leave little room for entrance to warehouses fronting on an enclosed wharf, and that any entrance from the bridge-approach to a Hall built forward of a row of Thames Street houses would come within four feet of the public water-stairs, an objection felt to be 'almost insuperable'. Therefore the advantages of building over the whole site were seen to be 'decidedly preponderant' and, while they were about it, the committee resolved to recommend that the company 'offer premiums for the three best designs' when the time came. To both recommendations the whole court devoted 'very long conversations' before shelving them. Three more years were to go by before such issues mattered.

But the Bridge authorities continued to be anxious to settle the general aspect of the Hall, so prominent it was in their grand design. Early in 1829 while a pending Bill for improving the approaches was at the committee stage in Parliament, the Fishmongers' Company discovered to its horror that the Bill contained powers to take the entire remainder of their Hall ground, and an immediate interview with John Rennie was demanded. He therefore brought Robert Finch Newman, solicitor to the Bridge Committee, with him to a building committee meeting at the old Hall (this being before the company's offices moved to Aldermanbury). Rennie now confessed that the Hall ground had been included in the land to be taken because 'his principal object was to secure in the erection of the Company's new Hall, such an Architectural front, as should harmonize with the style of Architecture of the new Bridge, and he urged the [company's] Committee to furnish some idea of the intended new Hall, which the Committee expressed their total inability to do' – this being two years before Rennie himself was ready to impart to them the precise levels for the new Hall's relationship with the approaches. Rennie had very likely been discussing all this with his new brother-in-law, the architect Charles Robert Cockerell.[5] At any rate, Rennie promised to submit to the company 'a sketch of an architectural front for the new Hall, but without at all entering into the subject of internal arrangement'. So Rennie and Newman came again, with sketch, and some horse-trading took place. To Rennie's proposal that the Hall be set back fourteen feet from the bridge-approach, the committee at length consented to ten feet, provided there should be no stairs to Thames Street next to the Hall – that is, steps from the viaduct to the street below should be on the north side of Upper Thames Street – with no curtailment of that corner of the Hall site. What was actually said, of course, minutebooks seldom tell, but the promoters of the Bill, that is the Bridge Committee, accordingly 'consented this day to omit in the Schedule to the Bill the premises described as Fishmongers Hall and offices'. How real the threatened appropriation of the whole ground was is debatable. The Chief Engineer's (or his brother-in-law's) drawing, whatever it dictated in the way of architectural style, seems not to have been preserved by the company, but might relate to some pencil sketches remaining among Cockerell's drawings in the R.I.B.A. collection. Those indicate a great propyleum mounted on the dry arch over Thames Street and forming a ceremonial entry to the City from London Bridge; although hand-some in a full-blooded Roman manner, that would have been even more of a nuisance to traffic than Wren's Temple Bar. But the Hall site on those sketches seems to be left blank.[6]

The offices were removed to Aldermanbury at the end of 1829, the remaining north and west ranges of the old Hall were pulled down early in 1830 and two more Thames Street houses early in 1831; the last three were not to come down until the spring of 1832. William Knight, resident bridge engineer under Rennie, lived or at any rate had his 'London Bridge Works' office at No. 112 during 1831, where he drew a competition design for the Hall under the pseudonym 'Pont'.[7] An Act of March 1831 authorized removal of the parish church of St Michael Crooked Lane, and in June the company burial ground there was sold to the City for £195, its site soon to lie in and beside the new road up to the Bank (Fig. VII). St Michael's exceptionally tall and graceful west tower with its 'spire' of three lead-covered stages and finial – one of Wren's best and a beacon in every former view (Frontispiece, Pl. 8) of the neighbourhood – did not stand in the way of anything at all, and could perfectly well be standing by the west side of King William Street still. A good deal of company property lay in the path of the approaches as these were defined and redefined between 1823 and 1834. Ground at the old Bridgefoot opposite St Magnus and beside the one-time ditch to the Gully Hole – part of it the old White Lion site where Thomas Lock made two houses 'with the chips that he pickt up at the Hall' – was surrendered under the initial Act of 1823 to become a temporary no-man's-land between the old and new bridgeheads, for the use of the bridge-builders; later this ground formed the site of the east side of Adelaide Place opposite the Hall, now of Adelaide House. After passage of the Act of 1829 authorizing the raising and lowering and arching-over of streets immediately adjoining the Bridge, there were many exchanges be-tween the company committee and the City committees and officials concerned, over the value of premises in Crooked Lane, Fish Street Hill, and Thames Street (the east end of Upper Thames Street now becoming the west end of Lower Thames Street with the westward shift of the Bridge). The details of freeholders', leaseholders' and subtenants' rights that filled the company minutebooks at this period were the same problems that filled them after 1666, in reverse, the destruc-tion coming after. In Thames Street property values had to do with the future of warehousing already affected by wet-docks downriver though not yet by railways, but sure to benefit from improved navigation through the new Bridge. In the nar-row side streets, the values in question concerned small shops and the living quar-ters of small shopkeepers. The Three Tuns inn, in an alley off Thames Street, finding itself the site of the eastern flight of steps from that street up to the bridge approach, was the subject of arbitration between the company as freeholder and the City by William Wilkins the architect as independent surveyor, as well as with the brewers Hoare & Co. and their surveyor Philip Hardwick, not to mention the publican's own claim for 'Loss of Beds etc.' The professional network of architects-and-surveyors to London institutions was as active as ever: Wilkins had University College and St George's Hospital behind him, the National Gallery still to come, and served as surveyor to the East India Company; Hardwick was also surveyor to the St Katharine's Docks Company and to various hospitals as well as to the Goldsmiths' Company and architect of their Hall by then in progress, his work at Euston Station still to come. A good deal of expertise was focused on ground near the Bridge in these years.

On the ceremonial day 1 August 1831, when the King came by water to open London Bridge, the Hall site beside the bridge-stairs where he landed was a piece of waste ground between the new granite cliff and the Shades tavern aloof in its second home. At the rear of the empty ground the windows of every remaining Thames Street house swarmed with guests' heads, and on the river the boats drawn up to channel the royal procession included the Fishmonger barge with 115 on board. The great structure officially begun in 1825 in the presence of the Duke of York was now declared open by his brother William IV, and there was a surge of feeling that a new era for the River Thames was at hand. Meanwhile, decisions for filling the empty site beside the northern approach to the Bridge were now in order.

CHAPTER 13

The Competition of 1831

IT WAS ONLY the second time since this shore was wharfed out and built upon in the early middle ages that the site had lain empty. Bounded as Walworth's ground had been on north, south and west by street, river and ancient property boundary, it had now lost some of the ground added after the Great Fire: the Hall's east boundary that had coincided with that of the parish from 1667 until 1827 now lay buried under the new public water-stairs. Once the last three Thames Street tenants' houses were removed, the site for a new Hall would measure about 185 feet long from the existing street frontage to the edge of the site for terrace and wharf, by about 95 feet wide on the river front without the ten-foot area to be left open on the east front but measured right up to the irregular west boundary. That ancient border was shared with two separate proprietors: No. 109 Upper Thames Street and its rear warehouses were owned and occupied by members of the interrelated Field and Ronalds cheesemonger families; and south of them was the Shades tavern on the waterfront with rear warehouses, all bounded on the far side by Wheatsheaf Alley (Fig. 7).[1] With such close neighbours on the west side, the Hall site was not an island. Of its three exposed sides, that on the still-narrow old street was the least exposed to view. The two main fronts were to be those visible from the Bridge and the envelope into which the company's business had to be fitted was to be, very much, part of the northern bridge-approach. Although, from 1829 on, the design of the approaches was under Smirke's official eye, his name was not mentioned in connection with the selecting of a design for the Hall.

Certain eager young architects had been passing around drawings long before time. For instance, there were Joseph Aloysius Hansom (later founder of the *Builder* journal and inventor of the hansom cab) and Edward Welch, whose joint design for Birmingham Town Hall was chosen in competition there in 1830: as eventually erected, that is a Corinthian temple, eight columns by fifteen, raised on a high platform. An unlabelled pencil-sketch of a Corinthian temple six columns by thirteen on a high base, shown on a site resembling the Hall's and now in this company's collection,[2] is probably explained by the following letter published in 1835 by Welch, who was conducting a running argument in print with his former partner:

The notes for Chapter 13 are on pp. 197-9.

It must be pretty well known, that the old Fishmongers' Hall, London, had been partly pulled down for some years; and that, although designs for a new hall were not, until recently, advertised for, it had been evident to architects that they would be wanted; and, no doubt, many young aspirants, like Mr Hansom and myself, were on the look out for an opportunity of showing what the Fishmongers' Company ought to have. Two years before the time when designs were required for the Birmingham Town Hall, I wrote to Mr Hansom from London on the subject (he being then at York), stating that I thought a temple mounted on an elevated basement would be a fine design for the Fishmongers' Hall, and would rise above the Thames and Thames Street with a proud outline, and would command considerable admiration. Mr Hansom then sketched out the design (he sketches better than I can), and soon afterwards gave his sketch to me. I put it into the hands of my friend, Capt. Freeman [probably Richard Freeman, clerk, of Bridge House Yard, Tooley Street, a freeman of the company] . . . for the purpose of introducing us to the Fishmongers' Company, when occasion might offer. That sketch [of 1828] was what Birmingham Town Hall now is.[3]

Hansom and Welch eventually entered the competition for the Hall, late in 1831 while work at Birmingham was hanging fire. A likely origin for their temple-on-a-high-base idea was the then unfinished Madeleine in Paris, taken over by a new architect in 1828. This and other designs bandied about at the time were more Roman than Greek, as the idea of an arched bridge was. However, the spirit informing the bridge-approaches – which were to include King William Street from the Bank to Adelaide Place in front of the Hall and, from 1834, the new street called Moorgate – was to be that of the Greek Revival.

Immediately after the Bridge was opened, during August 1831, the necessary decisions for rebuilding the Hall were taken. A committee resolution to keep the three remaining tenants' houses for the sake of their rent and to save paying £1500 compensation requested by Cope the glazier for surrendering No. 111, was overruled by a court vote to remove the houses, thus releasing about 2900 square feet for the northwest corner of the Hall. A sum not to exceed £50,000 was to be spent on the new building: funds already put into long annuities for the purpose included the compensation from the City expressly designated for the new Hall by the Act of 1827, purchase money for other sites taken for the bridge-approaches, money from the auctions of furniture and old building-materials, and profits from various estates. An architectural competition was announced in *The Times*, *Morning Chronicle*, and *Herald* on September 1, 6, and 10, designs to be submitted by December 13 (altered in October to December 31). Premiums of £200, £150, and £100 were offered for the three best designs, all entries to be signed by pseudonyms. With the Clerk's draft for this advertisement 'to Architects and others' lies a copy (written on paper with an 1830 watermark) of the announcement of the London Bridge competition of 1822, to which the wording is very similar. Architectural competition was not, however, then new in the City, as there had been a limited one for the Mansion House in the middle of the previous century. One wonders whether the idea of first, second, and third places came originally from horse-racing. Full particulars (including site drawings, for tracing by competitors' clerks from Suter's originals, which still exist) were available at the Aldermanbury office between 10 and 4. The particulars also included two pages of instructions drawn up by Suter and Towse, and containing a number of ambiguities that produced a flock of anxious letters from would-be competitors, so that a set of supplementary instructions had to be issued in October.[4]

The problem was not the easiest in the world to set clearly. The space was controlled by 'sundry heights' noted down by the Clerk early in 1831 : the wharf was three feet above high water, Thames Street was seven feet higher than the wharf, the bridge-approach was 22 feet above Thames Street, the Hall's entrance floor was to be six to eight feet above the bridge-approach, and so on.[5] The building was to have a dual relationship with riverbank-level and viaduct-level. Its substructure, almost none of it underground, was to contain at least two storeys, the upper one a 'basement' for the Hall kitchens and the lower for letting as 'Cellarage, Warehouses, or Offices' at 'Quay, or Thames Street level' and 'so designed as to produce in relation to the Wharf, the greatest possible Value or Rental'. There was no question of excavating for cellars below ground, only for foundations. Costs for the two main halves of the building were to be estimated separately, and also there were to be separate estimates for facing the upper half with Portland stone, with Bath stone, or with 'Compo' (cement or stucco composition), and the lower half with granite. That is, it was implied that the substructure in material as well as height might 'match' the Bridge. Yet oddly enough (to us), aside from requirements of position in relation to the Bridge, nothing whatever was laid down by the company as to harmonizing style or appearance with the Bridge or its approaches. As we have seen, Rennie more than once exerted pressure on the company in this direction. But the company's court, whether deliberately or not, left that aspect of the designs to the understanding of competitors, and to its own judgment in due course.

When the competition was about to be advertised, printing a hundred copies of the 'particulars' was thought to be enough (Suter to Towse: 'although you have as many as 100 I would not be too profuse in dealing them out at first'). After the advertisement appeared, demand was such that instructions had to be sent to 223 architects, not counting copies dealt out by members of the court. The list of interested enquirers that Towse carefully kept included seasoned practitioners like James Savage, James Elmes, Philip Hardwick, and Joseph Gwilt, rising young men like Charles Barry and Thomas Donaldson, and future mid-Victorians like Samuel Teulon (not yet out of his pupilage), Thomas Henry Wyatt, and even 'Mr Peto', possibly the young contractor (and future member of the court), besides a large number of nonentities eager to become entities. In this competition – the most publicly notable and numerously entered between the London Bridge competition of 1822 and the Houses of Parliament competition of 1835 – late Georgians and future Victorians met. That was not merely the position of William IV's short reign between the regency-extended rule of his brother and the long rule of their niece, but the character of a moment that seemed at the time a confused breathing-space or landing on the stairs, as it were, between the eighteenth century's aftermath and the upstart nineteenth century: the moment when the young John Stuart Mill wrote his papers on 'The Spirit of the Age' for the *Examiner* and Tennyson wrote the line, 'The old order changeth, yielding place to new'. In the end, there were eighty-seven entrants, of whom fewer than half besides the three premium-winners can be identified, from receipts signed for return of drawings or subsequent exhibition at the Royal Academy, or deduced in other ways. A number of letters received by the Clerk while the competition was open, from would-be contestants worrying over minor points in the instructions, also preserve a few names from the vast crew of the brilliant and the dull, seasoned or rising or only hopeful, that hovered around every architectural competition. A list of known entrants, enquirers, and hoverers is to be published separately – sources on architects' activities, just before the debut of architectural periodicals, being sparser than the Victorian oceans of print soon to rise.[6]

Most of the contestants seem to have taken the point of harmony with the Bridge, to the extent of casting their conceptions in one classical mode or another. Not that one or two aggressively Greek temples would have harmonized much. On a list of candidates' pseudonyms or mottoes, however, the Clerk has noted 'Gothic' beside nos. 47 and 60. Now, no. 47, according to the signed receipt for return of the drawings, was C. Fowler, with address on the initial list in Gordon Square, that is, Charles Fowler who had won the London Bridge competition before his design was set aside for John Rennie's. Best known in London for his Covent Garden and Hungerford Markets, Fowler seems to have used the Gothic style mainly for churches. Some variety of 'engineering Gothic' for the Hall seems unlikely, some Picturesque Tudor revival of the pre-Fire Hall possible; yet the Clerk may have misinterpreted Italianate arcades and towers (as in Fowler's unbuilt designs for Mamhead in Devon) as 'Gothic'.[7] No. 60 had a strange masonic-sounding motto: 'Glory to God ! ! ! 5555'; the design must have been very Gothic indeed and, with those exclamation points, by a very young man indeed. One almost wonders whether the young Pugin, newly married and needing to establish himself, and already soaked in Gothic architectural detail, hoped to impose his fiery vision on the Thames shore, but another young man, J. W. Johns, signed for return of the drawings.[8] Ten competitors submitted scale-models as well as drawings; for such a complex site it is odd there were not more models, for these were much used. Nevertheless, the company's offices at the end of December 1831 must have been chock-a-block with portfolios (a dozen drawings for each entry), framed and glazed views, and the ten models – to one of which a zealous competitor was allowed to come and attach miniature chandeliers omitted by the model-maker.[9] At a court meeting on 6 January 1832 the designs were opened and cursorily inspected, and it was directed that for two weeks, January 10–24, they were to be exhibited for 'inspection by Members of Court only'. And so for a fortnight the whole paraphernalia were laid out all over the small building off Aldermanbury, from courtroom to beadle's parlour, and the Clerk provided a synoptic table with all the estimates of costs for each design.

During this fortnight, more than one anxious letter was received. Two were anonymous.[10] One in block letters in two colours of ink urged the company to avoid 'the following Architectural Fornications . . . Columns placed in couples or pairs . . . Doric Columns with Bases . . . Classical architecture with arched Doors & Windows . . . Columns in the same front one above another . . . All manner of Gimcrackery above the order of architecture . . . In Gothic Architecture, arches of different proportions' – a splenetic purist. The other anonymous letter was malicious:

> Can it be true that the Candidates for Fishmongers Hall are to be decided upon by Interest, is it true as currently reported that many of the Drawings and Motto's are *known to private Friends on the Court*, that Fishmongers allow themselves *to be canvassed* and that partiality alone will determine against Merit, Are these things possible! as a return for Talent, Study, and private Expense of Architects, if so then may Professional Men bid adieu to all that is Honest in the City of London. . . .

Architectural competitions in the early nineteenth century invited spleen, the profession concerned was so far from secure, either professionally or socially. There was also a letter from Richard Suter, who had observed how other livery halls were still being rebuilt by their own company surveyors. For four years much of his time and study had been devoted to preparing drawings, estimates, and reports to guide the company in its decisions in the matter, and he had aspired to the honour as reward for his exertions. Now he said he was ready even to forego the priority of buildings to his own designs, if it were required that he should modify someone else's or even take the court's instructions as to the preferred features to be assembled from several of those submitted. A sad commentary, that, on what actually could happen: it was far from certain then that the winner of a competition would be allowed to oversee the building of his own design. Suter, unlike his predecessor Alexander, and unlike Hardwick at the Goldsmiths', had no other architectural works to sustain his reputation (except, so far, some chapels for the company's Irish estate); although, neither did the eventual winner of the competition. Suter was to write again at the end of February, before it was clear that the first premium winner was to be the chosen architect, pointing out his 'more than ordinary anxiety . . . considering the peculiar situation in which I am placed . . . on a question where the character of an individual [is] so materially concerned. . . . My professional character and reputation will be deeply affected by your decision'. As an officer of the company he may have refrained from entering the competition, but a drawing by him for the Hall was hung at the Royal Academy that summer.[11]

By February 2 the court had reduced the field to eight and then, it having been resolved that article 24 of the instructions (any departure from these instructions to disqualify) must be abided by, it appeared on careful examination that 'the whole of them are found not within the meaning of the 24th Article'. So another meeting was held on February 4 to 'rescind the said article No. 24' and ballot for the three best designs. For the first premium, design no. 43, two portfolios and model, motto *Mihi cura futuri*, was found to be that of Henry Roberts of 23 Suffolk Street, Pall Mall. The second premium went to no. 57, portfolio and model marked A.F.M., from John Davies of 4 Devonshire Square, and the third to no. 84, with design in gilt frame and portfolio marked 'Tobit' (with fish), by Lewis Nockalls Cottingham of 4 Basing Place, Waterloo Road. For Roberts' and Cottingham's designs, we have most of the actual drawings submitted; for Davies' design, only what he said of it in letters and in interview. All three designs were wholly classical if not wholly Greek. Roberts was the youngest and least experienced architect at 28, Davies was 36 with '10 years in business' and '3 in Italy' (the grand tour to Italy being still indispensable even if not extended to Greece), and Cottingham was 45 with nineteen years' practice as architect and surveyor in London. So what did these three have to offer above eighty-four others early in 1832?

Cottingham, in some beautiful drawings that deserved a better design, proposed a building with two domes, one externally visible over the great hall and one only internally visible over the grand staircase, with an Ionic temple frontispiece centred against the east side, and two terrace-levels facing the river. The trouble was, his saucer dome so fine on the entrance front would look comically off-centre from Bridge and river. His main entrance enshrined in the temple centrepiece was too near the top of the bridge-stairs, so that private dinner-guests would tangle with public-wherry passengers. His lower terrace was to be usable only from the kitchen-storey. Indoors, circulation was poorly arranged: space lavished upon the handsome staircase left none for a first-floor corridor reaching every main room. The great hall was given that excess of ornament better termed Grecian than Greek. It was all very expensive. Cottingham had been allowed in 1827 to draw the old hall (a set of six drawings of which one of the entrance survives) and had been 'a close observer of the nature of the ground . . . having noticed the peculiarities of the soil'. As surveyor to the Cooks' Company, to which Towse the Fishmongers' Clerk was also Clerk in his spare time, Cottingham had kept himself informed. He was even 'prepared to produce respectable builders' – his generation of architects saw nothing unprofessional in that – 'and in the event of your not employing your customary Surveyor, allow me to tender my services as architect.' Cottingham is known now as an antiquarian, as a restorer of medieval buildings, and for architectural publications, in short, as codifier and draughtsman.[12]

Davies' repertoire included the Greek Revival (his Highbury College of 1825, for training independent ministers, was an exercise in the Ionic style) and a tentative Gothic Revival white-brick 'Perpendicular' chapel style (as in his St Paul's, Winchmore Hill, of 1828). In the City, he was to produce elegant Grecian Doric offices for Rothschild's in St Swithin's Lane, and later the Italianate tower and rectory of St Martin's Orgar still standing in St Martin's Lane. It would appear from Davies' own comments on his design for the Hall, which are all we have to

go on, that he aimed to provide a Corinthian portico on the river front and possibly a colonnade on the east front as well. Quite likely he had in mind the Corinthian portico at University College, especially because Thomas Wilson – whom
Davies will have known as treasurer to the society of dissenters who founded
Highbury College – was, as we have mentioned, one of the founders of University College and probably brother to a member of the Fishmongers' building committee. The Hall's upper windows overlooking the river would have been shad-
owed by the entablature and roof of such a portico, as offices over the entrance
of the Tate Gallery are.[13]

Neither of these two designs seems to have been wholly thought out, nor likely
to have made a satisfactory building. One wonders if they were really better than
those of, say, Barry and Hardwick (if they did compete) or whether the point was
simply that Cottingham's and Davies' drawings contained more separate features
that more members of the court liked.

Roberts does seem to have thought it all out. There is a rational inevitability
about many of his arrangements, not all, for programme, site, and style combined
to defeat a perfectly rational solution. (And placing kitchen and banqueting hall
two floors apart, for instance, seems more irrational now that it did then.) His
design provided for a self-contained block, mainly rectangular on plan with north
and south ranges projecting westward. It was to have no protruding porches, the
only link with the bridge-approach was the short flight of steps at the main east
entrance, one arcaded extension of the substructure was to support the south terrace, and the cartway from Thames Street to the wharf was to be threaded through
the western projections of the substructure itself. Cartway-arch and terrace-arcade,
as if of a great basement storey, were to echo the 'arched vaults' under the bridge-
approach; the masonry of the Hall substructure was to be on the same scale as
the bridge-masonry; and the terrace substructure was to have a great dentil course
matching that of the pier already interposed between the company wharf and
the bridge-stairs (Pl. 9). Or, as Roberts put it, 'The character of the Bridge is here
preserved by a Terrace supported on a series of Arches, all the details of which
exactly correspond with those of the Bridge, and thus the otherwise objectionable
Pier at the foot of the Water Stairs becomes a connecting link.' His substructure
was to contain two warehouse-storeys, visible as such through the arcade, as well
as the Hall's kitchen-basement, sandwiched between the upper warehouse-storey
and the company's entrance-floor and lighted from areas on east and west. The
superstructure was to contain two main storeys of seemingly similar height, as the
old Hall had : Soane had commended the old Hall for that, in a lecture Roberts
probably heard;[14] and to Greek Revivalists, two similar storeys suited the proportions of classical orders better than the insertion of diminished top storeys inherited
from Palladian villas. There was more to Roberts' design than this.

The heart of a City company has traditionally been its high-roofed dining hall.
Before the Fire the Fishmongers' Tudor great hall had been visible to all as a
separate one-purpose space; at the opposite extreme, their next building gave no
sign whatever, on the outside, where the great hall was. That is, with the coming

of 'regular' architecture, the outward and visible signs of inner and spiritual use, as it were, disappeared. By the early nineteenth century, some architects were trying to feel their way back. Roberts, both by temperament and by training, was disposed to take a rational view. The great hall should have a central place and be seen to have it as much as architectural style allowed. So he centred that room, five windows long, on the upper floor of his east front and raised the roof, as if for an attic storey, for the greater ceiling-height there, bringing forward the great hall's two end bays as if to support and assert that height (Pl. 10–12). The recessed centre between these bays, with its pair of attached Ionic columns and company arms above, confirmed the symmetry necessary to classical style even though the building's main door – removed as far as possible from the common herd of the water-stairs – is in one of the side bays. At the same time, this entrance was centred on the widened road-bay or carriage-sweep between the viaduct arch and the top of the bridge stairs (Pl. 21a). And another virtue in moving a main entrance off the main axis of a building could have had to do with winds off the river. At any rate, the banqueting hall was to be suitably mounted. It was not quite so easy to be either symbolic or rational on the narrower river front. Having shortened the terrace at both ends, to avoid obstruction to Garratt's windows at one end and unseemly closeness to the bridge-stairs at the other, Roberts had a basis for a six-column Ionic temple front or, not approving of porticoes, an 'attached hexastyle' engaged in the building front. This gave seven windows to each storey and, with the rooms he had to plan for, no chance to express his internal planning externally there (Pl. 9). However, his giant order was to be rationally treated to the extent that antae (which are like square piers partly emerging from the wall) emphasize only corners, or implied corners, of the building, avoiding meaningless pilasters in between. Adapting 'pure' styles to single-front London street architecture (where all sorts of irregularity could go on round behind) was easy, but dealing with this site took a certain skill.

In Roberts' plan, the south end of the building was to be devoted to business downstairs and entertainment upstairs, the central portion mainly to grand staircase and great hall, while the north end was to be devoted to living accommodation for Clerk and Beadle and their families. Members of the court then familiar with the new West End clubhouses will have observed a resemblance, for example, to Wilkins' new University Club ('planned like a large country villa with the kitchens tucked into the basement', as Summerson put it, and with a grand central staircase).[15] Roberts' outer entrance hall was to lead to one side of a north-south corridor open to the main staircase-compartment through a four-column screen (Pl. 13, 17). The staircase – resembling that at the Athenaeum, opened in 1830 – was to begin as a single flight, then branch right and left against the west wall, and return in parallel flights against the side walls to finish on a long top landing leading centrally to the great hall and at one end to the livery drawing room, at the other by way of an adroitly irregular inner vestibule to the court dining suite overlooking the river. The provision of drawing room and dining room there, at the head of the great hall, signalled the social eclipse of the old word 'parlour'.

And finally, an old anomaly of the site was well-managed by Roberts: the open area or long light-well on the west side of the central 'waist' of the building.[16] Necessary to light the new grand staircase and the new kitchens, once it had been the Pepper Querne 'empty piece' of 1395 regained by the company in 1581, to be until the Fire a covered way through the great-hall cellars, and thereafter open above basement-shed level. Roberts brought the cartway from Thames Street to the wharf over this ground, through a vaulted way under the beadle's wing, into the open with the Hall's backside rearing up on the left and the neighbours on the right, and then through another vaulted way under the Hall's riverside wing to the wharf, where loading bays were to be protected from weather in the arcaded space under the terrace. That is, both streetside range and riverside range could go right up to the party wall. Certain other competitors in 1831, unable to cope with the light problem on the west side, ran an open area the whole length of the building there while bringing the required cartway through the centre of the building, thus wasting warehouse space. Roberts had thought it out.

Various little refinements in design that can be appreciated on acquaintance with the building may or may not have appealed to the building committee through the medium of scale-model and drawings, yet in total effect these may have influenced their verdict. Aligning the dentil course of the terrace with that of the adjacent bridge-pier brought the terrace several steps lower than the floor inside the windows, so ensuring that the bases of the columns and indeed the plinth of that entire entrance storey would not be hidden by the terrace parapet from the view of those aboard boats on the river – a point of view still then considered – and from any southerly viewpoint giving that temple front something to stand on (Pl. 9, 20). Another small point: the convention whereby window and door openings in the Ionic style diminished upward in width could be made ridiculous by heavy-handed or doctrinaire architects (in Cottingham's drawings, for example), but Roberts handled this as a barely detectable subtlety (a difference of one inch, according to working drawings for the upper windows). Still another subtlety with windows came not from the Greek but from Smirke in one of his more modern moments: the insertion of an extra sill within the frame of the lower windows. The year 1831 was almost the last moment in time when such understated refinements might be offered by a young architect or a competition won with their silent aid. Perhaps the publication of 1833 of J. C. Loudon's *Encyclopaedia of Cottage, Farm and Villa Architecture*, that manual in The Picturesque for proto-Victorians, was to mark the end of a taste for understated classical refinements in the young.

A more striking and allusive subtlety indoors, to which neither Roberts nor anyone else ever seems to have referred, may not have been appreciated at the competition stage: the curve of the great hall ceiling (Pl. 19). In its ratio of height to width of curve and in the ellipsoidal nature of the curve, it can be seen as a reference to that of the, then so new, London Bridge arches. This is not so fanciful as it sounds. In the years after the battle of Waterloo, the Thames was being bridged as never before, architects and engineers in London were fascinated by bridges. Even Canova the Italian sculptor said the sight of Waterloo Bridge alone was ample reward for a long and toilsome pilgrimage to England. A pair of young English architects, Lewis Vulliamy and T. L. Donaldson, in Florence in 1818 while on 'Continental Tour for professional improvement', eagerly measured the baffling curves of the Trinità bridge over the Arno with the help of 'men to manage the Boats, Cords, etc.' and Vulliamy published a slim folio when he returned to London, analysing the Trinità central arch as two intersecting portions of an ellipse.[17] We might take this further. Somewhere between the ratio of height to width of span at Waterloo Bridge (centre arch, roughly 7:24) and the much lower arch of the Trinità (roughly 7:48) came that of London Bridge (roughly 7:35 or 1:5). The ratio of height to width for the Fishmongers' great hall vault is $7\frac{1}{2}$ feet to 38 feet, or very roughly 1:5. At any rate, the general reference of the ellipsoidal form of the curve was enough to please quiet observers of such allusions while the Bridge of 1825–31 still stood outside the window. For contemporary inland comparison, the curve of the Salters' great hall vault, now gone, was segmental (part of a circle) and the Goldsmiths' great hall ceiling is flat.

Henry Roberts was born in mid-1803 the son of a City merchant resident after 1820 in Camberwell.[18] His father's City address was at first in Gold or Gould Square, later in Fen Court, Fenchurch Street, and at the time of the Hall competition Henry's brother was a dry-salters' broker in Jefferys Square, St Mary Axe; that is, Robert was quite familiar with the City. In 1818 he was articled to the architect Charles Fowler, who had just set up his own practice, and spent the usual seven years in that office, where he will have learned a precise and delicate mode of drawing. During part of that time Fowler was making his designs for the London Bridge competition. In or about 1825 Roberts entered the office of Robert Smirke (knighted 1832) whom he found a strong and congenial influence. Late in the 1820s Robert went off on 'an extensive tour in Italy and other parts of the Continent', and upon return in 1830 set up for himself, having 'under my direction several practical works', now unidentified. His first office was at 23 Suffolk Street, still standing on the north corner of Suffolk Place, off Pall Mall East between the Haymarket and Whitcomb Street: Suffolk Street and Place had been entirely rebuilt around 1823 by John Nash and friends, and lay just around the corner from that very new and still raw metropolitan improvement, Trafalgar Square. In this bright new environment, with Nash's Haymarket Theatre of 1820–1 behind, Wilkins' University Club of 1822–6 opposite, Burton's new shops on Pall Mall East, and Smirke's Union Club and Royal College of Physicians of 1824–5 nearby, young Roberts made his competition drawings for the prominent new livery hall at London Bridge.

The example of Smirke, then at the top of his profession in London, was paramount in Roberts' mind: to be able to say that 'a reference to Mr Smirke will no doubt be perfectly satisfactory as to my professional qualifications, having studied under him during the erection of the New Post Office, the British Museum, the restoration of the Custom House' etc., was to put one's best foot forward.[19] And references to Smirke's work crept into Roberts' description of his own design: to

the need for harmony with other edifices on the bridge-approach (under Smirke's
care since the Act of 1829); the fireproof advantages of iron plating between
warehouse and Hall storeys as 'over the Royal Library at the British Museum'
and under the Long Room at the Custom House (where Smirke went to the
rescue after it collapsed); and the confident promise that for the foundations 'an
artificial bed of grouted Lime and Gravel', that is, concrete, 'is much more secure
as well as less expensive than piling', Smirke being the best-known user of concrete
foundations of his day. As for the Hall's internal resemblances to Burton's
Athenaeum Club, Smirke had sat on the building committee there since 1824.[20]
And the Hall's two main fronts were to have their 'Smirkisms'. Although the river
front is patterned on the Palladian system of giant order on arcaded basement,
the order is a particular form of Ionic of which Smirke was fond. The heightened
centrepiece on the entrance front refers less to Greek origins (the monument to
Thrasyllus) than to Smirke's 'Graeco-cubic' style on the west side of Trafalgar
Square : a form of designing 'in Greek', a kind of synthesis, such as the better
Victorian Goths were to engage in when designing 'in Gothic'; a game of taking
old styles apart and putting them back together in a new way. (There was a strong
family resemblance, too, between the Hall east front and Francis Goodwin's
Manchester Town Hall of 1822–5, confirming the cross-fertilization that went on
among the Greek Revivalists.)[21] The temperaments of the eminent architect and
his young assistant were congenial : Smirke with his dignified reticence and
efficiency, Roberts 'a gentlemanly, religious, precise and quiet man' (as Scott was
to describe him), interested in modern techniques. Angry young rivals were quick
to assume that Smirke had put a word into the right ear. Whether or not he did,
Roberts' design might very likely have won this competition anyway. But Smirke
probably was consulted after the premium was awarded on February 6, before the
final appointment of Roberts as architect on March 10.[22]

Roberts acknowledged the first announcement by an anxious letter, hoping the
company 'would not deviate from the customary course on such occasions, but
confide to him the superintendence of the Building, convinced that no other
Architect could enter so fully into the spirit of the design; and that no remunera-
tion could compensate for the mortification of seeing another reap the benefit of
the study and labor bestowed in forming it; whilst the adoption of a contrary
course might, unintentionally, inflict a serious injury on the professional character
of an individual', etc. On March 1 he was interviewed by a special court and
gave precise answers to questions mainly related to possible reductions in cost.
By March 12 he was sitting with the building committee, receiving their instructions for 'certain alterations', and the long process was under way. In April Roberts
told them it would take three years, which it did. Five years from that spring of
1832, on the basis of this appointment, he was able to claim fellowship in a professional institution that did not exist in 1832 : the Institute of British Architects,
founded in 1834, was to require five years (later seven) as principal before membership as a Fellow.

These affairs did not take place in a vacuum. The winter of 1831–2 was a time of political crisis over the Reform Bill, with riots in many parts of the country in October. In February cholera came to London, where honest medical men already knew the Thames to be badly polluted.[23] Yet the determination of ancient institutions to reproduce themselves, allied with sheer London pride, was expressed privately by members of the Fishmongers' court such as William Smith the retired M.P. in this letter of 23 February 1832[24] to the Prime Warden :

> We are about to take a Step the Effects of which will, We *hope*, last for Centuries . . . We are about to expend a large Sum of Money, not *absolutely* our own, & I cannot but think that our Fellow Citizens, nay even in some degree the Public at large, may not unreasonably expect from us some considerable regard to the Improvement of the City to which We belong, – and our Building stands in so conspicuous a Situation that it must attract general Notice; to do this advantageously should then, as I think, be *a*, if not *the* primary Object. . . .

CHAPTER 14

Rebuilding, 1832-5

BUILDING GOES ON around us every day, and passers-by take it for granted. Yet, as every architect knows, that protracted period between acceptance of his design and the day the client moves in (not to mention discoveries afterward) is the crucial time. The story of those months or years of swarming activity on one piece of ground is part of architectural history. Yet, except among architects themselves, architectural history too often tends to be less a matter of bricks and mortar, more a matter of marks on paper – books, drawings, minutes, contracts, bills and criticism – aside from a few uncomfortable remarks about changes forced upon the original design during construction. For the building in question, certain bundles of papers of the sort generally thrown out long before a century has passed remain to reinforce with their immediacy the official minutes and accounts.

The year 1832 was not only a time of cholera and political crisis. Financially, it was bad for building, not as difficult as 1667, but the building-boom of the mid-1820s had subsided into a depression that was at its worst, for the London building trades, in 1832.[1] The fact that many major buildings were still under construction late in the 1820s after the collapse of confidence in the London money market in the banks crisis of 1825, perfectly illustrates the time-lag characterizing an industry so conditioned by the dimension of time. Even the big contractors found themselves hard pressed in the early thirties. As for the client, this rebuilding of Fishmongers' Hall begun out of savings and compensation for the purpose, was to be financed in its last year and a half of finishings and furnishings mainly from loans, and the first years of its occupation by the company saw 'moderate dinners' and retrenchment.

Three contracts were involved. A preliminary one signed in April 1832 and completed in August was for the concrete raft laid over the entire site. Then there was the first one for the Hall itself signed in August 1832 and completed early in 1834, that is, for the carcase (unfinished shell) of the building, with finishing of the warehouses underneath (prompt rent from below being vital, as in 1671). The last contract agreed in February 1834 and completed in May 1835 was for finishing the interior of the Hall. In 1834-5 certain specialists, upholsterers, and other tradesmen were dealt with directly for fixtures, fittings and furniture. All these operations were under the care of the architect.

The notes for Chapter 14 are on pp. 199-201.

First came the 'concrete bottom'. The Thames riverbank had been secured for large buildings in the eighteenth century by the Adam brothers for the Adelphi development and by William Chambers for Somerset House, apparently with some combination of timber rafts and piling with systems of arches of brick and stone, and various cements. In the period after Waterloo, Robert Smirke practised the laying of concrete platforms for such buildings in London : for Millbank Prison, for the Lancaster Place development near Waterloo Bridge, and for Sir Robert Peel's house in Whitehall Gardens, then a riverside site. In 1832 the word 'concrete' had only just begun to be used generally for this newly rediscovered material. Smirke in the 1820s spoke of a stratum of grouted gravel, and Roberts in the competition of 1831 meticulously called it an artificial bed of grouted lime and gravel, but everyone concerned at the Hall site in the spring of 1832 was calling the stuff concrete. The layer put down was not so much a 'foundation', as the Clerk continued to call it, as a platform over the whole ground, on which the footings of the building were to rest, except for wharf and terrace foundations already completed by Jolliffe & Banks. There is only one clue, in a rough note by the Clerk, to the depth of the concrete under the Hall : in March, Roberts thought it might go eleven feet below wharf-level; as matters went, its thickness is probably somewhat less.[2]

On April 14 tenders for the platform were invited from seven contractors with proposals due in five days. The six tenders received ranged in cost and time from £1590 for completion in two months to £2493 for completion in four months and £2593 for completion in fourteen weeks. A contract was signed on the 19th for the first-named sum and time with Samuel Grimsdell of Bell Lane, Spital-fields, who started excavating the ground in the last week of April. In early June Grimsdell's men were still removing earth and old rubble, part to be 'barged away' and part stored in the vaults under the bridge-approach for later use. As the excavation grew deeper, the neighbours grew uneasy over the gulf yawning beside them. Not least Sir John Rennie on the 12th when he examined these operations beside his new Bridge and Grimsdell's foreman told him 'that their bottom will be one foot below the foundations of the Piers of the Brick Arches of the Bridge Approaches and will come within three feet of them', and moreover that the whole space was to 'continue open in its present state' for at least a fort-night. To those who recalled the dismembering of the Hall for the rearing of the Bridge, now the shoe was on the other foot. Rennie thought the new works had 'certainly an injurious tendency', the Fishmongers' Company should be cautioned 'to fill up' as soon as possible. Whereupon Roberts examined the emerging founda-tions of the bridge-abutment, found them less deep than he had understood them to be, and on the 14th told Grimsdell to start filling in with concrete as soon as possible. The allover nature of that process, layer by layer over the whole ground, necessitated the settling of long-drawn-out party-wall differences with Ronalds the cheesemonger at the northwest edge where it was desirable to 'commence concrete'. And there were protests from the southwest edge where, according to Alderman Garratt's lawyers on the 15th, Grimsdell's men were digging below the foundations of the Shades cellars (where the wines had had four years to settle after removal from the brink of the bridge-excavations).

As the concrete-laying was about to begin, Grimsdell was asked to execute the drains that would have to be carried through it, in addition to his original contract, which suggests the empirical way in which drains were managed, almost as afterthoughts, although Suter had already arranged the outlet through the wharf-wall. By July 14 there had been several accidents among workmen laying the concrete, as reported in a petition for compensation written out for 'the bearer Timothy Kennedy who . . . could do no Work for 18 Days in consqunce having his finger Broke' and three other injured and 'ever humbel Servents'. Judging from accounts of Smirke's methods and from contemporary writings on concrete,[3] the process had its dangers : 'Thames ballast' or sandy gravel was mixed with ground lime and water, 'wheeled to the excavation, and thrown from a height of not less than 6 ft. . . . A man to be kept treading down and puddling the mass as it is thrown down'. The puddling by men in great boots and wielding shovels proceeded section by section across the ground : never more than an agreed thickness (twelve inches or less) was to be thrown in at a time, that layer to cover the whole area before a new layer was begun. Lime was to be fresh-ground daily at the site. Speed and planning were of first importance, although recipes varied in the proportions of gravel to lime, minimum heights from which barrow-loads of the wet mix where to be thrown, and thickness of layers and depth of the whole prescribed, as well as in the proportion of the site to be so treated. Smirke at this time, in June 1832, as architect for the bridge-approaches submitted to the City's Bridge Committee his specifications for neighbouring wharf-construction, in which he only required that the concrete bed should project two feet beyond the footings of buildings thereon. But Roberts, who probably consulted Smirke, was taking no chances and covered the entire ground here. The wet and unstable habits of the Fishmongers' ground that emerge from the company's older minutebooks suggest he was right to leave no margins unsecured.

An observant eye-witness here in June 1832 recalled twenty-five years[4] later that the concrete was poured on to 'a bed of muddy peat, in which there were a great number of old piles . . . almost entirely of oak, and they were in such a high state of preservation that the breakage of the grain from the force with which they had been driven was quite distinct; and on cutting the head of one of them it was found unaltered in colour and hardness . . . in fact, a nice fresh yellow colour just like a new piece of wainscot', preserved in the peat along with grass and nutshells – apparently the Tudor piling, unremoved and unreplaced after 1666, with grasses from windblown seeds lodged who knows where and nuts from who knows what dinners. (It may or may not be odd that no one ever mentions any blackened layer of Great Fire rubble here). At any rate, the Tudor piling presumably still rests below many feet of concrete : there is no record of the removal of any piles here whatever. This view of oaken piling in June will have been on the main body of the site, back from the river. Less healthy conditions revealed under Jolliffe & Banks's terrace foundations in July were another matter.

As we have seen (p. 121), when the 'wharf wall', that is, the whole structure of the wharf down to below river-bottom level, solidly rebuilt by them in 1828, had been extended inland to provide a base for the future Hall terrace, the great bridge contractors had found it unnecessary to take the additional work to the same depth as the wharf-wall, in spite of warnings from the company surveyor. Finding old piles there (probably less deeply embedded than the Tudor ones), they simply cut off their tops, packed in filling and a covering of 'grouted rubble' (a confusing term that did not mean carefully measured concrete, especially as the rubble here was mostly composed of old Shades bricks) with timber 'sleepers & planking' on top. Richard Suter, while officially not concerned with present affairs on the Hall site, anxiously reported to the building committee on July 5 that 'in witnessing the proceedings of the Works . . . I think it due to you and just to myself to suggest, that very great caution should be taken in using the present foundation for the future Terrace Wall, indeed, knowing the Way in which this is constructed I strongly recommend that no part of the new Structure be built immediately upon it.' So Roberts rushed down to look at it and reported that the 'brickwork' of the terrace foundation was defective to a depth of four or five feet, and subsequently it was agreed that this should be removed and the space filled with concrete as an extension of the concrete bed behind. The nature of the piling on which Jolliffe & Banks placed their inadequate brick-rubble is probably explained by the company's eighteenth-century minutebooks. In April 1753, when there had been serious settlement of the Hall's river front, and 'proper oak' was in short supply in London, the company's craftsmen declared that 'it had been found by experience that fir piles were as proper as oak & over a third less expensive' and Marquand the consultant surveyor agreed that fir piles would do if never out of water long enough to become dry.[5] No doubt that row of piles stayed wet between one tide and the next so long as the old Hall stood. But once Jolliffe & Banks, behind the protection of their coffer dam, rebuilt the embankment in 1828, the old fir piles left in place behind it dried out. (Which suggests what may have happened at the Custom House.) The emergency of July 1832 seems to have been the only moment, except for party-wall matters conveyed through the Clerk, when the company surveyor and the new architect several years his junior were in any sort of consultation.

Meanwhile, Grimsdell's 'two months' stretched to four. The eye-witness to the state of the ground in June, quoted above, was Roberts' new assistant George Gilbert Scott. In mid-May, when certain alterations to the original design had been approved and it was still imagined that Grimsdell might finish in June, so that building might then start, the committee expected Roberts to produce several sets of specifications and drawings to which contractors might tender in June. Final confirmation of the river front was delayed by an ancient-lights controversy between the company and the owners of the Shades (a question as to who were the owners of the Shades being then in Chancery) over the position of certain Shades windows which the company hoped to induce them to remove, and over the position of the new Hall terrace – considerably in advance of the old Hall terrace, what with the new embankment and arrangements with Rennie – with much holding up of tarpaulins beside the wharf to show that the new terrace would not 'deteriorate the value of the property' next door. By May 28 Roberts was 'confined to the house for a few days from the effects of over exertion in preparing the Drawings'. He must then have taken Scott into his office to help with the ensuing detailed drawings. Scott's later claim to have made 'all the working drawings' himself can perhaps be taken with grains of salt – though the fact that the greater number of surviving drawings seem to have Roberts' hand-writing on them could simply mean approval by the head of the office – but Scott the future arbiter of hundreds of Victorian buildings was given to making expansive statements. Eight years younger than Roberts, Scott had been articled for a few years to an architect and then in 1831 acted as building-contractors' superintendent on the works at Hungerford Market. By 1834 he was sharing rooms in Carlton Chambers, Regent Street, with Sampson Kempthorne who in 1830–1 had been assistant to Suter in the company surveyor's office; it was Kempthorne's subsequent practice designing workhouses under the new Poor Law that was to start Scott off on his own career, on his way to the Albert Memorial.[6] Meanwhile, he had two quiet, hardworking years of 'Smirkism and practical work' in Roberts' office until mid-1834. Scott was never once mentioned by name in the Fishmongers' Company records; he was not employed by them, nor did he presumably design anything himself. (The neat remark – long common currency on the historians' exchange – that, after Fishmongers' Hall, never again was Roberts so grand nor Scott so pure, does rather elevate Scott aged 21–3 beyond his station at the time, but so, one suspects, did Scott himself in retrospect.) At the end of the summer in 1832, Roberts moved office from Suffolk Street to No. 18 Adam Street, Adelphi, a building still standing just off the Strand at the corner of John Street.

On the Hall site in April, Elisha Bonner was appointed clerk of the works by the company on the architect's recommendation, at two and a half guineas per week paid every four weeks; a brick hut with chimney was made for him by the building contractors, who were also responsible for paying a gatekeeper twenty shillings a week, doubtless for tending the site entrance from Thames Street, where a hoarding was erected. Bonner's hut probably overlooked the wharf, of which free use was granted to the contractors, who were also to have the use of the five vaults under the bridge-approach, rented by the company from the City, for storage of materials as soon as they could be emptied of earth from the concrete diggings. Early in July, while the ground was still partly open, Roberts brought a well-digger to the site, Isaac Facer of Dog and Bear Yard, Tooley Street, whose proposal dated in August 'to bore the earth and to obtain a Spring of Soft water on the site' suggests that a preliminary pipe had been inserted in the con-crete for him; the well-boring was then postponed until the main Hall structure was built. A sad note from Facer in the summer of 1834 reported that it had taken him five months and more than the contracted £150, as he 'could not obtain a spring of soft water without going to the unusual depth of 230 feet', and he was granted £70 extra for it. This well was probably dug in the floor of the lower warehouse where a pump was installed and the tenant expected to allow access, though a well now exists beside the western cartway.

The firmness with which the Hall remained rooted in the ground beside the tidal Thames is due not only to Roberts' care and to the concrete layer underneath its cellars, but to the excellence of its builders. A 'cautious and excellent system recently adopted by architects in first selecting *known* and respectable, as well as responsible builders, to compete for the performance of the work' (as a book on professional practice was to put it in 1836)[7] was adopted here – unlike the free-for-all to architects in 1831. There were now in London a considerable number of firms ready to erect an entire building under one contract or, as one suppliant put it, 'possessing every means of conducting Works of Magnitude'. In mid-July, fourteen contractors were invited to tender by August 15, of whom eleven did. They were Atkinson & Brown of College Hill and Goswell Street, builders of the new Salters' Hall, Christ's Hospital great hall, and St. Dunstan's church, Fleet Street; Samuel Baker & Sons of Stangate Wharf, Lambeth, Baker being Smirke's brother-in-law and builder of many of his largest works including the British Museum; William Chadwick of Crown Wharf (Regent's Canal), New North Road, who was about to take the ground opposite Fishmongers' Hall on the east side of what was now called Adelaide Place for some speculative building; William & Lewis Cubitt of Gray's Inn Lane (later Road), separated since 1827 from the speculative building business of their brother Thomas and recently engaged upon Covent Garden Market for the Bedford Estate; Samuel Grimsdell, who was making the concrete platform; Grissell & Peto of Belvedere Road, cousins at the beginning of their partnership, lately engaged upon Hungerford Market and afterwards Barry's builders at the Reform Club and the Houses of Parliament, before Peto moved on to great railway works; Henry & John Lee of Chiswell Street, builders of the Travellers' Club; John Mallcott & Son of Newgate Street and Granite Wharf, Wapping, who had done stonework on Smirke's General Post Office and, though listed in trade directories as 'statuaries etc.', were not above paving the Hall wharf later on; Thomas Martin of Osnaburgh Street off the Marylebone Road, a neighbourhood of masons' yards; Thomas Piper & Son of Little Eastcheap, son and grandson of the Fishmongers' Company's mason concerned in the Hall building works of 1788ff; and Nicholas Winsland of Duke Street, off Great Russell Street, Bloomsbury.[8] The contract in question, for the main structure, faced with granite below and Portland stone above, and for the finishing of the warehouses, brought tenders ranging from Atkinson & Brown's £34,200 to the Cubitts' £27,750, which was accepted. Thereupon, on 24 August 1832 William and Lewis Cubitt signed the contract, their sureties being Thomas Cubitt of Clapham Common, builder, and William Scarlett of New Ormond Street, gentleman. William Cubitt was the partner most in evidence during the first year's work; when Lewis came to collect £5000 from the Clerk in July 1833, he brought a note of introduction from his brother. Their firm became one of the largest and most respected in Victorian London; from the 1840s Lewis also engaged in architectural works on his own, including King's Cross Station, and in 1854 William retired from business to enter public life, though the firm went on, eventually as Holland & Hannen and Cubitts.[9]

Roberts had arranged, when tenders were invited, that the quantities to be contracted for should be ascertained by two quantity surveyors – increasingly important figures on the building scene, much used by Smirke – one to be nominated by the tendering contractors and one by the architect on behalf of the company, their fees to be borne by the successful contractor. This was a world away from awkward conclaves of surveyors and measurers summoned by puzzled building committees a century earlier. Roberts and Towse had, however, forgotten to include an arbitration clause in the contract, as a joint statement signed by all the tendering contractors reminded them, while taking care 'to state that in so doing they have not been influenced by any want of respect for the Architect Mr Roberts, and they beg to express that from the personal knowledge of some and from all that has been heard of him by others they consider him well entitled to their personal confidence' – a personal knowledge that will have filtered through from Fowler's and Smirke's offices. A clause 'of the usual nature' was inserted, nominating Smirke, or Wilkins, or Hardwick to arbitrate in case of disagreement, though none arose. Nor was the winter of 1832–3 hard enough to invoke a clause that work might be stopped during December to February on notice from the architect; though he was to remark in January that the fixing of certain 'Stone and Iron work . . . is alone prevented by the state of the weather'.

Payment under this contract was made in five instalments, one-fifth after a quarter of the work was done (January 1833), one-fifth when up to the first floor 'and bearers fixed' (May), one-fifth when ready for the roof (August), one-fifth when roof, gutters and parapet were completed (September), and the remainder after the warehouses were finished inside in April 1834. There were occasional signs, to be expected in the economic climate of the time, that the Cubitts found themselves overstretched. In October 1832 they asked for a substantial advance and were allowed £2000 on account since they had brought materials worth more than that to the site; but in the following April, a request for an advance a month ahead of the second instalment was refused by the building committee after conferring with Roberts, although the building was by then over forty feet high and the masons had 'made considerable progress in the preparation of the Portland Stone at a prime cost of Eleven Thousand Pounds', William Cubitt said. Part of the third instalment was paid a month early because of the difference in roof heights, the upper walls of the great hall having to be brought up after the roofs either side of it were on. The entire shell of the building was just about completed by the end of 1833, Roberts certifying on 1 January that the Cubitts might have £5000 on account of the final payment. Possessing 'every means of conducting Works of Magnitude' could be a close-run thing on the basis of only five payments in twenty-one months. Thomas Cubitt, before the end of his partnership with William, had already evolved a system of monthly payments, but presumably Roberts had learnt the older method of management.[10]

When actual building began early in October 1832, the clerk of works was given £5 to be applied to treating the workmen on the occasion, although no inscribed stone seems to have been laid and no ceremony was mentioned : a utilitarian cast of thought governed all concerned. In any case, at this stage it seems to have been a matter not of laying the first stone but of laying a first course of cement for the footings. There had been other preparations in September. After Grimsdell's men left in August, the first thing the Cubitts' men had to do was restore the natural slope of the ground around the edges of the building-site. This was done by bricklayers using the earth temporarily 'deposited under the Arches of the Bridge Roadway' and ramming it down over the concrete bed to form 'an inclined plane from the Level of Thames Street to the Wharf level on the exterior of the Building', also bringing up a flat base 'to receive the paving of the lower warehouse on the interior' (Roberts' specifications).[11] The actual footings, with four courses of Roman cement under six courses of bricks laid in cement, were laid directly on the concrete. It was only in October that a certain process was fixed upon for treating the timber 'chain-plates through the footings'. Having at first specified a previous coating with 'Boyd's antiputrescent Tar mixture', Roberts was introduced by Smirke to John Howard Kyan, who explained to him the secrets of a new method 'for preserving timber from dry rot, fungus and decay' by immersion in a solution of corrosive sublimate in tanks installed at Grosvenor Basin, Pimlico, 'Patronized by His Majesty's Royal Architects', and citing Smirke, Soane, Wyatville, and 'the Navy Board at Woolwich Dock Yard 1828–31'.[12] Although the (now obsolete) Kyanizing process for destroying or neutralizing 'the Vegetative property in Timber' cost an extra £150, certain members of the Hall building committee and the Clerk could probably recall very well the dry rot that rose again in 1796 and 1813, and so it was agreed.

The shell of such a building consisted of a frame of brickwork, ironwork, and some timberwork clothed on the main fronts in a stone skin about a foot thick. The floor structure of the central portion of the Hall at entrance-level (entrance hall, corridor, staircase compartment), of brick arches in cement between iron bearers, the brick arches levelled to receive stone paving, was to bear up well in 1940. Walls of best stock bricks, in the 1830s the local yellow brick of London, lie behind the white Portland stone on three sides of the upper building, with brick facing on the west side. The brickwork of the warehouse storeys was faced with granite from the quarries in Devon of the Haytor Granite Company, a firm with offices in Broad Street Buildings and a wharf on the South Bank, from which much granite for the new Bridge came.[13]

Roberts included in his internal brickwork a feature variously called pot-tiles or hollow bricks : 'Tiles resembling the form of a garden-pot, closed at both ends, have long been applied to the turning of floor arches', he wrote in 1850, adding that he had used them 'when building Fishmongers' Hall in 1833' and that the ceiling of St George's Hall, Liverpool, was later vaulted with them. Smirke's fireproofing arrangements at the General Post Office had included 'hollow bricks turned in flat arches and closely cemented together'; Soane had used pot-construction to lessen the weight of his domes and vaults at the Bank of England; and there are said to have been similar usages by Nash at Buckingham Palace and by Wilkins at the National Gallery. Such methods seem to have come to this country before 1800 from France – used there especially in new fireproof theatre construction, and in a sense reviving Early Christian methods of vaulting in Rome and Ravenna. As when some medieval builders inserted jars in church walls for resonance, any 'pot tiles' in the vault over the Fishmongers' banqueting hall may have made some difference acoustically (concerts with a small number of instruments sound especially well there). Although nineteenth-century architects were aware that empty champagne bottles could withstand structural stress if so used, there is no record that the steady supply available here was drawn upon.[14]

The combined use of hollow-pot vaulting and shallow brick arches with iron girders on iron columns had appeared in English mill-building by 1800, usages hastened by the Albion Mill fire at Blackfriars in 1791.[15] At the Hall, to save money, the fireproof floor required between warehouse and kitchen storeys was brick-vaulted on iron columns, omitting the 'arched iron plating' originally intended, which may have been just as well. There was a good deal of ironwork in the Hall, both cast and wrought, made by the Dewers of Old Street who were later to execute the *tour de force* of the Coal Exchange. Roberts had apparently been concerned in or close to the construction of Smirke's King's Library at the British Museum, where the use of cast-iron beams of exceptional span (58 feet and 41 feet) in the ceiling was quite revolutionary in urban building at the time. The longest iron girders at Fishmongers' Hall are the pair, just under forty feet long, supporting the centre of the banqueting hall's west wall, themselves partly supported by the two pairs of columns confronting the foot of the stairs.[16] At first Roberts designed those columns as slim iron cores to be coated with scagliola, the popular substitute for marble; the fact that a surviving drawing for these shows naked iron columns means only that the drawing was for the structural contract and the scagliola was to be added at a later stage. But for such an obviously structural position, he suggested after building had begun that solid granite would look more honest, or as he put it, any imitation 'in a situation where it will be apparent that a considerable weight is borne, must convey an idea of weakness'. Moreover, scagliola (being just a polished mixture of marble chippings in plaster of paris) 'in so exposed a situation' and 'especially in the Grecian Doric order, which does not admit of the introduction of a marble base', would be liable to damage. Finally, he said, 'an edifice which probably presents in its exterior a far greater display of Granite than any other in England' could with 'peculiar propriety' exhibit some inside. Doubtless inspired once again by the King's Library, he recommended red Aberdeen granite: the working of this stubborn material had only been perfected about ten years before. The Stirling Hill quarries near Peterhead, north of Aberdeen, supplied the shaft of the Duke of York column at the foot of Regent Street, the four columns at the centre of the King's Library in the British Museum – and the pillars and pilasters at the foot of the staircase in Fishmongers' Hall.[17] Anxiously pointing out in December 1832 that it could take a year to prepare the granite, Roberts estimated four fluted Doric columns and four pilasters 12 feet 8 inches high at £516, against £200 for scagliola, and the court turned him down; but with a new estimate for plain unfluted shafts at £420 and the backing of the Prime Warden, committee and court changed their minds. By May the Cubitts had undertaken to do both shaping and fixing for £432, including cost of the stone, and by the end of 1833 polished pinkish-grey granite from the northeastern edge of Aberdeenshire replaced scaffolding as part of the structure of the great hall above them. In a way (whether or not consciously designed as such) this triple-spaced colonnade alongside the passage from Clerk's house to courtroom and athwart the approach from entrance to great hall, repeats the idea of Jerman's portico. That had been an arcade on single shafts, while now the shafts are paired under a flat lintel, yet a certain precedent seems to have been observed.

The roof, as with the old hall, was a series of roofs: now there were low slate-covered hip roofs over riverside range and Thames Street range, a lead flat over the grand staircase, and copper over the great hall roof, all over trusses of timber. The 'best malleable copper, laid on Borrowdaile's Patent Felt', was supplied and apparently applied by R. & E. Kepp, coppersmiths of Chandos Street, Covent Garden, whom Smirke regarded as the only workers in this 'rarely used' material worth considering for the roof of the British Museum. At the Hall, Messrs Kepp were paid £100 as a separate item not part of the Cubitt contract.[18] James Kepp of the same address had done minor repairs to the copper roof on the old riverside range in 1819; and so the continuities of London crafts went on.

Another extra, the balustrading before the Hall's entrance front, involved an inordinate amount of conversation with the Bridge authorities because it stood upon City-owned pavement and was part of the bridge-approach (although neither the parapet of the Bridge itself nor of the dry arch over Thames Street had balustrading then). Roberts had to submit a drawing for the approval of Smirke as architect for the approaches, to show the two rows of open balustrade either side of the front steps (as in Pl. 10); approval also for the pair of pedestals flanking the steps as they too stood partly on the City's pavement, and for the extra support-wall under the bottom steps against the bridge-abutment. Although the two balustraded parapets were to cost over £350, the City's Bridge Committee refused to contribute more than £100, since the company would have to enclose its front basement-area somehow. It was not until late 1833 that the Cubitts' price for the balustrade was settled, and then there was a delay in the supply of granite for the steps, so hoarding will have masked the east front until well into 1834. The Cubitt masons also carved the company arms crowning the east front and the flanking sea-horse relief panels. Passers-by sometimes ask what the sea-horses 'mean': they are simply marine motifs like dolphins on furniture, jolly mythical creatures like the sea-horses in the round over the Admiralty gateway in Whitehall. At Roberts' suggestion, the year of construction was carved in a blank space below the company arms: A.D. MDCCCXXXIII. And Hancock & Rixon supplied the pair of gas lamps (then in keeping with those on the Bridge) still in use on either side of the front steps.

While the shell, or carcase, was being completed towards the end of 1833, with the warehouse-finishing of that contract still to be done, specifications for finishing the Hall interior were drawn up. Court and committee had imagined that this like the earlier contracts should be put out to tender from a selected list of builders, including the Cubitts, possibly with separate tendering for the plasterwork. Upon inviting these tenders, around December 1, they were surprised at an immediate reply: the Cubitts 'declined to enter into any competition for the same'. That is, a building begun by them would be finished by them, or not. And so, on 31 January 1834 their tender for finishing the Hall for £17,500 including plasterwork, and considerably under Roberts' own estimate, was accepted and Lewis Cubitt signed the initial agreement.[19]

Roberts' concern for the continuity of operations had appeared in October when he asked that the Cubitts be authorized, 'before winter comes . . . to fix proper frames covered with Canvass or Calico . . . to exclude the weather' from the new window-openings, which explains an odd item, 'Calico lights', in the accounts. London weather in 1834 was dry from February to June, followed by a wet summer, though by then the window-glass decided upon in March would have been installed. The south and east fronts were glazed entirely with the more expensive new plate-glass instead of partly with crown-glass: 'the appearance of the Building and the obstruction of external noise would be materially improved thereby', said Roberts. It is likely too that wind-resistance, and the window-rattling gusts this site is subject to, were considered. Through the river-front's upper windows in October 1834 there will have been a dramatic distant view of the fire that destroyed the Houses of Parliament.

Ancient and modern techniques were mixed at the new Hall, as befitted an age of transition. For example, old-fashioned views on heating prevailed. Various central-heating systems then being applied in new buildings, such as the several versions of piped hot water circulating from great boilers, were too new to have been thoroughly proven (one Dublin architect complaining of these systems' 'present many inconveniences', confessed in 1835 that he had 'put more people in hot water than any other person in this country').[20] Smirke had used a number of different systems in his public buildings. But the Fishmongers firmly intended to rely upon open fires in the latest grates set into one or more chimneypieces in each room. Early in 1833 Roberts hopefully recommended heating the two-storey grand staircase space and adjoining ground-floor corridor by 'warm water which at a very small expense might be introduced from a boiler in the Kitchen to two ornamental Pedestals placed one on each side of the Grand Staircase'. But the court preferred fireplaces, one under each of the niches that were eventually to hold statuary, like the niches over fireplaces in the entrance hall at the Athenaeum. Fireplaces were therefore installed, each with arched niche above and flanked by pairs of granite pilasters complementing the screen of pillars (Pl. 13, 17), and these fires warmed the plaster goddesses installed in 1840 above them – if not the whole two-storey space between them – until 1898.[21] The only (apparently) original heating appliance not embedded in a chimneypiece is the handsome register stove still standing (though now unused) in its place in the entrance hall, described in an early inventory as 'Polished Steel (isolated) Stove, blower, Cast iron and bright bars with bronze Ornaments' and costing about £60 – more than the other grates as a free-standing piece – from Bennett of Aldersgate Street, iron-monger. The thought of this entire building with its high ceilings and exposure to the river, heated like its predecessors only by open coal-fires – cheerful though those must have looked – implies different ways of eating and dressing in the winter from the way we live now. Not to mention the Hall chimneys' contribution to the coal-laden air outside. One wonders how the 'hot closets' installed in 1835 in the first-floor serveries for the two dining rooms were heated, perhaps by a coal-fired boiler connected with the fireplace in each servery or with a small coal-fired kitchen range. The kitchen equipment in the basement, down to 'jack-chains, trivets for charcoal stoves, lark spits' etc., was presumably the latest available. A history of the kitchens of the City of London, and how they compared with Alexis Soyer's imminent improvements at the Reform Club, would be a subject for connoisseurs.

A temporary heating question arose in November 1834, when Cubitts requested that they be allowed to keep fires going in all the main rooms, lest the joinery (dadoes, doorcases, shutters, etc.) they were about to put up should suffer 'great Injury from the damp Atmosphere' of winter. Roberts confirmed the importance of this measure for finishing the contract on time in May, while judiciously commenting that there was always a risk of shrinkage for joinery fixed in winter unless an artificial 'atmosphere' were created, that is, the Cubitts in arranging their work and the amount of their tender should have allowed for it, in which latter view the building committee concurred, seeing 'no necessity to interfere in the Contract'. But after a talk with Lewis Cubitt, by then as active in the contract as his brother, they changed their minds. 'Fires' will have meant free-standing coal stoves brought in by the contractors, since all the marble chimneypieces were 'guarded by casing' immediately after fixing. The weather of early 1835 was milder than expected and by June two and a half tons of the Cubitts' coals remained in the Hall cellars for company use at a reduced price. Fire insurance had been carried by the contractors from July 1833 when the walls were roof-high until May 1834 after completion of their first contract, when the company took out its own insurance, dividing the risks, at the Union Assurance Office's suggestion, by insuring warehouses, 'north portion' (Clerk's and Beadle's houses), and Hall separately.

There were other risks than fire in 1834, year of labour unrest in England. In the wake of working-class discontent with the results of the Reform Act, a Grand National Consolidated Trades Union, active from February to August, made a series of aggressive and unsuccessful attempts to promote a general strike for an eight-hour day. In the summer the firm of John Mallcott & Son were engaged to pave Fishmongers' Wharf and the cartways from Thames Street while the Cubitt men were busy inside. Apparently the strike-promoters tried to get at both groups. By July 19 Roberts was asking Towse for a copy of a clause in the Cubitt contract whereby work could be suspended 'in the event of a general Strike amongst the workmen'. This clause, inserted as a rider before the second contract was approved in draft by the Cubitts in April, stipulated that the contractors should not be penalized for delay 'occasioned by the refusal of the persons employed by them to continue the said Works' provided that refusal was 'in pursuance of a general agreement or Combination among them & for the purpose of accomplishing some unreasonable object'. (In fact, the labour situation may have been the reason why this contract, under which work was already proceeding, took so long to be signed.) In September, Mallcott reported to Roberts that 'we have had to fight through the difficulties of Unionists & sometimes at the risk of our lives'.[22] And that is all we know of the matter, the only fighting reported from this ground since the Fishmongers' Company came to it, whatever disturbances medieval fishmongers made in the streets outside.

There was no serious delay, however, in the Cubitts' orderly progress. A few jobs were done by specialists paid separately, such as the interior bell-hanging which Roberts found he could get done more cheaply by Mr Barrow, probably John Barrow, smith and bell-hanger of East Street, Manchester Square. Then there was the yellow scagliola, for two columns in the staircase window and pilasters deployed on the top landing, in the drawing room, and around the great hall, from Joseph Browne's Scagliola Works in University Street, Fitzroy Square (Browne being apparently the man who had executed the Marble Arch, under difficulties, for John Nash at Buckingham Palace).[23] And there was the 'stained glass' by Hancock & Rixon, 'lamp, lustre & glass mfrs' of Cockspur Street (better known for their chandeliers), whose designs were based on sketches and instructions from Roberts, in preference to those of Thomas Willement (heraldic artist to George IV and best known for his 'medieval' glass, who sent in designs characterized by Roberts as 'partaking more of the Roman than of the Grecian style'). There were three sets of ornamental windows: a triple set on the staircase with 'elaborate Grecian enrichment in enamelled glass' in the centres surrounded by borders of 'stained glass with a rich Grecian pattern'; a vestibule window with 'neat enamelled pattern' and similar border; and two heraldic panels one in each lunette at either end of the banqueting hall, apparently of painted glass and each 10 by 6 feet 'with Copper bars fitted into a Wood frame prepared for illumination at night', the royal arms at one end and the company arms at the other end, as once painted on the end walls of the Tudor great hall, but with 'a highly enriched Grecian border' (Pl. 19). [24]

The chief building-trades involved in interior work – carpentry and joinery, marble-carving for chimneypieces, laying cantilevered stone steps for the staircases, plastering, plumbing, glazing and painting – were performed by the Cubitt firm from their workshops in Gray's Inn Road. All timber used was either oak or 'best dry Memel wood', all the oak had been sawn at least two years before, and 'no American wood of any description' was to be brought on the premises – a reflection upon 'Canada timber' which the *Architectural Magazine* noted was 'much more liable to decay than that . . . of Europe', although Smirke had used some American oak flooring at the General Post Office. The floors of the best

rooms at the Hall were dowelled together with 'dry old Ship dowells'.[25] Mahogany
doors carefully saved from the old Hall fitted nowhere and had to be disposed of.
Marbles used for the best chimneypieces included white statuary marble for the
court drawing room and black marble for courtroom and banqueting hall (black
chimney-pieces were often preferred in this period in rooms used for serious
business). A drawing for the first-floor vestibule chimneypiece is marked for 'Red
Mona Marble', apparently the Welsh serpentine or streaky marble. Twenty-seven
sheets of drawings for Grecian chimneypieces, measured or sketchy or unused
alternatives, survive.[26]

The purity of Roberts' translations from the Greek was maintained on the
principal fronts of the building (except for the Roman-looking arcaded warehouse-
base hinging the whole to the Bridge). But inside, various concessions had to be
made where the full Greek rigour did not suit company traditions. There was at
first some doubt whether the statue of Sir William Walworth, his robes still
brightly coloured, should 'be placed in the new edifice'. Then Roberts recommended that 'a nitch be formed on the central landing of the principal Staircase
immediately beneath the large Window – this position though a prominent one
will be so much in shadow that the Statue will not have an obtrusive effect', and
suggesting that the colouring of the drapery be toned down. A prominent recent
example of the niche with figure on the landing of such a staircase was that of the
Duke of York in the United Services Club, and a similar position, higher up, was
occupied by the Apollo Belvedere at the Athenaeum. And so Peirce's gesturing
figure, after spending about 140 years dominating the old high table, now dominated the new staircase. But it was less easy to accommodate Peirce's 'Shield of Arms
taken down from the Old Gateway' to Thames Street, with its jolly merman and
mermaid and general air of flutter once so suited to the unrefined bustle of that
street: the only place where it could 'with propriety be introduced' was high
above the west warehouse door on the backside of the building (in fact, almost
back to back with Walworth on the stairs) where at that time it was scarcely
visible, 'skied' like a picture at the Royal Academy and a bit vulgar compared to
the aristocratic merman and mermaid being carved for the east front. The rest
of the gateway, originally embedded in one of the Thames Street houses, went in
1834 to a rural retreat in South London, in the garden of a company tenant,
Daniel W. Richardson, off the Walworth Road, until 1861 when the carved gate-
posts were removed to St Peter's Hospital at Wandsworth; their fate when that
ground was sold in 1923 is unknown.[27] The Coade stone statue of Charity, dating
only from about 1790, did not suit the new Hall either, and was relegated to St
Peter's. As during the drastic redecoration when the Charity group was acquired,
there was in 1834 the urge to make all new and, even more than in 1790, there
was a conscious regard for 'propriety', for furnishings 'in keeping' with the
building.

One change made from Roberts' original design went only from one Greek
form to another, when he realized that the row of prime wardens' shields to be
hung like an extra frieze in the banqueting hall would outshine the very plain

pilaster capitals he had envisaged there : 'with so rich an heraldic decoration, it would be requisite in order to preserve a sufficient prominency in the architectural features . . . to substitute the Corinthian for the Ionic Pilaster & entablature.' He therefore adapted for that room the Corinthian order (lacking the lower leaves of the capital) of the little Monument of Lysicrates in Athens, that staple cliché of the Greek Revival which, because of the small scale of the original, was approved by revivalists for (blown-up) interior use.[28] To emphasize certain points in the room Roberts used overlapping pilasters, as Smirke had at the British Museum (for instance on the grand staircase), or for that matter as Wren had on St Paul's – a mannerist device, but useful. The fact that Roberts' pilasters almost disappear in a rather furtive manner into the corners of the great hall must have been partly the result of changing classical orders in midstream, after plan and dimensions were settled.

From the first, the great hall and certain other rooms were lighted by gas, with all the subsequent problems of that then still new technique. In recommending it, the architect pointed out that 'it has been invariably introduced into the Club Houses recently erected' – a clinching reference to the most modern London palaces. One eager tradesman of an Oil & Gas Lamp & Chandelier Manufactory in Great Peter Street, Westminster, explaining that by the meter system 'only so much Gas will be registered as is actually consumed', claimed that he had not only lighted noblemen's houses, the kitchen and offices of St James's Palace, and the General Post Office but was about to lay the pipes for the new City Club in Broad Street. Another interested firm, of brass founders in Creed Lane, were able to cite the livery halls of the Ironmongers and Cordwainers, East India House and the Mansion House, the Royal Academy and St Paul's Cathedral. Gas had arrived. Not only gas fitters but gas suppliers (the City of London Gas Works near Salisbury Square) wrote in. The Clerk's files in 1834 bulged with trade circulars and letters offering, 'with all due difference' as one Staining Lane water-gilder put it, to supply goods and services. In the end, Mr Deville's tender for certain gas fittings was accepted, apparently that of James DeVille, lamp manufacturer of 367 Strand also operating as brass founder, presumably the same man who supplied a brass rail placed around the great hall (to protect walls and scagliola from diners and waiters) and a staircase railing – presumably the 'bronzed balusters' of the main staircase, for James DeVille in 1834 was also making bronzed stair balustrades for Buckingham Palace.[29] But the rosewood hand-rail-capping fitted so nicely to the hand was apparently made in the Cubitt workshops (section, Pl. 13). Gas was laid on for entrance hall, central corridor, back staircase, basement passage, kitchen, scullery and basement entrance, while the great hall and grand staircase were to be lighted with 'portable Gas' – that is, supplied in some limited form for occasional use. The chandeliers for the court drawing and dining rooms were made for candles. These and the principal chandeliers for gas and oil were supplied by Hancock & Rixon as 'being more in taste with the general appearance of the Hall' than those offered by other firms : including the eight brass 'chandelier gas burners' in the great hall (Pl. 16) and a 'chandelier for ten oil lamps' in the livery drawing room. A pair of bronzed lamp standards were fixed in the scrolls of the handrail at the bottom of the staircase (Pl. 17). Their light was multiplied by the great mirror in the corridor opposite the bottom of the stairs, 'a silvered plate glass' about ten by five feet in a 'veined marble recess' framed, as now, like a doorcase. Lamps in the main corridor were reflected by small mirrors applied to certain door-panels that would otherwise be dark; for example, the doorway opposite the entrance hall, now leading to a large cloak room, then contained a false door against the wall of the upper space of the kitchen. The Hall's large single-sheet glasses reflected the same pride in the newly possible size of plate glass as those shining in new shops and gin-palaces; and the small reflector-panels mirrored a popular fashion for reflected vistas. The popular mode for mirrors did not attain such sophisticated ambiguity of light-sources as in Soane's museum of a house, but was part of the Picturesque taste that affected even the strictest Greek revivalists. It was only in 1898, after this part of the building was first lighted by electricity, that the little mirror-panels were ordered removed from those doors : the Early Victorian love of looking-glass vistas had a good deal to do with the gentle luminosity of Early Victorian oil and gas lamps.

The court drawing room at the southeast corner of the first floor became an exceptionally felicitous example of Late Georgian/Early Victorian marine-villa decoration. This room has two south windows immediately overlooking the Bridge and the river above-bridge, and three east windows overlooking the bridge-approach and the Pool below-bridge, then busy with shipping. By 1840, looking glasses were hung on all four walls of the room : three panels on the chimney-piece wall flanked by pilasters as now and one at the north end as now (Pl. 22); and gilt-framed pier glasses on the window-walls, two on the east side, and the one between the south windows in two pieces combined with a marble slab (console table) on gilt supports and rosewood base. The floor-length pair of mirrors between the east windows were added at Roberts' suggestion, to give an effect of widening the room. The furniture was of rosewood upholstered in the green silk tabaret of the window curtains. 'Tabaret' as supplied by Messrs Wilkinson of Ludgate Hill (who spelt it 'tabrait') was woven in alternate stripes of watered silk and damask weave, a striping only of weave and texture; a crimson piece survives, marked 'to be of green colour' for the drawing room, and probably representing the red curtains hung in the court dining-room.[30] 'China Vases' in both rooms may have been 'the Jars' reserved in 1827 from the court parlour of the old Hall, possibly eighteenth-century blue-and-white ware. Wilkinson also supplied mirrors and furniture, and other furniture was supplied by Webb & Cragg of Old Bond Street – who said they had furnished Crockford's, the Travellers' and the City of London clubhouses – and by William Hunter & Son of Finsbury Place (the rosewood furniture), also by Taylor & Fisher, tenants of the Fish-mongers' Company in Fenchurch Street (the courtroom's fitted furniture). Roberts even handled orders for brown holland covers. Early inventories for the present Hall list an array of protective materials suggesting to what a fine pitch good housekeeping had been brought in England in the 1830s.[31] For the drawing room alone there were listed brass protecting rods in front of the pier glasses between the windows overlooking the entrance front (windows much used by spectators of eminent arrivals), drugget and damask cover for the Persian carpet and hearth rug, oil-cloth covers for tables and chimneypieces, and holland covers for chandeliers, chairs, sofas, glasses, and curtains. Upholsterers' men were engaged to bag and unbag the curtains, and lampmakers' men to cover and uncover the chandeliers, as necessary. Probably ever since Evelyn had pointed out what coal smoke was doing to London furniture and hangings, coal smoke and dust-covers had both flourished. There were also holland inside blinds on all the windows, and outside blinds on the south-facing ones.

Downstairs, all the offices and entrance hall had 'fly wire blinds' or screens. In the outer office the desks were enclosed by a wainscot dwarf partition with brass trellis work along the top. There were 'office lamps', probably oil lamps, and taper stands (probably for sealing-wax), but the Clerk's private office contained no inventoried light fittings or lamps; Mr Towse, born in 1760, very likely preferred candlelight, or small lamps brought up from the lamp room in the basement. This was also the case in the courtroom. Overlooking the river as the company's Tudor courts had, it was a smaller room than now, with two windows, and approached through a waiting room from which the central window on the river front, with dwarf doors under, opened to the terrace steps. (Roberts in his cautious way offered to put a railing on these steps 'to prevent accidents', but no one was interested.) More than any other room in the building the courtroom looked backward, with its traditionally fixed seats raised on a platform around an inner space set off by a low curtained partition, with the prime warden's chair between the windows.[32] The seats on carved dolphin supports were covered with purple leather stuffed with horsehair, the backs were of wainscot, a rail for hats ran underneath, and the oak platform was carpeted. Here for the first time the court met on 15 June 1835, ten years to the day after the first stone was laid for the new Bridge that had caused so much upheaval and renewal. This day in 1835 also happened to be that of the first meeting of the new Institute of British Architects, perhaps a symbolic coincidence for a building that embodied so much of past and present and for a while in 1831 had deeply concerned a sizeable segment of the now newly organized profession.

The profession and its hangers-on, predictably, both praised and damned the new Fishmongers' Hall. No doubt the competitors of 1831 and their friends were the ones who liked it least, especially those future Victorians who were busy breaking away from the language of Sir Robert Smirke. For in a sense – although the Greek Revival went on in certain quarters – the Hall was one of London's last large buildings, except for the National Gallery and that earlier-begun long-playing performance the British Museum, in the style. Early Victorians of the late 1830s criticised the Greek Revival for its 'flatness and want of light and shade' (W. H. Leeds in 1838 on the Hall's exterior).[33] A new optical sense was developing, demanding bolder shadows from more beetling cornices and deeper porches (the

Hall suffered from 'the want of greater boldness and richness in the cornices of the pediment', said Leeds). Architecture in a time of transition is bound to be controversial, and a style so universal in one decade loathed in the next. Yet Leeds, a critic who was to condemn the Greek Revival more than most, saw much to admire in the new Hall, finding it a better building than Smirke's dual building on the west side of Trafalgar Square : 'the whole is in far better keeping, and free from that intermixture of enrichment in some parts and nakedness in others' observable in Smirke's work – a stick to beat Smirke with could be found even here. Leeds also preferred Roberts to Hardwick and saw in the Fishmongers' main staircase 'simple dignity' instead of the 'pomp and variety' at the Goldsmiths' – partly because the Fishmongers hadn't finished painting and gilding yet (walls and ceilings will have had an unintended coldness here at first), partly because Hardwick was a much less austere architect than Roberts, who would have been temperamentally incapable of the 'Euston Arch'.

What pleased Leeds most at Fishmongers' Hall was the succession of state rooms, beginning with the vestibule (called at first by the Clerk 'the announcing chamber' or anteroom) to the right at the top of the stairs : the deft advantage taken of its irregular plan (Pl. 11), a square crossed like a T, the square part under a circular ceiling penetrated by a little skylight, the oval-centred cross-piece with one apselike end and one windowed end (where the space over the window then contained a mirror). Not only did this vestibule 'acquire a decided and peculiar character' by its irregularity, but by communicating with all three of the principal rooms 'it may be quoted as one of those happy instances where convenience and architectural effect go hand in hand', he thought. The court dining room was 'a very noble apartment' with its four windows overlooking the river, and its chimney-breast mirrors at opposite ends reflecting 'almost interminably the splendid silver chandelier'. With the 'rich but simple' furniture, all this had 'an air of grandeur tempered by sobriety', while the drawing room next door might 'pass for magnificent in comparison with many a "west-end" saloon'. The climax was the great hall, where this critic found 'variety of surfaces' and liked it better than the Goldsmiths' gorgeous banquet room. Thus one articulate critic in 1838. Earlier, under another hat (writing as Candidus in the *Architectural Magazine* in 1836, probably before he had been inside the Hall), Leeds included it in a list of 'some of the very finest opportunities that ever presented themselves [which] have of late been quite thrown away'. But James Noble in his book of 1836, *The Professional Practice of Architects*, said that the City 'derived considerable architectural importance' from the new halls of the Fishmongers and Goldsmiths.[34] Noble was assistant to C. R. Cockerell, and it is through some comments by Cockerell on Smirke that we may see how Roberts' Hall interior succeeded in pleasing even such a crusty anti-Greek as Leeds. Cockerell thought Smirke's ceiling decoration rigid and mechanical, with 'no coves, circles nor any of those floating amiable forms, in which the 17 & 18 [century] schools abounded'; ignoring the circular ceiling panels in the King's Library, Cockerell saw in Smirke's entirely rectilinear ceilings 'unmeasured trabeation' in a 'single unbroken sheet' threatening 'to crack over us'.[35] But when Roberts applied Smirke's rectangular bands and coffers to the Fishmongers' banqueting-hall ceiling, it was to a curved surface. The vestibule introducing his state rooms (Pl. 11) is roofed by a variety of 'floating amiable forms'. Roberts did not take Smirke straight.

Two other London buildings come to mind, apparently designed at the same time as the Hall, Lewis Vulliamy's Law Society in Chancery Lane (without its later north wing) and Cockerell's Westminster Life Office in the Strand (demolished 1907 for Rhodesia House). In quick external comparison with Vulliamy's neat but toneless building, the livery hall at London Bridge has a crispness, with the slight vibration set up by the fluting of the columns and the greater air and light around to define its edges ('one of the few buildings in London that can be viewed from a distance without losing definition in its detail', it has been called in this century).[36] On the other hand, in comparison with Cockerell's concentrated sculptural quality, the Hall has a bland uncomplicated character; Cockerell's work was exciting and scholarly, Roberts' dignified and reasonable. Charles Barry's nearly contemporary Travellers' Club design (1829) for the first Italianate *palazzo* in London marked the beginning of the end of the Greek Revivalism epitomized in Fishmongers' Hall, even before the latter was designed.

Certain critics not in a position to know complained that the Hall cost far more than the limit of £50,000 set in the competition.[37] Strictly speaking, that rule did better than most such, although the whole cost of rebuilding here depends on what costs you include. Roberts drew up one summary in October 1835 that included the concrete contract with extras, the carcase contract with extras, the finishings contract with extras and sundry fixtures, the separate bills for granite columns, scagliola, stained glass, brass interior railing and copper roofing, while allowing for painting and gilding not yet done and omitting fittings and furniture, and excluding his own commission and the clerk of works' salary, to arrive at a total of £51,533 for the three years 1832-5. This compared well with his original estimate, including granite facing below bridge-level and Portland stone above, of £58,500.[38] An undated sheet drawn up by the Clerk, summarizing the building fund accounts for the eight years 1827-35, before all the Cubitt bills were in, includes many items that were not or not entirely the architect's concern, such as shoring up the old Shades, the embankment of 1828, extra fees to Suter, compensation to Thames Street tenants, premiums to Roberts, Davies and Cottingham, Facer's well-boring, Mallcott's wharf-paving, and so on: without some large sums listed by Roberts and without furniture and fittings, but including his commission and Bonner's salary, this total came to £55,092.[39] However, costs strictly related to the unfitted, unfurnished building were indeed below the architect's first estimate, it would seem; the entire series of operations involved in the rebuilding on that site were another matter. For comparison with Roberts' figure of £51,533, the Athenaeum clubhouse opened in 1830 – with no deep concrete raft or warehouse storeys below its cellars – cost £43,101 with furniture and architect's commission. The more elaborate Reform Club was to cost, including fixtures, fittings and furniture but not the architect's fee, £78,650.[40] Roberts' fees at five per cent were paid each time the Cubitts' and other bills were paid. The only questioning of his fees arose in October 1835 when he presented his account for five per cent on the furniture bills. He replied, to the court's satisfaction, that 'the charge is a customary one where, as is usual in Public Buildings, the Architect superintends the furnishing. . . . The trouble attending the various and minute arrangements connected with the greater part of the furniture and fittings', he said, were greater than directing similar expense on the building, peculiar care being needed to preserve 'uniformity of character' between articles from different suppliers. He had prepared many drawings and specifications, compared tenders and communicated with 'upwards of twenty different parties who have been employed', and the tenders would show how much money he had saved; that is, everything from carpets to plate-warmers had been under his eye. No drawings for furniture survive (though quite a few for fixtures and fittings, e.g. Pl. 14, 15), but some of the furniture does.

It was Roberts' last as well as first such elaborate commission. In January 1835 he appears to have been offering his professional services for part of London's first modest railway terminus to be built at the other end of London Bridge, where none of his work now remains.[41] Also in 1835 he became honorary architect to the Destitute Sailors Asylum in Well Street, where his Sailors' Home of that year was a prototype for the model lodging-houses he was to design for a housing society in the 1840s, for his pioneering block of workmen's flats in Bloomsbury, and for his little block shown at the 1851 Exhibition: ancestors of all Victorian workmen's 'dwellings', his prototypes were humane in scale. Meanwhile in 1834, while work at the Hall was still in full swing, he designed a Collegiate School at Camberwell in the Tudor style thought appropriate to grammar schools. After the Fishmongers moved into the Hall, he was kept busy with post-mortems and after-thoughts, and in 1840 with completion of the decoration. In 1837 he was elected Fellow of the Institute of British Architects, in 1838 he became a Fellow of the Society of Antiquaries, where one of his proposers was Sir Robert Smirke, and in the Royal Academy summer exhibition of 1838 were three drawings by Henry Roberts, one for a country house in Devon, one for a chapel in Manchester, and one of the Fishmongers' banqueting hall.[42] Between the ages of 28 and 31, Roberts produced in Fishmongers' Hall 'a very skilled building by anyone's standards, in terms of planning and handling of classical elements', as one young architect put it in 1975. That this type of commission did not arise again for Roberts was probably more than partly by choice. As time went on, until an independent income enabled him to retire to Italy, his bent was increasingly toward rationally designed humanitarian improvement.

The two Cubitts, soon after their contract was completed, were elected freemen of the company and taken on to the livery (William eventually becoming Prime Warden, as well as Alderman, Member of Parliament, and twice Lord Mayor). And on 1 August 1835 the first court dinner was held at the new Hall beside the new Bridge with guests that included His Majesty's Ministers. On the brink of a new age, the company was once again well and prominently housed. But life on the brink of the Victorian Thames was not going to be easy.

CHAPTER 15

Victorian Gilding and Riverside Smoke

LONDON'S PALL of coal-smoke thickened with the swelling fleet of Thames steamers. The single waterman sculling Mr Pepys, quietly reading a book, up to Barn Elms and back had been replaced by steamboat captains and their crowds of passengers chugging from pier to pier. The river-water itself, laden with sewage, hardly bore thinking about until, in the hot summer of 1858, it was forced into public notice. Even while sheets soaked in anti-putrescent substances draped the windows of the Houses of Parliament to enable members to legislate without choking, it appears that at Fishmongers' Hall English phlegm and a stiff upper nose were enough : no complaints appear in the minutebooks for that summer. As private dwellings were replaced by great warehouses on the City's riverbanks, the river itself could be sinister, as in the opening scene of *Our Mutual Friend*. Habit, however, as installed on Walworth's old ground in Roberts' comfortable Hall, seems to have found nothing sinister there. The smoke nuisance did greatly offend the new building's owners when they first moved in; it took them about six years to come to (commercial) terms with it – a period wonderfully illustrating Thames-side accommodation to new sources of smoke, as ever since William Harrison noted new chimneys there in Elizabeth I's time.

At first, possession of a private wharf meant that smoke came only from vessels moored or passing nearby. In March 1834 negotiations were opened with the Dublin & London Steam Marine Company for grant of a lease to them of the warehouse space under the Hall, on condition that 'no Steam Vessel shall be moored at or near the Wharf', the firm's agent assuring the court that business would be 'carried on entirely by Lighters nor will our Vessels come nearer than their present Moorings' about a mile below-bridge. The Thames Street end of the warehouse storeys was to be fitted up as an agent's residence, no cattle or pigs were to pass over the wharf, and no horses would 'pass or repass up or down' the ways beside the Hall – conditions soon relaxed after much talk to allow six horned cattle at a time and 'horses belonging to gentlemen' to be shipped from the wharf. But each party then added so many prohibitions inadmissible to the other, the subject was dropped until the wharf-paving and labour troubles of that summer were over. In December 1834 wharf and warehouses, with five vaults under the bridge-approach leased to the Fishmongers' Company by the City, were agreed

The notes for Chapter 15 are on pp. 201–4.

to be let to Messrs Jones Bros, provision merchants of Abchurch Lane, a firm that was to occupy this space under and beside the Hall until 1888. At first they worked entirely from barges.[1]

Soon after the Fishmongers' Company moved in upstairs in the summer of 1835, steamboats plying from Adelaide Wharf and Fresh Wharf just downstream past the bridge were causing 'great damage' to the company's new furnishings 'by the quantity of Smoke constantly coming into the Apartments'. Accordingly complaints were sent to the directors of the steamboat firms concerned, some of whom replied that burning only coke while lying alongside would prevent them from 'getting the Steam up'. During the next five years the Clerk complained to twelve steamboat companies plying from this neighbourhood to Richmond, Greenwich, Woolwich, Gravesend, Herne Bay and other popular ports. From 1837 one could go from London Bridge to Westerminster Bridge by water, avoiding the traffic of the Strand and Ludgate Hill, for fourpence. By 1839 steamers using the Shades wharf next door to the Hall brought revenue to the wine tavern and more dirt to the Hall. The revenues from steamer passengers were now such that several riverside neighbours talked of uniting to make a steam wharf all the way along to Old Swan Stairs, but their hope that the Fishmongers' Company would join them was disappointed. The watermen of London Bridge stairs prayed in vain for the company's consent to their 'affixing a float' for steam vessels there in 1840. Meanwhile Messrs Jones asked the company to join them in the passenger-wharf business: in July 1839 a committee of five wardens, seasoned men and all former members of the original building committee, decided that the company should reconsider its attitude, a process that lasted until the spring of 1841. Jones Bros having offered to take on the entire management of the new sideline in spite of inconvenience to their regular trade and to pay the company extra rent or a proportion of 'the Head Money', the court finally agreed to permit use of Fishmongers' Hall Wharf by steam vessels 'on board of which there shall not be consumed any Coals which shall be prejudicial to the Company's building', the intended steamboat line to furnish a list of the types of coal to be used. It was, of course, soon discovered that relaxing this condition to the extent of demanding use of only 'the least prejudicial' coals meant merely, as the harassed Messrs Jones explained, that all coals were prejudicial to the Hall.[2] No white building there and then could 'abide white', in the words of the young New Yorker Herman Melville arriving in November 1849, a little like Macaulay's New Zealander, to see

the greatest everyday crowd which grimy London presents to the curious stranger : that hereditary crowd – gulfstream of humanity – which, for continuous centuries, has never ceased pouring, like an endless shoal of herring, over London Bridge.

Hung in long, sepulchral arches of stone the black, besmoked bridge seemed a huge scarf of crape, festooning the river across . . . eastward toward the sea, tiers and tiers of jetty colliers lay moored, side by side, fleets of black swans . . . As ant-hills, the bridge arches crawled with processions of carts, coaches, drays, every sort of wheeled, rumbling thing, the noses of horses behind touching the backs of the vehicles in front, all bespattered with ebon mud. . . .[3]

No view of the Hall since it became part of the bridge-approach is complete without that ebb and flow of crowds. And not only over the Bridge, for 'an ant-hill swarm of spruce clerks' landed every morning at Old Shades Wharf, 'scuffling and pushing; the quivering old barges, moored in the mud . . . swaying and groaning beneath trampling feet' on their way to Thames Street and 'insatiable counting-houses', as George Augustus Sala saw them around 1859.[4]

A week before Melville's visit, the new Coal Exchange in Lower Thames Street was ceremonially opened by Prince Albert, an event accompanied by one of London's last great river-processions. The Fishmongers brought out their gilded barge (which they had been talking about disposing of since at least 1836), hired a steamboat for large numbers of liverymen, and put up awnings and special seats on the Hall terrace for spectators, with music and champagne ashore and afloat. In spite of the late cholera epidemic and the murky state of the river, the throngs that came that day wished to see what might be the last day of its kind. Although this company's barge last appeared in a Lord Mayor's water-procession in 1854, its last big ceremonial year was 1849, not only in October in City waters but in June when the company went to Wandsworth to lay the first stone of new buildings for St Peter's Hospital, moving from its old place at Elephant and Castle (once 'a place in the country, and not what we now see it, a noisy, crowded, smoky place in the very heart of a dense population', said the Prime Warden). When the new St Peter's was finished in 1852, as usual after a large building-programme there were moves for retrenchment and renewed suggestions that the barge, much in need of repair, be sold. The ninth of November 1854 was positively her final appearance. In 1855, when the bargemaster said he would rather not take her out in the state she was in, she was offered as a gift to the Crystal Palace at Sydenham, but regretfully refused. In the summer of 1856 someone paid £20 for her, minus the heraldic sternpiece 'and the several carved Devices constituting her Pageantry deckings' which were retained.[5] The sternpiece, the gilded St Peter, and the two 'figures of fame sounding trumpets' all deck the Hall now.

Interior painting of the Hall was not finished before it was first occupied in 1835; postponing final touches while the fabric was new and internally damp was an old habit in the building trade, and suited the company financially. In April 1840 the final painting and gilding was begun by the Cubitts under Henry Roberts' supervision. Court and committee will have been aware of the latest club-house decoration, as in Smirke's Oxford and Cambridge Club where Russell Gurney of the Fishmongers' court, and later Recorder of London, sat on the club committee, and in Barry's Reform Club of which Sir Matthew Wood was a founder. Yet decoration at the Reform, barely under way in the spring of 1840, was to inaugurate that elaborate series of club interiors of the Forties, at the Con-

servative Club, the Carlton, the Army and Navy, while Roberts' scheme will
have been more in keeping with the quieter and less expensive elegance of the
Athenaeum and the Oxford and Cambridge. No specifications or drawings remain for this work of 1840,[6] and Roberts' drawings of 1834 show only structural
colour. But the general hue preferred can be deduced from Smirke's doubtless
influential King's Library at the British Museum : a restrained warmth of tawny
and cream tones and white, with delicate touches of gilding – the ivory-and-gold,
or chryselephantine, image of Greek art. The bronze-painted metal stair railings
and the bronze ornament on polished steel grates already installed at the Hall
had been popular enrichment in the pre-Victorian period, and the hue of the gilding on ceiling and wall mouldings probably tended toward bronze. What were
later to be slightingly referred to as the 'dim cream' tones that Owen Jones replaced by strong colour in 1865 were the background tones of the Greek Revival :
on a lesser scale, when Suter was supervising the decoration of the Aldermanbury
offices in 1829, he told the painter he would need 'drab, fawn, salmon, grey, tea,
stone, buff, white or others of similar value'. Roberts' banqueting-hall pilasters,
with their siena-yellow marbleized shafts, probably had white capitals. Thirty-
nine gilt shields from the company's traditional collection were hung on the walls,
with thirteen more in the gallery. Although male evening dress in the 1830s and
after was entirely black and white, a great dinner there then could have a quiet
splendour (Pl. 16). For ten whole years after 1835, no entertainment whatever
was 'given to the Ladies' at the Hall.

Sculpture and paintings were added in 1840. For the lunettes at either end of
the great hall, in the side spaces flanking the heraldic glass windows, Roberts
produced sketches, and models of vaguely marine reclining figures were commissioned from the sculptor William Frederick Woodington, who had modelled the
Coade-stone brewery lion on the South Bank and was soon to execute the bronze
relief of the Battle of the Nile for the pedestal of Nelson's Column. From his
models for Neptune and Amphitrite at the Hall two pairs of 'Basso Relievos' in
papier maché were made by C. Bielefeld.[7] To fill the two niches at the foot of the
grand staircase, two plaster copies of classical works were ordered : the familiar
'Diana Robing' for seven guineas, and 'Libra' for six, from Loft & Co. of Dean
Street, where James Loft sculptor also carried on a plaster-figure business.[8] Such a
Diana stands in a similar setting at the Athenaeum. Libra, carrying the top bar
of her scales, nicely symbolizes both balance and the pound sterling.

Until 1840 no portraits were hung in the great hall, there being two chimneypieces there and only one painting of a suitable excellence and size – Beechey's
Earl of St Vincent, then hung in the first-floor vestibule. And so two more portraits
by the late Sir William Beechey were obtained from the painter's family, of the
Queen's father the Duke of Kent and her uncle the Duke of Sussex, both honorary
freemen of the company since 1816. It was now felt that a portrait of the Queen
herself would be appropriate. Opportunely, the matter was raised with Prince
Albert, who received the honorary freedom of the company in August, and Her
Majesty, who was expecting her first child in November, granted several sittings

at Windsor to the young artist commissioned by the company, Herbert Luther Smith (selected because he was related to the recently knighted Sir William Charles Ross, who had painted a miniature of the Queen in 1837). A suit by Dominic Colnaghi the well-known print-dealer to obtain engraving rights to Smith's portrait – regarded in palace circles as an excellent likeness – was decided by the Vice-Chancellor in favour of the Fishmongers' Company and the portrait was delivered to the Hall in February 1841, to hang at the south end of the great hall as it has ever since.[9]

With the advent of gaslight upstairs and more advanced kitchen equipment below-stairs in 1835 came problems of ventilation. Not only were 'the effluvia from the dressing of the dinners in the Kitchen spreading over the entire building' but, owing to fumes from the range of charcoal-fueled stewing stoves, early in 1836 'three of the Head Cooks and the Woman attending fainted' – a matter of particular concern to Alderman Samuel Birch, whose family catering firm had been dressing the company's dinners for many years. (Earlier in the century he had even been allowed use of the old Hall ovens for baking his own Twelfth Day cakes, a practice stopped in 1809.)[10] There were also complaints during the first winter of 'the great heat caused by the use of gas in the Great Hall' and anxiety about escaping gas. During 1846–9 they tried out the new 'Bude-light' in the great hall: it was brilliant and not too hot, with new air-shafts through the roof, but did cause considerable draughts and the apparatus was not handsome; and so the original 'rich and elegant pieces of Garniture . . . in strict Keeping with everything around them' (Pl. 16) were rehung, and in 1850 new gas 'sun-burners' applied to the existing lights. Meanwhile, the application of vents above and below-stairs was a continuous vexation inherited by the company surveyor from Roberts after 1840.[11] Keeping the courtroom warm in its exposed position facing the river was another problem: in November 1839 Roberts recommended following 'Dr Arnott's principle' with heating pipes brought up from a stove in the basement which would, incidentally, also make the basement corridor 'much less cold than it is at present [for] the domestics of the establishment'; but the court contented itself by placing thermometers in the courtroom and eventually installing a new grate there. Still another modern gadget of the inventive Thirties proposed by Roberts, 'a Machine for taking the Dinner upstairs' (probably a manually operated serving lift) was declined, and again in 1845, as expensive and inconvenient.[12] So the human stream continued to bear the dinners up the back stairs from two floors below. As for drainage, when the City Sewers Act of 1848 suppressed cesspits and compelled connection with sewers, all of which then ultimately drained into the Thames, the Hall as a modern building already drained directly into the river; and the company contributed to expenses incurred by its tenants of older premises (such as John Ruskin's father the wine merchant in Billiter Street in 1853) in making themselves drains.[13] Water pressure at the Hall was not strong and use of facilities by visitors to the office was discouraged. Dinner-nights must have been, in many ways, triumphs of tradition over technology. Progress in a great city in the nineteenth century seemed a series of mighty improvisations, sometimes helping and sometimes hampering one another, so that for every three steps forward there were two steps back.

The company held its first ball in a generation, and the first one at this Hall, in June 1859, when the City was beginning to feel more prosperous. That evening must have been a triumph of skilful navigation over the preposterousness of fashion : seven hundred people were invited in that year of most gigantic skirts – how many crinolines could dance at once on a ballroom floor was a nice Victorian point. The drinks estimate from Messrs Ring & Co. (Birch's successor, later Ring & Brymer) included 'Wenham Lake & Rough Ice', a luxury brought in straw-lined holds of fast ships from the ponds of Massachusetts.[14] The six-light brass 'oil chandelier' in the first-floor vestibule or 'Announcing Chamber' was converted to gas, and extra chandeliers, rout seats and cheval glasses were hired. The courtroom served as cardroom, and midnight supper was served in the court dining and livery drawing rooms. So the pattern for Victorian balls here was set. In May 1870, eight hundred and fifty invitations were sent (it was a curious feature of these balls that a far greater number of dance programmes were invariably ordered for ladies than for gentlemen). By 1876, the arrangements included a marquée on the terrace with mirrors and chandeliers, for an extra supper room. On a series of such occasions, Messrs Coote & Tinney provided the band, Mr Cutbush the flowers, and Mr Harker announced the guests.

In the Sixties, with general prosperity and the City building boom, the company was enjoying increased income and importance; 'the property which they hold in London . . . is rapidly augmenting in value', said *The Times* when the company conferred honorary freedom on the Duke of Cambridge, and others so honoured during 1863-4 were the Prince of Wales, the Earl of Shaftesbury, Sir Rowland Hill, and Garibaldi. (The period, that is, when London's prime monuments, according to *The Bab Ballads*, included 'The Church of St Paul, the Fishmongers' Hall, and the Angel at Islington'.) A number of men especially deeply concerned in City developments of one sort or another sat on the company's court : Baron (Lionel) Rothschild M.P., the former building contractors Alderman William Cubitt M.P. (died 1863) and Alderman William Lawrence M.P., the railway contractor Sir Samuel Morton Peto M.P., and the textile magnates George Moore and Samuel Morley M.P. Peto only sat on the court for four years before his firm's involvement in the crash of Overend Gurney & Co. made it necessary for him to resign in 1867, but in 1865 he obtained the services of the architect Owen Jones – who was decorating the Peto mansion in Kensington Palace Gardens at the time – for the redecoration of Fishmongers' Hall.[15] For some years it had been felt that 'the present state of the Hall' inside was dingy, although London fogs and smoke were of course facts of life. (In 1863, after considerable argument,[16] the new Thames Conservancy had built a long steamboat pier parallel to the shore, centred on the former Old Swan stairs and lying out in the stream, the downstream end of it in front of Fishmongers' Wharf; and Cannon Street Railway Bridge was built just upriver in 1865.) In many interiors, the more powerful light cast by the newest gas sunburner gave a taste for more intense colour to

Victorians now more familiar with Indian art and with the new colour plates in books. For a few discriminating people, the latter included Owen Jones's great folios of the 1840s on the Alhambra.

Owen Jones's father had been a Welsh furrier and antiquary of Thames Street about two hundred yards west of the Hall.[17] Like Inigo Jones two centuries before, Owen Jones (1809–76) had been a local boy. By 1865 he was well known as a decorator, especially for his Greek Court in the Crystal Palace at Sydenham in 1854, and for his influential book *The Grammar of Ornament* first published in 1856. Fishmongers' Hall enabled him, fairly late in his career, to demonstrate in a different milieu from Sydenham his theories about colour in Greek art. Traces of paint on ruined Greek temples had helped to fuel a controversy among architects and archaeologists as to whether the pale ivory-and-gold image of a proper Greek Revival interior were false, and the use of strong reds, blues, and greens with much gold more true to ancient Greece.[18] Jones's designs for redecorating the Hall's grand staircase and state rooms were approved in June and Thomas Kershaw's estimate for doing the painting and gilding accepted. The old silk tabaret curtains and Persian carpets in the court dining and drawing rooms were sold and Jones designed new ones, as well as certain new grates and new door handles. His feeling for total design was expressed especially in his carpets which reflected the lines of Roberts' ceilings (a dual mode first practised in this country on a large scale by Robert Adam): the three coffers of the drawing room ceiling, the central circle and side coffers of the dining room ceiling, and especially the elegant concourse of circles, ovals, and spandrels of the vestibule. The present vestibule carpet is thought to be the original Jones piece, made by Templeton of Glasgow – although today too faded to give a true idea of Jones's colours, reflecting the ceiling curves as elegantly as ever. A number of Jones's sketches and finished drawings for the Hall are in the Victoria and Albert Museum, the sketches in blocks of intense colour, the finished designs of a lower-keyed but more subtle and complicated richness. The ceiling panels and coffers contained a good deal of Jones's 'peculiar blue', as contemporary comment called it, light but with the intensity of a Mediterranean sky, always with little areas of white in it, sometimes like very small broken clouds, sometimes like Islamic tile patterns, bordered by gilding that was not heavy-handed but interwoven with flecks of red and blue. The Corinthian capitals of the great hall pilasters were gilded, with 'the hollow parts' painted crimson, 'and the soffits in the same colour all round the cornices, giving a peculiar depth and richness in conjunction with the gold work upon the prominent parts. . . . this use of red brings the whole together', explained the *Daily News* (19 January 1866).[19] An extra painted frieze of honeysuckle ornament was stencilled on the walls of the great hall level with the capitals, below the moulded entablature. The wall colour here, described later as green, Jones explained as a substratum for the ceiling colours. For the walls of the court dining room, one restrained design shows panels of luminous blue against an ivory ground and the doors and dadoes apparently of polished oak as before. There seems to have been an aquamarine waterside emphasis in the corner drawing room with

its multitude of windows and mirrors: a carpet in which blue and green predominated, curtains called 'deep blue' after renewal in 1881, and the furniture
upholstery (until 1926) still green, with the white marble and dull yellow scagliola
of the chimneypiece wall, and 'a delicious sense of coolness'. Downstairs, in the
court waiting room even the oak frames of the eight fish paintings – made sober
in 1835 – were now gilded, so were the 'sombre bronze' railings of the grand staircase, and over Sir William Walworth's head, between the pillars of the grand
staircase window, stood the gilded figure of St Peter from the barge.

On 18 January 1866 a banquet was held in honour of the new decoration. In
proposing a toast to the architect, the Prime Warden was pleased to take credit
for the company 'for having allowed the artist to exercise his discretion', and
Jones replied that 'these halls had afforded him the opportunity of realising his
conception of Greek art. That was the style in fashion when the building was
erected, as the Gothic was now; but it had lacked the all-important element of
colour which he had ventured to supply'. He did not claim credit for creating
anything new here, but 'for having brought into life that which, without the aid of
colour, would have lain dormant'. As the *Daily News* put it, 'The art of an
archangel would not have availed Mr Owen Jones if he had not found [Roberts']
admirable solid ornament to work upon'. In contrast with the generation before,
when Lewis Cubitt dropped around to the Clerk's office to pick up several
thousand pounds, presumably in banknotes, Kershaw was paid by cheque on
the English Joint Stock Bank in which Samuel Rogers' old bank had merged.
The cheque, dated 8 May 1866, was presented for payment on the 11th – Black
Friday in Lombard Street – when the bank had just suspended payments;
Kershaw was paid again without fuss as soon as the Fishmongers' Company had
opened an account with the Bank of England.[20]

The outside of the Hall was washed down occasionally. Soot accumulated
early: a passerby wrote to the Clerk in 1839 to point out that the company motto,
'All Worship Be to God Only', carved with the coat of arms over the Hall's east
front, was already 'rendered . . . totally inevident'. In 1855 the Clerk enquiring
about 'washing down the fronts of the Hall by means of Fire Engines' had some
correspondence with James Braidwood, head of the then Fire Engine Establishment, as to using 'the Steam Floating Engine' for this purpose, but nothing came
of it. On three days in May 1869, however (three years after the company had
entertained Braidwood's successsor, Captain Eyre Massey Shaw of the reorganized
Fire Brigade, at dinner), the main fronts were washed down by firemen under the
superintendence of Shaw himself, by permission of the Metropolitan Board of
Works. Again in May 1881, Captain Shaw, now C.B. and a popular figure in
London (not quite yet immortalized in *Iolanthe* nor yet made K.C.B.), came with
his men to wash the Hall.[21] Whether they used Thames water, and whether that
did much good, is not mentioned: Victorian photographs suggest that the peculiar ability of Portland stone to stay white where most exposed to wind and rain,
kept the corners of the Hall clean while grime collected among columns and
cornices. Until the so-called Clean Air Act of our day, in fact, this could be called,

Pl. 17 The main staircase in 1896, showing north fireplace before changes of 1898, and stair-rail lamp standard by Hancock & Rixon (pp. 147, 152). Photograph in Fishmongers' Company collection.

Pl. 18 The banqueting hall as hospital ward, drawing by Randoll (?), September 1914 (p. 171). Fishmongers' Company collection.

Pl. 19 The banqueting hall in c. 1920, as redecorated in 1898, showing south window with heraldic painted glass designed by Henry Roberts and furnished by Hancock & Rixon 1834 (pp. 149, 177). Crown copyright, National Monuments Record.

Pl. 20 Fishmongers' Hall and wharf from London Bridge in June 1914, showing Seal House at left and original scale of bridge-approach at right. Crown copyright, National Monuments Record.

Pl. 21 The neighbourhood before 1940. (*a*) Air-view *c*. 1923, while Adelaide House was being completed, before rebuilding of Fresh Wharf at right, and before removal of Old Swan Pier at left. Fishmongers' Company collection. (*b*) Old Swan Pier in 1904, showing Adelaide Buildings at right, Fishmongers' Wharf, steamboats, and smoke. Crown copyright, National Monuments Record.

Pl. 22 The court drawing-room, (*a*) in 1940 and (*b*) in 1952 (pp. 176-7, Pl. 14). Fishmongers' Company collection.

Pl. 23 The court dining-room, (*a*) in 1940 and (*b*) in 1952 (pp. 176-7). Note wartime view of Bridge and Southwark Cathedral, a view also once including Kent and Surrey hills. Fishmongers' Company collection.

Pl. 24 Upper Thames Street, looking east in 1920, after demolition of Adelaide Buildings and before erection of Adelaide House, with Fishmongers' Hall at right, the 'dry arch' under the bridge-approach ahead, and St Magnus temporarily re-exposed; showing the width of Thames Street, seemingly increased here by north setback of Hall, from 1830 to 1970. Crown copyright, National Monuments Record.

as it was by the *Architects' Journal* in 1924, 'a grand dirt-stained building'.[22]

During the decorating of 1865, the great hall's 'gas chandeliers' were replaced by three of the latest and most powerful sunburners – so that for spring balls in, for example, 1876 and 1885, glass shades were hung under them 'to modify the excessive heat arising therefrom', doubtless warming the copper roof on those nights. Ventilation during the gas era was one of the company surveyor's continual headaches. (The company's Victorian surveyors were: Richard Suter, retired 1867 fifty years after being assigned to the company's work in Alexander's office and forty-five years after officially becoming surveyor; and Thomas Chatfeild Clarke, who died in office in 1895, succeeded by his son Howard.) In 1865 gas was at last laid on in courtroom and offices, and the oil lamps relegated to the lamp-room in the basement, candles remaining only in the court's drawing and dining room chandeliers. The Early Victorian interior was now almost entirely Mid-Victorian. Its Late Victorian translation was intended to coincide with the arrival of electricity.

Various modern techniques penetrated the Hall after 1870. An overdue improvement installed apparently in the 1870s was a form of partial central heating by hot-water pipes from boilers in the servants' hall. In 1885 it was agreed to introduce a telephone (Jones Bros had installed one in the warehouse below in 1882); the Hall telephone was glassed-in in the entrance hall by 1897, when the number was Bank 909 – few other livery companies were on the telephone then.[23] Upon the death of William B. Towse in 1889, after forty-nine years as Clerk, it was decreed that henceforth the Clerk and his family should not live on the premises, thus adding to the Hall much-needed office space and a few bedrooms for the wardens' and the Clerk's occasional use (although for some years thereafter the north end of the Hall was still called 'the house', probably because the Clerk until 1921, Sir J. Wrench Towse, had been born there). During 1894–5, as prelude to a planned programme of redecoration, the whole building was wired for 'the Electric Light'; only the great hall and courtroom were connected at first, and then certain other rooms, though not the kitchen storey. The Hall's sanitary arrangements were suddenly called in question in December 1894 by the serious illness, probably typhoid, of the company beadle and his wife, who had continued to live at the Hall. It became immediately necessary to connect the Hall drains properly with the main drain in the street nearby; whatever the Hall's basic relation with the river had been since the City's main drainage was done, it had certainly suffered from repeated floods – in the usual ancient tidal manner.[24] Wholesale alteration of the Hall's drainage system took about six months, until early 1896. In 1897 extra expense was centred on the Diamond Jubilee. Finally in 1898 the planned redecoration took place, according to some preliminary suggestions submitted in 1894 by Bodley the eminent architect, who sat on the court (Prime Warden 1901–2).

George Frederick Bodley (1827–1907, A.R.A. 1882 and R.A. 1902, R.I.B.A. Gold Medallist and F.R.I.B.A. 1899), architect of Late Victorian Gothic churches and sensitive designer of church furnishings, was a descendant of George Bodley,

gold laceman of Lombard Street (Prime Warden 1800–2), and also related to
Thomas Bodley (Prime Warden 1824–6) whose portrait now in the courtroom was
painted by a nephew of a member of the Lombard Street firm, William Etty.[25]
G. F. Bodley became Gilbert Scott's first pupil about a decade after Scott's stint
in Henry Roberts' office, so there was a sort of preordained rightness in Bodley's
attention to the Hall, and his report of 1894 was another milestone along the
course of Victorian taste. The paint and gilt of 1865 were blackening in spite of
the usual maintenance and something had to be done. To those traditionally-
minded members anxious to preserve the status quo, Bodley did not mince his
words :

> Owen Jones, to come extent, aroused a feeling among us in England for a
> greater interest in decorative work. . . . at a time when art was at its lowest
> depth. The results of his work, however praiseworthy, were never, to an
> artistic eye, at all satisfactory. I had almost said not tolerable. It was work
> that had no artistic breadth whatever . . . not in accordance with the prece-
> dents of better days of art. What he did in the Hall cannot be called artistic –
> it is disjointed and inharmonious, like a series of experiments. . . .[26]

But Jones's work on the riverside rooms was not substantially changed. The great
hall and its approaches were what Bodley chiefly had in mind, and these were
redone in 1898 by the firm of Messrs Crace of Wigmore Street under John Dibblee
Crace (1838–1919), supervised by the company surveyor, Howard Chatfeild
Clarke.[27] The walls of entrance hall, front corridor, and lower staircase compartment became a 'lively Pompeian red' with the pilasters painted stone-colour, the
walls of upper staircase and great hall were in tones of 'quiet green', the hall
ceiling coffers were a 'soft blue' instead of 'peculiar blue', and there was more
gilding than ever. Colours that were 'warm and hospitable', dispelling an existing
'coldness', were the theme, a Greek livery hall at this date was impossible. The
'plastic figures' at the foot of the stairs, too, were replaced by a very different pair
of statues commissioned 1899, displayed (one of them) at the Royal Academy in
1901, and installed in the Hall niches (which also lost their fireplaces) in 1902 :
large marble figures of a 'Fisherman' and a 'Fisherwoman' by a young sculptor
Alfred Turner (1874–1940).[28] Instead of the fireplaces, 'Finsbury radiators' were
fixed and connected with the 'hot water circulation system'. Leaded stained glass
with heraldic and fishy motifs, provided by Messrs Crace (whether to Bodley's
design not said) was installed on the grand staircase and in the first-floor vestibule
and ground-floor corridor windows, replacing 'embossed glass', the enamelled
glass of Roberts' day. A marble floor with white and black squares was laid in
the south corridor, for which a pair of benches were ordered and apparently
designed by Bodley, presumably the balustraded benches there now. In 1904
the positions of the courtroom and its waiting-room/luncheon-room were reversed
–to bring the one nearer to the Clerk's office and the other nearer to the southwest
kitchen stairs – according to a plan made in 1900 by Bodley.[29] Regard for the
Greek Revival was at its lowest ebb around 1900 : there were (rejected) proposals
by Crace and Clarke in 1898 for new courtroom wainscot in the 'freer classic style'

of Wren, with steep pediments over the doors and an open arcade along the traditional dwarf partition like a City church screen. In 1905 more comfortable courtroom seating around a T-shaped formation of tables replaced Roberts' traditional wall-seats and their platform was taken out. There was to be only brief interest in a more formal seating design made by Goodhart-Rendel about 1938.[30]

The Hall had multiple uses during the Victorian period, as it has had ever since, not only because its owners have been readier to lend it than in the days of earlier halls, but because the number of benevolent, civic, and cultural organizations in London multiplied so greatly in the nineteenth century: public-health congresses, dinners to benefit asylums for idiots, exhibitions of ship models to encourage craftsmen, presentation of student prizes, board meetings for the protection of fisheries, and so on and so on, took place here. Not all requests could be accommodated and some, such as one from the Cannon Street Ladies' Bible Association, were declined as unsuitable.

The Hall's immediate surroundings did not change much in the Victorian years, except on the west side. Until our own day the east front had a special 'presence' because it was set back from the main road by a shallow carriage-sweep or widened roadbay (Pl. 21a). A public coach-stand was placed there in 1843 by the City, in defiance of the first London Bridge Act of 1823 (no hackney coach chariot cabriolet etc licensed to ply for hire to stand within 100 feet of the Bridge), and not even the strongest complaint to the Court of Aldermen could remove it for many years, except by arrangement on nights of large entertainment at the Hall. The instructions on ball invitations in 1859, 'Carriages to set down with the Horses' heads towards London Bridge' – against the stream of traffic – must have added to traffic congestion. In 1865 Gladstone was late for dinner when his carriage was 'blocked up' in traffic on the Bridge (the short way from Westminster was and is via Westminster Bridge and Southwark). The Hall's presence as chief building in the neighbourhood was unchallenged while Adelaide Buildings, occupied as offices and warehouses, of similar height but weaker classical character and of no particular distinction (stuccoed, probably), stood opposite until after the 1914–18 War. For many years until 1893, Kitty Curran kept a fruit stall near the Hall steps. Also part of the scenery, up the hill at the head of the bridge-approach, where Cannon Street, King William Street, Gracechurch Street and Eastcheap met, stood a statue of William IV on the site of Falstaff's Boar's Head Tavern.

Between 1863 and 1879 the company acquired the freeholds of Nos 107–8 and 109 Upper Thames Street, and of the Old Shades site, subject to the tavern's lease which the company finally bought in 1882, when the Old Shades was taken down as out of date and inadequate of improvement. The wine tavern that, during some seventy-five years in the old Hall basement, had been the 'local' for nearby residents of standing in the City, had become, during the half-century or so on its second site, an increasingly shabby stop for steamboat-passengers. The present premises of the Old Wine Shades north of Thames Street at No. 6 Martin's Lane, although a much older building, has been occupied continuously as a wine tavern only since the early nineteenth century: possibly founded there in rivalry to the original Shades during the latter's move from the old Hall basement to Garratt's premises next door.[31] In 1889 much of the combined site of No. 109 and the Shades became Fishmongers' Hall Street (closed 1975), by arrangement between the company and the Commissioners of Sewers, with the closing of Wheatsheaf Alley west of the former wine and cheese warehouses and the resulting provision of a building site that no longer impinged directly on the Hall. In 1899 along the west side of the new little street an office building called Seal House (demolished 1975) was begun for the Pearl Assurance Company, the Fishmongers' lessees. A little farther west and unseen above-ground, the world's first electric-traction Tube was constructed in 1886 under Old Swan Lane for the City of London and Southwark Subway, as it was called then, on its way under the river toward Elephant and Castle.[32] As for company reaction to other neighbourhood activities, the Chartist march of '48 and a Fenian attempt to bomb the bridge in '84 were ignored, but the dock strike in '89 led to strengthening of locks at the Hall, as in previous centuries and previous halls, against Gordon rioters and Cromwell's soldiery.

There were during Victoria's reign more triumphal marches over the Bridge, in 1863 and 1897. Princess Alexandra's entry into London on 7 March 1863, three days before her marriage to the Prince of Wales, proceeded from Bricklayers Arms railway station in the Old Kent Road, then the suitable intermediate point between the Channel ports and a London street procession. The Prince having been made an honorary freeman of the company the month before, the Hall put on all its pomp. Nine hundred people were invited to view the procession from banks of seats constructed over the entrance-front area, a platform on the terrace, the Hall windows, and the roof. The building was decked with British and Danish flags inside and out, and a military band played on the front steps. Four wardens including William Cubitt went in carriage and four with postilions and escort of Doggett Coat and Badge men and staffmen with silver-topped beadles' staves to breakfast at Guildhall before returning with the Lord Mayor to welcome the Princess on her entry into the City from the Bridge, which was decorated with great gas burners shaped like antique tripod lamps. When the procession had passed, all nine hundred privileged spectators went into the Hall for a champagne lunch, and afterwards the tables were removed for dancing. In the evening the building was illuminated by gaslit devices in the form of plumes, laurels and stars.[33]

The even more deeply felt occasion of the Diamond Jubilee was similarly staged, but with the Queen's carriage coming down from St Paul's to cross London Bridge to the sound of guns from the Tower, church-bells, steamboat whistles, and high-pitched cheers from Bridge Ward's charity children ranged in front of the Hall's spectators, and roars from roofs black with people on both sides of the river. This time there were bagpipers with the band stationed at the Hall, and that evening 'Greek vases of gas' flared at three corners of the roof while ruby, amber and green lamps formed a great crown flanked by V.R. The Hall fed about a thousand people that day, the caterers being instructed to supply 'Boars heads if practicable', not for the first time on this medieval site.

CHAPTER 16

Beside the Bridge, 1901–75

BETWEEN 1800 AND 1914, in the interests of traffic-movement on, across, and alongside the river, many visionary town-planning schemes dressed the north shore of the Thames between Blackfriars and the Tower with visionary structures, on paper. These included several bold schemes made around 1800 for rebuilding London Bridge, such as Thomas Telford's single-arched iron bridge, with a long shoreside ramp leading to new quays downstream and cutting off the existing Fishmongers' Hall from the river; and George Dance's twin bridges, upstream and downstream of the old bridge-site, approached from a huge crescent-shaped open space centred on the Monument, and requiring rebuilding of Fishmongers' Hall as part of a uniform block. And numerous schemes were produced for the bridge-approaches around 1828, all of which included a new guise for the Hall: George Allen's published *Plans and Designs for the Future Approaches to London Bridge* put a great portico on the Hall; and an elaborate plan by Peter Jeffery provided for an Ionic livery hall and ramps for carts from Thames Street to the Bridge. Colonel F. W. Trench's scheme of 1827 for a Thames Embankment from Charing Cross to Blackfriars was extended in 1841 (on paper) to London Bridge with the addition of an overhead railway. Later there were H. V. Lanchester's plan of 1910 for a direct road from Euston Station to Waterloo Station, and the much-discussed St Paul's Bridge scheme intended to cross just downstream from Blackfriars. And there was a scheme drawn up by W. D. Caröe in 1910 for the north approach to London Bridge, dressing Fishmongers' Hall with an extra storey and Gallic bull's-eye windows, and duplicating it with a twin building opposite. None of these projects materialized, though they foretold a good deal.[1] But changes actually made in London Bridge itself during 1902–4 and 1968–73 were of close concern to the Bridge's closest permanent neighbour.

The widening of the Bridge carried out between the spring of 1902 and the spring of 1904 added little to the bridge-carriageway, being done primarily to broaden the footways so that each could take phalanxes of office-workers marching eight abreast, Citywards in the morning and trainwards at night. It will be remembered that the architect of Fishmongers' Hall had a hand in the assembling of London Bridge Station south of the river, first of the tidal railway-heads pouring workers into the City and sucking them back, part source of the hereditary

The notes for Chapter 16 are on pp. 204–5.

gulfstream of humanity Melville saw in 1849 and main source of the crowd
flowing over the Bridge in Eliot's *Waste Land* of 1922. The bridge-works included
the suspension of temporary covered footways while massive granite corbels were
inserted underneath, and improvement of the road-surface with a concrete bed
under great granite setts because, as the *City Press* put it (30 March 1904), 'there
is no place in the world where the traffic is of such a destructive and grinding
character as that which ceaselessly passes to and fro over London Bridge'. The
noise of that traffic is seldom remembered now. The bridge-works were no obstacle to the new Sovereign's progress through the City in October 1902 after his
postponed Coronation, for which Bodley had designed festoons of June flowers for
the Hall with the motto 'O'er land and sea the Empire's voice is greeting thee';
in October, at any rate, the 'pendant chains and hooks of the travelling cranes
were touched with flowers' and the roadway full of colour against the scaffolds
on either side and the dark waters below. The bridge-alterations, while narrowing the public water-stairs beside the Hall, had no effect on the Hall site. It was
at this time that the bridge-parapets were balustraded, in keeping with Roberts'
balustrades in front of the Hall.[2]

The fruit-merchants then occupying the wharf and the warehouse under the
Hall were Messrs Knill of Fresh Wharf, the firm of Stuart and John Knill, father
and son, each successively alderman of Bridge Ward and subsequently Lord
Mayor (1892, 1909) and baronet. They also sublet Fishmongers' Wharf to steamboat companies, as in 1888 for a line of small steam launches plying from there
to Oxford. Old photographs show casks on the wharf (Pl. 20), and managers of
Thames lighterage firms today recall the smell of apples there. As early as 1844
Jones Bros, the Knills' predecessors at the wharf, had asked permission to enclose
the arcaded space under the terrace and insert an extra floor in it, for handling
more goods. While inadvisable 'in point of Taste', the company surveyor observed,
if commercially necessary it could be done 'without making any great Blot upon
the Architecture', the court thereupon refusing the request, but later the extra
flooring was allowed without the enclosure. Similarly in 1900 the Knills proposed
a new hydraulic luffer crane with a long jib, much needed at such wharves for
landing goods 'from an outside barge' and so tall enough to rise above terrace-
level. As that would have made a blot upon 'the architectural appearance of the
Hall', the court decided that the company surveyor should design it, on a sunk
base. Life at a trading waterside was a continual exercise in English pragmatism.

A period of special links between the Fishmongers' Company and the Royal
Navy began during the Napoleonic wars with a series of awards of the honorary
freedom of the company to eminent naval officers, notably that proposed for Sir
John Jervis in 1795 for gallantry in the West Indies, two years before he earned
his earldom at Cape St Vincent, although he was only able to come to Fishmongers' Hall for the freedom ceremony in 1801; his portrait painted for the
company by Beechey in 1805 now hangs in the entrance hall; his colours were
flown on the company barge in Nelson's funeral procession up the Thames from
Greenwich.[3] At a great Nelson Centenary banquet held at Fishmongers' Hall in

1905, celebrating also the recent Anglo-Japanese alliance, a telegram was read from Admiral Togo professing his devotion to the hero of Trafalgar. By October 1914 the entrance hall, which had been used briefly in 1903 as a recruiting station for the Royal Naval Volunteers, contained a field gun and a bomb-fragment; the captured Maxim-Nordenfelt gun and carriage given by Major-General W. E. Blewitt, Prime Warden 1913–14, was given away early in 1940 to the Royal Artillery Institution for the Rotunda Museum at Woolwich; the bomb-fragment, shown in October 1914 for a fee for the benefit of Belgian relief, had been dropped by Zeppelin on Antwerp. The risks from the air being demonstrated from the first in 1914, the Hall and its contents were insured with Lloyds against air raids and the most valuable pictures stored in a vault at Hibernia Wharf across the river. And the Kaiser's name was removed forthwith from the company's list of honorary freemen.

The most immediate decision, however, was taken two days after war was declared in August, to offer the main floors of the Hall for use as a hospital.[4] This the War Office accepted for the care of wounded officers, the hospital was run by the Red Cross, City of London branch, and much of the expense during most of the war was met by an anonymous donor, later known to be Mr Henry Hirsch, while the Fishmongers' Company provided heat and light (heating by electric stoves with Zeppelin-like globes, said the *Morning Post*). The wards were in three large state rooms on the upper floor – the great hall with five two-bed cubicles partitioned off along the window wall, and other beds in the two riverside rooms – twenty-five beds in all at first, later thirty : by the end of the war a total of 1,100 patients had been cared for here. One room was fitted up as an operating-theatre, probably the present 'Gold Room' at the northeast corner of the building (once the Clerk's drawing room, later a library, now a committee luncheon room). The livery drawing room to the left at the top of the main staircase, now the banqueting-hall servery, was used by the patients as a smoking room. Straw was spread on the Bridge to muffle the noise of traffic. 'Healthy breezes' off the river being thought beneficial for septic cases, the Fishmongers' Company installed a curtained shelter on the terrace for open-air treatment in the summer of 1916, when casualties were coming from Verdun and the Somme. In July 1917, with increasing air raids on London, it was suddenly decided on medical advice to close the hospital immediately, because of its exposed position and the harmful effects of air-raid warnings on patients, but it was reopened in September. One who was a patient here in May 1915 still recalls waiting on the train at Charing Cross with other wounded, hoping for consignment to the Duchess of Westminster's glamorous hospital in the West End, only to feel 'shattered when the man labelled us "Fishmongers Hall, City". We thought this was the End' – but not after they found themselves being efficiently tended in the gilded banqueting hall; 'quite often we had wine from the Hall cellars'.[5] The hospital was finally closed in February 1919, its installations were removed by April, the company's pictures came back unscathed from storage, and a great luncheon was held in the banqueting hall for troops taking part in the Victory March on July 5. In May, at the first company ceremony held after the Armistice, the Prince of Wales was admitted freeman by patrimony.

Now came the first marked change of height in the neighbourhood with the erection of Adelaide House opposite the Hall. Redevelopment of the site had been pending before the war, when Adelaide Buildings were occupied mainly by the Pearl Assurance offices, with a steamer wharf. Caröe's layout for the bridge-approach, shown at the Town Planning Exhibition of 1910 and mentioned above, had seized the chance afforded by the prospect of rebuilding there. The historic locality between St Magnus Martyr and the Hall at the threshold of the Bridge was, as the editor of the *British Architect* then put it, 'bound to Londoners and indeed all Englishmen by the strongest sentiments of our national life', although it was 'hemmed in by buildings of the poorest class, out of date and even squalid',[6] that is, in the Lower Thames Street, Pudding Lane, Fish Street Hill area, like survivals of Todgers' boarding-house. In 1913, just before the Adelaide Buildings site was due to be auctioned in 1914, the remaining inhabitants of Bridge Ward at their annual wardmote held, as for centuries, in Fishmongers' Hall on St Thomas's day, aired their fears of an unworthy building that would 'alienate users of the river'. But, thought the ward committee, from the advertising point of view (that twentieth-century consideration), London Bridge was the world's greatest thoroughfare and ground rents here would be too high for building meanly. After the war, the structure for which heavy pile-driving began late in 1920 was to be, for a time, second only to St Paul's in height: 120 feet or so above Lower Thames Street, 100 feet or so above Adelaide Place (to the Hall's 60 feet from the pavement of Adelaide Place to the top of its east parapet). During 1921, at the corner of Lower Thames Street and Fish Street Hill opposite the building site, the walls of the Steam Packet Hotel began to bulge and buckle, 'not being built for an earthquake country' (*Evening News*), and successful suit for damages against the building contractors was brought in 1922 by the brewers Hoare & Co., the Fishmongers' Company's lessees of this ground beside the old Three Tuns site given up for the 'dry-arch' stairs in 1830.[7] By early 1924 a letter to *The Times* signed 'Facit Indignatio' was complaining that the enormous pile of Adelaide House blotted out St Magnus and the Monument and dwarfed Fish-mongers Hall (Pl. 21 *a*). Large buildings rising in King William Street were also raising light-and-air questions in relation to property in Upper Thames Street. The equation of mass and space that Rennie and Smirke had worked out lasted not quite a century. By 1926 professional eyes considering interior redecoration of Fishmongers' Hall noted that the great new building opposite 'cast strange lights' into the rooms it faced. The somewhat Egyptian form of Sir John Burnet's Adelaide House, with a twentieth-century arrogance of bulk that seems less startling now than it must have in 1926, increased by contrast the delicate Ionic austerity of the Hall opposite. The Thames Street neighbourhood down at the feet of these two buildings, below the 'dry arch' of the bridge-approach, went on being its battered unbowed self (except the Steam Packet Hotel, which had to be rebuilt), Wren's St Magnus retired gracefully behind Burnet's enormous pile, and the sky was no longer a large part of the Hall's eastward prospect (compare Pl. 21, 24).

In the spring of 1926, during the nine-day General Strike, there were other prospects : eighty Oxford undergraduates bedding down every night in the banqueting hall and marching off over the Bridge every morning to be volunteer dockers at Hays Wharf. That past, plans for a major redecoration, the first since 1898, were made for the summer. The architect in charge was H. S. Goodhart-Rendel (1887–1959), and the firm of decorators Messrs Campbell-Smith of Newman Street. From the front door, between 1898 and 1926, one walked into a dark Late Victorian interior. The most advanced taste of the Twenties aimed to lighten Victorian darkness wherever found. Goodhart-Rendel was one of those who took part in a rather glossy Regency-revival remodelling of London early-nineteenth-century house interiors so congenial to that taste – for example, in his own house at 13 Crawford Street – but he was also a sensitive analyser of Victorian architecture who liked finding out how Victorian architects worked : he appreciated his predecessors better than they appreciated theirs.[8]

For example, Henry Roberts' reaction to relics of the seventeenth and eighteenth centuries had been to put Peirce's sub-baroque statue of Walworth on a shadowy landing, to sky Peirce's gateway coat of arms on an unseen wall, and to dispense with the carved chimney-piece of the 1740s and the Bacon-Coade 'Charity' of the 1790s altogether. Owen Jones's opinion of Roberts' decoration was that it 'lacked the all-important element of colour', it was something to build upon, it needed Jones; whereas Bodley's opinion of Jones's work was that it 'had no artistic breadth whatever', was almost 'not tolerable'. More tolerantly Goodhart-Rendel's view, published in 1953, of Bodley's 'sensitive and fastidious manner of design' was that 'as a colourist . . . he had a great reputation, although one difficult now to account for', and that 'he delighted in brownish tones'; his decoration surpassed Pugin's 'in what the Victorians called "refinement"; and what is thought of it will depend upon what is thought of that quality'. Others more critical in the 1920s said of the Victorian Hall that it had been 'as carefully obliterated as only a building of consummate simplicity of design can be obliterated under layers of undiscerning paint'. And so, in 1926, taste came almost full-circle, back toward Roberts' idea of decoration, almost but not quite. *The Times* (2 August 1927) described the new work at the Hall as 'more in the nature of restoration' of the 'William IV' work, an uncovering of Roberts' 'splendid detail' overlaid by Crace under Bodley's advice (nobody remembered Owen Jones in the 1920s), a return to the original scheme but with slightly gayer colours owing to 'the difference in the London atmosphere' – thought to have been so pure a century before. Actually there was something of Jones and something of Bodley and Crace in this restoration.

In the great hall Goodhart-Rendel repeated the 'soft green' walls and 'sky-blue' ceiling coffers of the previous work, while modulating the gilding with several different shades and finishes of gold leaf, or *ors variés*. The tight row of shields hung like a continuous frieze (or a poulterer's display) in 1898 was separated into clusters. New blue damask in the drawing room toned down Jones's play of blues and greens, though the idea of blue panels in the ceiling had first been Jones's. In the vestibule, frescoes in grisaille of water-nymphs by Colin Gill were added, in poses emulating Woodington's recumbent figures of 1840 in the great hall; Gill's work did not survive the war as the latter did. The entrance hall and staircase compartment were now painted in lighter tones more nearly like those of Roberts' day. Diana and Libra returned to their niches – lined with stone colour after a 'fluted background' recommended by the architect was rejected – and the marble fisherfolk so out of scale with such niches stood sturdily in the corridor for a while. Around the foot of the staircase a mosaic floor installed in 1886 to replace Roberts' stone paving (and extended in 1898 to main corridor and entrance hall where it still is, a Victorian version of Roman work) was now replaced by a much more sophisticated floor of Belgian black marble, veined with white and bordered with gilt mosaic, a floor newly revealed by careful cleaning in 1975. A 'gelatinous gloss' removed in 1926 from the pink granite columns suggests in the vocabulary of the Twenties a condition bound to be Victorian and therefore nasty, although Roberts stipulated 'polished granite' there in 1833 – when the technique of polishing such hard stone had only just been mastered and was therefore interesting. Some of Goodhart-Rendel's suggestions were too much for the committee of wardens to swallow, such as a turn-table pedestal for the statue of Sir William Walworth, then being divested of his old coats of paint : neither his pose nor the space would have allowed him to revolve with any dignity on dinner-nights.

Various modern improvements of a more practical nature gradually accrued at the Hall. What appears to have been the office's first typewriter was bought in 1902, an addressograph in 1910, and by 1913 the staff included three women typists. A tenant's departure from offices on the upper warehouse floor entered from Thames Street made it possible to move the company's fish-inspectors' office into the building in 1927, and in 1928 a working museum was made there, stocked with models of all the common food fishes to be encountered at Billingsgate Market, for the use of food inspectors taking examinations for the Royal Sanitary Institute; for a while, there was also a 'tank room' with small fish-tanks in it. By the 1930s there were two service lifts from the kitchen floor to the dining floor. In 1930, horizontal separation of the upper kitchen-ceiling space made a large cloakroom beside the grand staircase. On the other side of the staircase, the one-time pensioners' waiting room – relic of days when charity had to be seen to be done – was redecorated in 1936 as a committee room, using the remains of the elaborately carved chimneypiece made by Easton in 1741 for the old court parlour.

The odyssey of that early Georgian chimneypiece reserved from the auction sale of 1827 is a little history of taste : until 1839 it languished in a stonemason's yard in Eastcheap, during the 1840s it seems to have been inventoried on the back stairs of the Hall as 'several pieces of sculptured marble', in 1850 it was installed in reduced form in the library of St Peter's Hospital at Wandsworth until that was closed in 1923, when Goodhart-Rendel advised that such a piece could not 'without detriment' to Roberts' interior be incorporated anywhere at the Hall (an opinion Roberts would have endorsed), but a committee decided nonetheless to put it in the livery smoking-room, then occupied by the Association of British Fisheries; relegated next to the basement, in 1936 it rose again – as if at the approach of the Georgian Group – on the advice of the architect H. Austen Hall, who designed a plain shelfless base for the carved upper panel and fixed it in the committee room (now the library) where in 1940 it stood surrounded by war wreckage, and finally in 1949 he was able to design a more impressive base for it in the new courtroom where it now triumphantly stands.[9] Good original work in the great hall also survived an unsuccessful move to substitute for Roberts' black marble chimneypieces a carved oak pair in the 'free classic' style of 1908.

Down on the wharf in the 1930s old and new conditions required attention, by the raising of flood defences and by the widening of lorry-access from Fishmongers' Hall Street. Old Swan Pier had been removed, but the greater bulk of steamers moored at the new Fresh Wharf on the down-stream side of the first bridge-arch made trouble with their long mooring-chains for users of Fishmongers' Hall Wharf. And pigeons then 'congregating in the vicinity of the Hall' to the disapproval of the City Medical Officer were to return undeterred by six years of war; treatment of the south front with a repellent tested on St Paul's was to be necessary in the 1960s.

In October 1937, air-raid precautions were discussed, and again in April 1938. In September, after Munich, a plan for removal not only of records and silver but of offices and staff from London was seriously considered. In the spring of 1939 the Prime Warden, Lord Hollenden, offered the use of his house, Hall Place at Leigh in Kent near Tonbridge, a Victorian Tudor brick mansion designed by the architect George Devey for Lord Hollenden's grandfather Samuel Morley M.P., also a member of this company's court. In the City, the family textile-warehouse stood on the site of the company's sixteenth-century armourer's house in Wood Street.[10] On the outbreak of war on Sunday 3 September 1939, two pantechnicons laden with records, silver and other valuables rolled down to Kent, while paintings were protected at the Hall. And for about three months the staff ran the office from Hall Place, while courts and committees continued to meet at Fishmongers' Hall, but soon in that quiet winter the staff, with current papers, were moved back to the Hall. Their war, as for the rest of London, began in September 1940. In June that summer little ships from the upper Thames will have passed the Hall on their way to Dunkirk.

At about 3.30 a.m. on Monday morning, 9 September 1940, an incendiary bomb fell on Seal House next to the Hall on its west side, while a heavy bomb dropped near the Monument and King William Street just up the road – part of an attack aimed at London Bridge, the waterside warehouses, Cannon Street Station, or even Bankside Power Station. Inside the Hall electric and water power and window-glass had already gone when sparks from a fierce fire at Seal House caught the Hall roof. The company steward W. L. Roberts (successor to the old beadles), on fire-watching duty, found his tubs of water useless and the nearest firemen powerless with a single hose until reinforcements arrived from another fire, 'and they certainly looked very tired men'. By that time the south side of the Hall roof was well ablaze, though Roberts stoutly insisted afterward that with 'half a dozen hefty soldiers' in time he could have saved it. But now that the Blitz had begun there were more fires than men. Fishmongers' was the first City company to suffer, as on that other September morning 274 years before – the penalty for its brave site by the river. The ruin was not complete this time, as the Hall itself had not been bombed, but bracketed between blast and fire. The riverside range was gutted from the ground up, its shell left open to the sky. Charred fragments of the roof-structure dangled from the remaining floor-boards of court drawing and dining rooms and vestibule, and the grand staircase was roofless too (Pl. 22, 23). There was doubt about the stability of the southwest corner of the building. Damage to the great hall was slight, apart from blasted windows including the heraldic pair in the end lunettes. In the central 'waist' of the building Henry Roberts' brick-vaulted floor construction was intact. The grand staircase itself – with its stone steps and the top landing on iron cantilevers – was safe. Walworth, swaddled like a mummy, stood his ground and behind him, on the wall outside, Peirce's merman and mermaid watched the interior of Seal House burn for four days. The pictures, wrapped and stored in the basement corridor, had wisely been placed on wooden supports that held them above the water washed down from the firemen's hoses; they were now removed to a Buckinghamshire rectory made available for storage.[11] The gilded shields went to Bray. The silver and old records were in Kent, but current records and much other valuable material were rescued from the Hall, while the fire still burned, by Francis Pester the company accountant – like Thomas Tanner before him, but this time not into a barge but into barrows that were trundled over to Billingsgate Market for temporary storage. In a few days the company offices were comfortably established in borrowed accommodation at Clothworkers' Hall, and there remained until that hall was destroyed eight months later in the great air raid of 10 May 1941. Some of the more recent minutebooks consulted for this book were found intact in the strongroom there, as the oldest ones had escaped in 1666. Meanwhile, out in the country in November 1940, in a disastrous fire at Hall Place, the old court books and title deeds stored in the cellar were damaged by water. These, together with Munday's pageant scroll of 1616 which had suffered at the Hall, were immediately sent for restoration to the British Museum, where in 1941 they were endangered, though not further damaged, by enemy action there and were eventually safely restored by delicate conservation work. Both Martin's Bank in Lombard Street and Hambro's Bank in Bishopsgate, through their directors who sat on the company's court, made their strongrooms available for valuables. Many of the company's properties in the City were of course badly damaged, or about to be.

By June 1941 the Clerk had established the offices in undamaged rooms at the northeast corner of Fishmongers' Hall. The banqueting hall and kitchens were now requisitioned by the London County Council for a communal feeding centre, as one of the British Restaurants that fueled London office-workers for the rest of the war at prices of a shilling or so for a meat-and-two-veg lunch, the Council paying rates but no rent. This restaurant was open from June 1941 until early 1950 (with a special caution to the L.C.C. by the company to take full responsibility for the building on the day of the Victory March in June 1946 – but that lunch was more austere than the Victory March luncheon in 1919). By late 1941 discussions of the postwar planning of the City had already begun, but the immediate issue for surveyors of damaged buildings, as in 1666, was the shoring-up of ruins and assessment of stability. Now there was the War Damage Commission to appeal to for compensation, the Hall site being regarded as already fully developed and requiring full reinstatement.

Five years after total destruction in the Great Fire of 1666, this company had had a new building. During and after a twentieth-century war, it took rather longer to mend one. Restoration at the Hall was done in four stages over fourteen years: emergency first aid until 1943 and then structural work including new roofs until 1948, by Holland & Hannen and Cubitts, business descendants of the Hall's builders; and two stages of restoration and redecoration by Messrs A. E. Symes of Brentford from 1949 to 1951, with further specialists' work on into 1954. This long programme of work was hampered by all the wartime and postwar delays in finding materials, especially steel, and the issue of Government licences to use it; hampered during 1944–6 by dry rot, caused by water poured in after the fire in 1940 and apparently retained in 'tiled channels' of the floor structure; and hampered by the war itself, with more damage from flying bombs falling in Thames Street in the summer of 1944. By 1942 the Hall had three fire-watchers nightly, including Roberts the Steward, who died in 1943 after fifteen years of service to the company. The company surveyor since 1936 was (Sir) Edward Gillett, knighted in 1948 and made a Commissioner for Crown Lands in 1956.[12] He collaborated in the reconstruction of the Hall with Herbert Austen Hall, who was appointed architect in 1943.

Besides completely new roofs and floors, the interiors of the two riverside state rooms and the complicated ceiling of their vestibule had to be entirely rebuilt (Pl. 22, 23). The original white marble drawing-room chimneypiece could be restored, but not those in the court dining room where the black marble originals with their shelves on paired columns had to be replaced, this time with simpler pieces in white marble.[13] On the ground floor instead of reinstatement there were certain changes. Early in the century the courtroom and its waiting room, each with two windows overlooking the river, had changed places; in 1949–50 these became a three-window courtroom and a one-window office with a little lobby. In the banqueting hall, the old painted-glass heraldic windows in the north and south lunettes were not restored. From the first these had been illuminated at night from the outside by protected gas lamps; that light by night and the natural light, however foggy, filtering in by day through these upper end-windows (Pl. 19) are now a missing element in the character of the room, like two eyes closed. But their position made upkeep difficult: long before the bombing, first one, the south one of course, and then the other needed protection against weather, like the 'skreenwork' protecting the old Hall's armorial glass against southwesterly gales in the seventeenth century. New armorial glass designed by Hugh Easton was inserted on the grand staircase, at the west end of the south ground-floor corridor, and in the upper vestibule. The door-furniture renewed throughout in 1950 may still follow Owen Jones's design for handles and plates mentioned in an order of 1865 from Messrs Jackson & Graham to take the place of the original ones in the principal rooms and probably duplicated in sets ordered for corridors in 1898. (Roberts' original door-handles may have been brass rosettes like those still functioning in the British Museum, though the lack of remark on them in the very full records of his work at the Hall suggests something cheaper.) Light-brackets incorporating a Greek-urn motif, placed on the grand staircase in 1950, were designed by Goodhart-Rendel for the banqueting hall in 1926. The opportunity was also taken during the restoration to instal central heating at last.

The Coronation ball held at the Hall on 28 May 1953 was a double celebration in honour of the new Queen and for a blessing on the company's house restored. After some initial anxiety over the stability of the dance-floor in the great hall, engineers guaranteed it safe for at least six hundred people, and the Georgian Group was allowed also to hold a ball on it in July; with respect for Roberts' girders, however, these were the last dances to be held here. For the Coronation the river-front was floodlighted, as in 1937. With the new forty-foot flagstaff of British Columbian pine put up in 1951 above the pediment, the illuminated building by itself is festive enough (as we can now see it every night in the year) without further decoration by the symbolic festoons of little lamps of oil or gas added in 1838 and 1897. In 1954 a portrait of Queen Elizabeth II was commissioned for the Hall from the Italian painter Pietro Annigoni and delivered in 1955, in continuance of the tradition carried on by the company's portrait of her great-great grandmother, and earlier royal portraits in earlier Halls; and subsequently, from the same artist, a portrait of the Duke of Edinburgh, Prime Warden 1961–2.

There were later improvements to the buildings, such as the passenger lift put in in 1954, the more extensive residential accommodation for wardens and staff added at and above the north end in 1961, and the conversion of the former Assistant Clerk's office to the court's private sitting-room, or Walworth Room, in 1965. The circular internal window above the door to that room from the corridor appears to be part of Roberts' original design – though no drawings for it survive – and its glazing bars, suggesting a simplified Greek rosette, could be based on an austerely classical design often seen in ironwork of fifteenth-century Florence, a place and period as congenial to Roberts (who retired to Florence) as fifth-century Greece. In 1960 the grand staircase handrail, admired by architectural visitors in 1924 as 'ebony', was stripped of black paint – applied who knows when – to reveal the original rosewood shaped in the Cubitt workshops in 1834 to lie upon DeVille's metal balusters. In a sense, the restoration of an historic building is a continuous performance.

The events that close this account concern London Bridge as the present Hall's beginnings did. Although earlier buildings on the Hall site were much affected indirectly by the medieval Bridge, they were not cheek by jowl with it; but in 1832–3 what might be called a party-wall relationship was set up, or, rather, as between built-up ground and a highway, a street-frontage relationship across a front-basement area, like a moat, in the London manner. In 1925, when the London County Council proposed to abolish the street-name 'Adelaide Place' and list Fishmongers' Hall in King William Street, the company's court – with a more realistic grasp of the situation – requested the address 'London Bridge', and so it became. The bridge-widening of 1902–4 left Hall and area exactly as before, narrowing only the public bridge-stairs. Early in 1962 came news that a pending London Bridge Improvements Bill allowing the City Corporation to widen the Bridge further, both for pedestrians and for motor traffic, would bring the up-stream bridge-parapet to within a few feet of the Hall, raise the pavement-level halfway up the Hall's front steps, and throw into the roadway the whole of the Hall 'loading bay' or 'carriage sweep'. Such a widening (not then to be a rebuild-ing) was to start in 1964 and take two years. After discussions between the com-pany and the City, reminiscent of those with Rennie in 1829, certain concessions were promised, such as double-glazing for the Hall's south and east windows, no pile-driving at night, and a clause protecting the company's interests to be in-cluded in the Bill, in return for which the company withdrew opposition to the Bill. After trial-boring by engineers in the summer of 1964, however, it became clear that using the old bridge-foundations was not feasible and in 1966 a Bill was brought in to rebuild the Bridge entirely. At least there was now to be no rise in pavement-level in front of the Hall, a change that would have destroyed the building's architectural relation to the bridge-approach : it will be remembered that a new Hall could not be designed at all until Rennie had settled the pavement-level, and it is somewhat surprising that such potential vandalism was even considered in 1962. Motorways were uppermost in the early 1960s.

The building of the new Bridge, designed by the City Engineer, Harold Knox King, was managed so as not to interrupt weekday traffic throughout construction, the two outer lanes being built first. The width of the Hall 'loading bay' was lost, of course, as were the old bridge-stairs, little used since the days of wherries and then of arguments over passenger-approaches to steamers. Rennie's 'pilaster', the much-discussed pylon that originally gave the bridge-stairs architectural import-ance, was embedded in the new structure; on its wharf face this remnant of Rennie's Bridge still bears the Fishmongers' Company's painted inscription, 'Less Noise Please Consider Offices Above', relic of the commercial uses of wharf and warehouse discontinued in 1968 and a poignant notice during the years 1968–73. Pile-driving was entirely at night, for minimum interference with traffic; so far as staff and wardens in permanent or temporary residence at the Hall were con-cerned, the City Corporation paid for hotel rooms on the worst nights and promised no 'undue' noise on the other nights. As for the bridge-works by day, the years 1968–71 must have been, in the company's offices, like the years 1825–9 before the retirement to Aldermanbury. In 1973 there was a trying period after the main bridge was done, when the narrow old 'dry arch' over Thames Street at the northeast corner of the Hall had to be replaced and a Bailey bridge took traffic across while construction went on underneath. On this temporary metal affair, traffic-blocks of buses and lorries perched at odd angles while mechanical diggers fingered the edges of tunnels far below and pedestrians in Indian file on narrow catwalks were suspended in noise and space; on the site of the new subway stairs near the Hall front steps, a half demolished mass of brickwork from the old abutment of 1829, riddled by the summer rains of 1973, subsided one day with a shaking roar. But that already seems long ago, and the new six-lane Bridge has at least a quieter road-surface than its predecessor. Its three great arches, instead of Rennie's five, and the somewhat Stonehenge-like parapet – dwarfing the odd little obelisks added to the bridge-piers, for ornament or to hitch a boat to – are even out of scale with Adelaide House. The only near neighbour on the scale of the new London Bridge is Mondial House, a telephone exchange for giants erected by the Department of the Environment nearby in Thames Street, just downstream of the Cannon Street Station railway bridge. Thames Street itself is now a boulevard (compare Pl. 24), accommodated by the greatly widened 'dry arch' of the bridge-approach and baring more of the Hall's plain north front than was intended, although its proportions carry the new isolation well enough. Henry Roberts' building would seem to be more and more isolated in the giant vice of a new City of London. Rebuilding on the Fishmongers' Company's ground between the Hall and Old Swan Lane, begun in 1976, was designed in the office of the distinguished architect Lord Holford (died 1975) to be in scale with, though not in the style of, the Hall. With the new public riverside walk, a civilised pedestrian version of the old Thames Quay idea, this may yet remain an oasis in the new City.

Meanwhile, beside the giant causeway, the Hall's chalk-bedded 'barge lay-by' is visible at low water, fenced by campshed piling against tidal erosion in the old way. Young watermen annually compete on the river for Thomas Doggett's scarlet coat and silver badge in England's oldest sporting fixture, administered and celebrated in the Hall as usual. Bridge Ward continues to hold its wardmotes at the Hall, according to an ancient tradition, whereas the lending of the Hall to charitable organizations for the benefit and pleasure of many people continues a tradition of Victorian origin, a benevolence characterizing this Hall rather than its predecessors. Hospitality to organizations interested in the fishing industry goes further back, to guests such as Lord Maltravers, John Rushout, and Samuel Pepys in the seventeenth century, and doubtless to friends of Lovekyn and Walworth in the fourteenth. Today the company's inspectors still exercise their very ancient powers at Billingsgate, as the company beadles inspected the fish markets long before surviving minutebooks begin. Every other June, newly elected wardens accompanied by the court proceed on foot to St Magnus' church for an election service – silver-tipped beadles' staves carried before them and constables parting the rude traffic of Thames Street – and return for the election dinner in the great hall. Fishmongers' Hall for all its heirlooms is no museum, for it houses an institution in full tide of civic, charitable, educational, business and social existence, resembling in its well-regulated domestic machinery one of London's grander pre-war town houses. This particular piece of ground seems to nurture a gift for selective, robust survival.

Sources

AT FISHMONGERS' HALL are kept charters, the company's book of ordinances begun in 1508, transcripts and abstracts of wills and leases, certain planbooks and views, certain working drawings for alterations to the present structure, court and committee minutebooks for the past century, and newspaper-cutting albums. Since the last war, the company has deposited most of its records and drawings at Guildhall Library by agreement with the City Corporation. Thus the manuscripts section and the prints and drawings section of the Library hold between them a hoard of this company's papers, from which I have drawn upon the following types of material, more precisely listed in the notes that follow.

Minutebooks. Court minutes 1592–1664, saved in the Great Fire (rebound since; two sets of typed and indexed abstracts at the Hall, made in the 1930s, are useful but not infallible; old indexes, made in the early nineteenth century, use different numbering due to rebinding). Court minutes 1666–1872 (old indexes as above). Later court minutes at the Hall (some twice rescued in 1940–41, chap. 16). Committee minutes: a few included in court books; one sheet for September 1666; a set for 1712–30; committee minutebooks 1731–1870, also with elderly indexes; later committee minutes at Hall. Building committee minutes 1826–36 bound separately.

Accounts. Prime wardens' accounts 1636–1784, made up in two-year periods June to June, begun 1639 with 1636-8 account, pages 1636–66 rescued in the Great Fire. Miscellaneous accounts cited below; annual accounts bound with later court minutes, and accounts committee minutes.

Title deeds, leases etc., 1391–1882, cited below. Also: letterbooks, inventories and auction particulars, architect's and surveyor's reports; registers of apprentice bindings, freedom admissions, and elections to livery and court; barge papers, and other loose papers cited below.

Drawings. Planbooks of 1686, 1772 and after at the Hall; pair of *c.* 1726 at GL, all including ground-plans of Hall and/or environs. At GL: 50 loose drawings or sheets of drawings, 1618–1830, relating to predecessors of the present Hall; 209 sheets of drawings, 1831–5, from Roberts' office for the present Hall; also 16 sheets of competition drawings by others, 1831. Miscellaneous later drawings at the Hall.

Printed books given shortened references in the notes:

Beaven, A. B., *The Aldermen of the City of London*, I, 1908; II, 1913.

Bell, W. G., *The Plague in London of 1665*, 1924; *The Great Fire of London in 1666*, 1951.

Brazell, J. H., *London Weather*, 1968.

Colvin, H. M., *Biographical Dictionary of English Architects, 1660–1840*, 1954.

Graves, A., *The Royal Academy of Arts; Dictionary of Contributors and Their Works, 1769–1904*, 1905–6.

Gunnis, R., *Dictionary of British Sculptors, 1660–1851*, 1953.

Pepys, S., *Diary*, ed. R. Latham and W. Matthews, 1970ff.

Reddaway, T. F., *The Rebuilding of London after the Great Fire*, 1951.
Salzman, L. F., *Building in England down to 1540*, 1952.
Sharpe, R. R., *London and the Kingdom*, I, II, 1894.
Stow, J., *Survey of London* (1598), 1603, ed. C. L. Kingsford (1908, 1927), 1971.
Woodhead, J. R., *The Rulers of London 1660–1689*, 1965.

Notes

Dates in text and notes are in modern style. Manuscript numbers, assigned at Guildhall Library, refer to papers held in the manuscript section there. Where these numbers are not repeated for every reference to the minutebooks, they can be ascertained from the 'principal sources' at the head of each chapter's notes. Abbreviations: GL, Guildhall Library; CLRO, Corporation of London Record Office; *DNB, Dictionary of National Biography*; *OED, Oxford English Dictionary*; RIBA, Royal Insetitute of British Architects.

Chapter 2
The Circumstances before c.1525

Principal sources: Book of ordinances and transcripts of wills at the Hall; Aldermen's Court records, CLRO (see n. 30 below); company title deeds, GL (nn. 26–8 below); Stow.

1. Yeveley is named twice, as property-owner in Thames Street and as witness, by Lady Walworth's executors in a deed of 1391, Ms. 6707. In general on Yeveley, J. Harvey in *Archaeological Journal* vol. 108 ('1951') 1952 p. 108; references in E. M. Veale, 'Craftsmen and the Economy of London in the Fourteenth Century', *Studies in London History*, ed. A. E. J. Hollaender and W. Kellaway, 1969, p. 145.

2. On the Thames rowing race, England's oldest sporting fixture, see Ms 7269, Doggett Race papers 1721-1832, also court minutes generally on or about August 1.

3. On the Gully Hole, planbook at Hall, 1686, fo. 4; deeds 1766, 1828 (Mss 6256–7) to ground abutting on common way from Gully Hole to river; and two of the company's 18th-century drawings at GL showing open drain; also H. T. Riley, *Memorials of London . . . 1276–1419*, 1867, p. 616 on water-course 1415 to Oystergate.

4. *Rape of Lucrece* v. 1667; *Coriolanus* V iv. 51–2.

5. John Rennie, *Autobiography*, 1875, pp. 174–5, 192, 407–8.

6. William Harrison, 'Description of England' in Holinshed's *Chronicle*, 1577.

7. Less than that by 1779 according to 'A Table of Distances . . . upon the River Thames . . . with the usual time of Navigating loaded Barges' (sheet at CLRO, Small Mss) but earlier, from Isleworth to Maidenhead could take three days to a week (B. Dunning in *Country Life*, 19 April 1973).

8. Stow, *Survey* I. 83.

9. Wharves 1584: B. Dietz, ed., *The Port and Trade of Early Elizabethan London*, 1972, pp. 158, 160, 162, 163. Stow, *Annales*, ed. Howes, 1614, pp. 503–4.

10. W. Whitaker, *The Geology of the London Basin*, 1872, p. 483 on boring here to 237 feet; Facer in 1834 said he went to 'the unusual depth of 230 feet' to find water, Ms 5843 file 6.

11. Waterfront remains: R. Merrifield, *The Roman City of London*, 1965, gazetteer nos. 306–7; J. Schofield on Seal House excavation 1974, *Current Archaeology* no. 49, March 1975, p. 54, and verbal comment during contractors' diggings, early 1976.

12. Clerk's rough notes, 'Sundry heights' (1829–31), Ms 5843 file 2; drawing, 12 September 1816, southwest basement plan from surveyor's reports, Ms 5862-A.

13. Shoreline 1395, see p. 15; 1667, see pp. 67, 87.

14. Grassy banks: two watercolour views of Hall, dating between 1790 and 1830, in GL's own collection. Drain-mouth: Clerk's rough notes, 17 July 1833, Ms 5843 file 1.

15. Map drawing at British Museum reproduced in Reddaway opp. p. 54, related to Darlington and Howgego no. 21.

16. Typical lease, court minutes 3 December 1593, p. 29; complaint 1 June 1602, p. 313.

17. Stow, *Survey* I. 213

18. A reference used by Stow (Harley 541 f 225 v) on the company's three halls dates from 1483–5 or earlier (kindly given me by Dr Caroline Barron).

19. 'Glasiers Plott' (Pl. 1): Fishmongers' Company court minutes 16 March 1618, p. 275; schedule, lease of 1601 with Glaziers' Company Ms 5758 deed 6 at GL. On Chancery suit Fishmongers' Company *vs* MBW 1865, Ms 6761 with plans.

20. Charter 8 February 1433, confirmed 3 July 1508: Book of Ordinances and transcripts vol. 66 at Hall.

21. Lovekyn: reference to 'our said tenement where John Lovekyn was living' (transl.) in deed of sale next door December 1395, Ms 6697. Walworth: reference in same deed to his water-tower; on his library S. Thrupp, *The Merchant Class in Medieval London*, 1948, p. 161; also references by Barron and by Coleman in *Studies in London History* and by Harvey (n. 1 above). Askham: reference to 'all the great Tenement . . . which formerly belonged to Sir William Walworth and in which William Askeham . . . dwelt situate in Thames Street', will of Henry Preston, dated February 1435, proved November 1438, copy in transcripts vol. 66 at Hall.

22. Botiller: W. Herbert, *History of the Twelve Great Livery Companies*, 1836–7, II.61 (although on early company deeds in general Herbert badly needs disentangling); Botiller was at any rate one of the 19 names concerned in arrangements recited in Preston will (n. 21).

23. Compton Reade (with Earl of Liverpool), *The House of Cornewall*, 1908, chap. x with Fanhope will of December 1443, proved January 1444, bequeathing to Blackfriars rent-charge due from Fishmongers' Company. Copy of separate will of April 1437, proved November 1444, on 'annual rent forever' for Askham's former tenement, is in transcripts vol. 66 at Hall; Preston will (n. 21) holds Askham's former tenement 'for the life of Lord Fanhope'. On such devices see also B. W. E. Alford and T. C. Barker, *A History of the Carpenters' Company*,

1968, index, 'testamentary devise'.

24. A tenuous connection, as the 'late Countess of Arundell' must have died in or before 1429, when her husband John Fitzalan VI (declared Earl 1433, died 1435) reached his majority and began claiming the earldom, as his second wife bore his only heir in 1429 (*DNB*).

25. Committee minutes 7 May and 6 July 1841, pp. 466, 480.

26. Pepper Querne: deed 1395, Ms 6697, recites a surprising 'total longitude from the road to the Thames 233 feet' (transl.) and specifies component parts including wharf. (I am grateful to Mrs M. J. Post for help with this deed.) Also five deeds 1403–64 in Ms 6688. In Ms 6707, six deeds 1523–5, one 1548, five 1573–93, last including sale to Thomas Ware, his bequest to the company (will 1573, death 1592), his confirming bond of 1581, and widow's release 1593. Premises first referred to by name in 1523.

27. Nun's Head: court minutes October-December 1593, pp. 25, 29, 34, 51; 24 December 1599, p. 225. Bond of 1641 in Ms 6429 gives dimensions south half of ground. Two leases 1652 in Ms 6973. Earlier references in deed to neighbouring premises (Mss 6704–7) without name.

28. Flower de Luce: court minutes 22 October 1592, p. 7, and November 1604 to June 1605, pp. 406–32 *passim*. Three leases 1649–55 in Ms 6973. Earlier deeds of 1424–74 in Mss 6704–7 without name. First reference to former Stockfishmongers' Hall in connection with this ground is in court minutes for November 1603, p. 352.

29. Charter 1399, authorizing *inter alia* all fishmongers to sell saltfish in Stockfishmongers' Row, recited in *inspeximus* 1427, Book of Ordinances at Hall.

30. History 1504–36: the Act of 1504 required submission for royal approval of all institutional ordinances; the Fishmongers submitted theirs in October 1508, approval granted following February (Book of Ordinances, pp. 16 ff). Relevant aldermen's court records at CLRO include Repertories 2 (1508–14) fo. 55, 101, 134–6, 142, 169; Rep. 5 (1522) fo. 271; Rep. 9 (1536–6) fo. 142, 172–5; Journals vol. 11, 1509–10. Sharpe, I, 338, 367–9.

31. Knesworth will 1513: transcript vols.

65, 67 at Hall; original of separate will or deed of trust 1511 is at Hall. (Copy of former made in 1814 when Porter's Quay was sold also includes a final bequest to the company of 'two Table Cloths of Diaper with true loves', vol. 65.) Knesworth executors' account is Ms 9277. See also Beaven.

32. Ground west of Pepper Querne, waterside end, i.e. alongside the 'little wharf' ('the stone house on the west side of Mr Trattle's', court minutes 23 June 1659, p. 828): see chap. 6, n.i. and Pl. 2–4, Fig. I.

33. Glass roundel: court minutes 3, 17 July 1930, pp. 115, 127; committee minutes 3 July 1930, p. 256.

34. Southwark Cathedral: Royal Commission on Historical Monuments, *East London* (including Southwark), 1930; Survey of London, vol. 22, *Bankside*, 1950.

Chapter 3
Buildings and Repairs c.1525–1666

Principal sources: court minutes 1592–1664 (Ms 5570, vol. 1, 1592-1610; vol. 2, 1610–31; vol. 3, 1631–46; vol. 4, 1646–64); prime warden's accounts 1636–66 (Ms 5561, vol. 1, 1636–58; vol. 2, 1658–82); Stow; Salzman.

1. 'Master' was an older term in this company, succeeded in the 17th century by 'Prime Warden'. On Porter: Dietz, *Port and Trade* (chap. 2, n. 9 above), p. 162. Thwaites: court minutes 6 April 1596, p. 98; Alderman for Bishopsgate, he lived in the parish of St Mildred Bread Street (will proved 1598, unnumbered transcript vol. at Hall); renewal of the Mermaid lease involved amicable debate during 1595–9 between the company as freeholder and two Williamsons, vintners, on the tavern's extension to Friday Street; but see Schoenbaum, *Shakespeare's Lives*, 1970, on the Mermaid legend. On Penington, *DNB*.

2. 'Concealments': court minutes 8 March 1594 concerning deeds delivered by Queen's patentees William Tipper and Robert Dawe; two deeds, of 1591 and 1593, are in Ms 6708; others in Ms 6762.

3. F. Braudel, *The Mediterranean*, I (1972), 621–9, e.g. cargoes of *pesci stockfiss* to Leghorn.

4. Court minutes 26 June 1592, p. 2: 6 cups, 1 salt, 1 nest of bowls, 1 garnished (sil-

ver-mounted) nut, 1 basin and ewer, only.

5. Early surveyors: court minutes 3 December 1593, p. 30; 27 February 1598, p. 161; 20 October 1600, p. 264; 10 June 1605, p. 431; and prime warden's accounts *passim*. Directive 1643; court minutes 1 May 1643, p. 657.

6. Inspection fee: court minutes 18 October 1647, p. 49. Company plasterer: Richard Barfold or -feld (court minutes 29 March 1602, p. 306; also in 1597 offering for a lease); a plasterer of that name worked on West Horndon Hall, Essex, 1577–94: A. C. Edwards, 'Sir John Petre and Some Elizabethan London Tradesmen', *London Topographical Record*, vol. 23, 1974, pp. 72–3. List of 118 leases: front pages, court minutebook begun September 1666 (Ms 5571, vol. 1).

7. Deed 5 March 1474, Ms 6707.

8. Court minutes 29 November 1608 and 8 May 1609, pp. 543, 551.

9. Entry paving: court minutes 31 March 1600, p. 236; *OED* gives 1612 for tarras as imported waterproofing cement, but also 1485 for tarras as plastering, probably related to medieval 'terryng' (daubing with earth) in Salzman, pp. 189–90. Turned pillars: court minutes 13 August 1649, p. 153; accounts 1648–50, p. 282.

10. Salting meat, etc.: January, March 1630, pp. 781, 790; November 1640, April 1645, pp. 478, 829; May, October 1647, November 1662, pp. 25, 51, 1038.

11. Court minutes 7 February 1594, p. 34.

12. Winchester House: Survey of London, vol. 22, *Bankside*, 1950, pp. 46–56, pl. 44–53, and remains in Clink Street. Cromwell House: A. H. Johnson, *History of the Worshipful Company of Drapers*, II, 1915, 279–81. Protective boards: court minutes 31 January 1642, p. 573.

13. 'Inner Buttery next the Parlor', court minutes 24 October 1654, p. 455. Great chamber: court minutes 27 October 1595, p. 83; 11 April 1636, p. 257. On Ludgate Prison, Stow I. 40. Clerk's brooms: accounts 1636–8, p. 15, and thereafter.

14. Glass sundials, Pre-Fire: ordered by court 23 March 1646, p. 900 (accounts too dim to confirm); at Lambeth Palace, see Royal Commission on Historical Monuments, *West London* (including Lambeth), pl. 3; after the Fire, Fishmongers' Com-

pany paid 46*s* to Mr Dutton, glass-painter, for 'a Dyoll in the Court room' (accounts 1676–8, p. 324), probably in an east window; Custom House: Survey of London, *All Hallows Barking, Part II,* 1934; Weavers' Hall: drawing in F. S. Eden collection, Guildhall Library, 5.29; Pewterers' Hall: Royal Commission on Historical Monuments, *The City,* 1929, p. 171. In general, Maurice Drake, *History of English Glass-Painting,* 1912, p. 94.

15. Ogilby (1600–76) was described in one of Aubrey's *Brief Lives,* and a biography by K. S. Van Eerde is due in mid-1976 (Dawson); on the Ogilby-Morgan map, see p. 87 below.

16. References to the company armoury at the Hall in November 1599, p. 222; August 1601, p. 292; May 1613, p. 82; July 1628, p. 692; and to the armourer's house in Wood Street as early as November 1593, p. 28, and as late as March-April 1607, pp. 493, 495.

17. But the first and only references in the pre-Fire court minutes to a 'long gallery' (in April 1660, p. 863, and June 1662, p. 1013) seem to imply the re-flooring of an existing room; the joiner was paid in the latter month (accounts 1660–2, p. 62).

18. Former chapel as office, court minutes 2 June 1606, p. 464, 31 October 1639, p. 384 (also 14 October, p. 378 on lost key and confusion left by previous Clerk); chest in treasury, accounts 1636–8, pp. 12, 60, etc. Dust from ceiling, 9 August 1658, p. 663; chalk, A. Clifton-Taylor, *The Pattern of English Building,* 1972, p. 63.

19. Lee family: parish registers St Michael Crooked Lane, Ms 11,367, GL. Clerk's two storeys over the office: court minutes November 1639, pp. 391–2 on rooms 'two stories high' and 'two stairs high'; also February 1626, p. 576, and February 1631, p. 883.

20. E.g., 'Mr Carill' in 1654 and 'Mr Calamy' in 1656: on Joseph Caryl and Edmund Calamy the elder see *DNB* and W. Wilson, *History and Antiquities of Dissenting Churches,* 1808–14.

21. Dimension of halls: Margaret Wood, *The English Medieval House,* 1965, pp. 62–6.

22. Hearth tax: accounts 1662–4, p. 105. 'New ovens & chimneys': court minutes 10

June 1605, p. 431. Cook's gear: 24 October 1653, p. 395; boiler: accounts 1656–8, p. 458.

23. Carved mermaid-vane: accounts 1638–40, p. 76.

24. Sir Nikolaus Pevsner has kindly reminded me of the Sidney Sussex window (described in his *Cambridgeshire,* 1954, illustrated in Royal Commission on Historical Monuments *Cambridge*). The Hampton Court window is in the Watching Chamber.

25. Brass laver: accounts 1656–8, pp. 458–9. Chairs: court minutes 10 May 1624, p. 522. On Baldwin, n. 30 below.

26. Title deeds to the Star Inn, one of Knesworth's arranged 'bequests' of 1511, are in this company's Mss 6696, 6711 at GL.

27. Munday's pageant scroll at the Hall was reproduced in a folio published by J. G. Nichols, *Chrysanaleia, The Golden Fishing,* 1844. Cf. S. Orgel and R. Strong, *Inigo Jones, The Theatre of the Stuart Court,* 1973, cat. no. 84, Indian torchbearer 1613, drawing at Chatsworth. Extra barges, court minutes 11 November 1616, p. 196. Both the scroll and various court minutes refer to pageant figures kept as ornaments in the great hall, but only Herbert's *Twelve Great Companies,* 1836–7, to their hanging from the beams.

28. On Arundel-Fanhope connection, chap. 2, n. 24 above. One Jones drawing for Lothbury is dated 1638: J. Summerson, *Inigo Jones,* 1966, pp. 114–5; J. Harris *et al.,* exhibition catalogue, *The King's Arcadia,* 1973, pp. 187–8. The Lothbury development was continued by Sir William Petty, who bought the ground in 1659 and continued building operations, already probably influential on Mills and possibly Jerman (*The Petty Papers,* ed. Marquis of Lansdowne, 1927, vol. 1, part ii, ed. introd. to sections 9ff).

29. C. & P. Cunnington, *English Women's Costume in the 16th Century,* 1970, p. 70.

30. For information on Baldwin prior to publication of *The History of the King's Works,* vol. 3 (1975), I am grateful to Sir John Summerson. Court minutes 12 May 1623, p. 481; 1 December 1628, p. 705; 17 October 1631, p. 932.

31. On Gayer see Beaven and Sharpe. His connection with St Katherine Cree may be one reason for the placing of this com-

pany's badge on the nave ceiling. Lee had been clerk to the Deputy Town Clerk at Guildhall: court minutes 24 March 1635, p. 210.

32. Hall repairs: court and committee minutes 11 March, 7 May, 13, 19, 27 August, 30 September, 16 December 1639, pp. 358, 364, 374–7, 396–7; accounts 1638–40, pp. 61, 75–7. Wade: Alford & Barker (chap. 2, n. 23 above); list of Fishmongers' Company leases (n. 6 above), and court minutes 15 November 1652, p. 355.

33. August 13, Window-grates ordered removed; August 27, mason ordered to take down and rebuild part of wharf-wall; September 30, more of wharf-wall to be taken down and rebuilt; accounts not helpful.

34. Jerman family: Carpenters' Company court minutes (GL Ms 4329), vol. 3, January, February, December 1604; vol. 4, September 1652; Colvin; P. E. Jones and T. F. Reddaway, introduction to *Mills-Oliver Survey of Building Sites after the Fire*, vol. 1 (1962), pp. xi–xv, xxvii. On Edward Jerman's appointment and pre-Fire employment by Fishmongers' Company: court minutes 24 April, 22 August 1654, pp. 430, 448; 14 May 1655, p. 500; 20 June 1661, p. 952; also chap. 7, nn. 5, 7, 8 below, 35. Lock family: freedom and livery lists, Ms 5576, vol. 1, 1621, 1655, Ms 5587, vol. 1, 1642; Thomas taking apprentices from April 1655, court minutes p. 495; accounts 1654–6, pp. 408, 411, 1656–8, p. 448, 1658–60, pp. 17, 33; Colvin; chap. 8, n. 11 below.

36. See Woodhead on Hayne and son-in-law Francis Griffith. A note of 1668 from the latter on a company case is in Ms 5857. Copy of Hayne's will in transcripts vol. 67 at Hall.

37. Repairs 1660: accounts 1658–60, pp. 33–5; court minutes 16 April, 18 May, 5 June 1660, pp. 863, 868, 874–6, courts (also funeral and wedding receptions) being then held at the garden-house (chap. 4). Pepys, 21 July 1662, ed. note on price of beer. Payment of £30.8.11 to Thomas Bedford, John Colt, Richard Crooke, masons (compare £304 for carpentry) precedes payment of £133 to a carver, and suggests repair of battlements etc. Garrett or Gheeraerts family: Mrs R. Lane Poole in Walpole Society vol. 3, 1914. One member of the committee

for obtaining 'the King's picture' in 1635 was Isaac Penington, member of the King's tribunal in 1648. On royal trumpets, C. C. Oman in Royal Academy catalogue, *The Age of Charles II*, 1960, no. 120, quoting Lord Chamberlain's accounts at P.R.O.

Chapter 4
The Great Parlour in the Garden

Principal sources: court minutes and accounts as chapter 3; planbook 1686 at Hall.

1. Knight's will: transcripts vol. 67 at Hall. Tiptoft's Inn: C. L. Kingsford in *London Topographical Record*, vol. 12, pp. 43–4. By 1686 there were four houses, later Nos. 44–7 Lime Street.

2. No non-culinary plants mentioned.

3. Court minutes 30 September 1630, p. 832. For information on the Carter family prior to publication of *The History of the King's Works*, vol. 3 (1975) I am grateful to Sir John Summerson.

4. Court minutes, October 1623 and October 1624, pp. 490, 538.

5. Specifications for gallery: committee minutes in court minutebook, 24 February, 8 March, 16 August 1631, pp. 883–4, 922. Exterior of Carpenters' Company 'great room as drawn *c.* 1830 is in Alford & Barker (chap. 2, n. 23 above), pl. 3.

6. *DNB*.

Chapter 5
River, Wharf, and Drains

Principal sources: court minutes and accounts as chapter 3.

1. 'Water carpenter' and 'tide carpenter' were standard terms around the river-wharves and London Bridge.

2. Freedom registers, Ms 5576, vols. 1, 2; court minutes 26 April 1647, p. 21; accounts accounts 1660–2, p. 74.

3. Drawing dated October 1833 in company collection, GL; building committee minutes, Ms 5837 vol. 2, 6 July–24 August 1833, pp. 66, 70–1, 74, 75–6, 80; chap. 2, n. 14 above; committee minutes in court minutebook 31 January 1642, p. 573.

4. Act of Common Council, 30 Henry VIII 1538, reinforcing Act of Parliament 27 Henry VIII 1536 (CLRO, P.D. 10.46, 4.28).

5. On wharf masonry 1639, court and committee minutes 13, 27 August, 30 September, pp. 375–7. Portland stone at Goldsmiths' Hall: John Newman, 'Nicholas Stone's Goldsmiths' Hall', *Architectural History*, vol. 14, 1971, p. 38, n. 20. On Seal House excavation 1974, chap. 2, n. 11 above. Tower Wharf 1389: Salzman p. 469, no. 42; Tower Wharf 1631–5: *History of the King's Works*, ed. H. M. Colvin, vol. III, 1975, p. 276.

6. Company market conduits: court minutes, 12 September 1659, p. 836. Walworth's water-tower: deed of December 1395, Ms 6697. Pump and cistern on Pepper Querne 'little wharf', earliest reference, court minutes, 26 January 1605, p. 416, tenant to pay half and company half. Morris waterworks: court minutes, 8 April 1661, p. 935. On post-Fire water supply, p. 85 below.

7. Company's fire engine: court minutes, 26 October 1646, p. 953, 7 July 1656, p. 573; accounts 1660–2, p. 73.

Chapter 6
Neighbours, Plague, and Fire

Principal sources: court minutes and accounts as Chapter 3: Bell, *Plague*; Bell, *Fire*; Pepys; Reddaway.

1. The 'stone house west of Mr Trattle's' stood well forward of the parlour block as parts of Seal House did until 1976 (chap. 2, n. 32 above); on timber house behind it, alongside the company's great hall, see ancient-lights agreement 1612, Ms 6705, continued in arrangements with Lamott in 1673 (p. 88 below).

2. On drying-out of piling 1827–32, see pp. 121, 140.

3. Rebuilding of Stockfishmongers' Hall: court minutes, 29 July, 12 August 1616, pp. 179–82, 10 March, 7 April 1617, pp. 217, 223, 7 December 1618, pp. 312-13.

4. White Lyon, Thames Street, 'at Watergate', St Magnus parish (cf chap. 2, n. 3), lease 1655 to R. Shelberry, Ms 6973; and later to Thomas Lock, p. 72 below. The company had two other properties called White Lyon; on one also in Thames Street, chap. 7, n. 14 below.

5. Schedules with leases of 1650 (Flower de Luce) and 1652 (Nun's Head), chap. 2, nn. 27, 28.

6. Bishop's Head lease, 1656, with schedule of fixtures, in Ms 6973.

7. Reddaway, p. 221, cites also Evelyn's plea for beautifying the City, in GL Ms 94.

8. Acts of 1662, 14 Charles II, c.ii.2.2, c.vi.6.28.

9. Burial register 1665, St Michael Crooked Lane, Ms 11, 367, GL.

10. Tanner: accounts 1666–8, p. 164. Jekyll: see chap. 7, n. 1 below. Dawkes: court minutes, 27 November 1666, p. 22; accounts 1666–8, p. 173.

Chapter 7
The Circumstances, 1666–8

Principal sources: court minutes September 1666–October 1668 (Ms 5571, vol. 1, 1666–83); sheet of committee minutes, 21 and 28 September 1666 (Ms 6762); prime warden's accounts 1662–8 (Ms 5561, vol. 2, 1658–82); Pepys; Reddaway; Woodhead.

1. On these people see Woodhead; also, on the Jekylls, *DNB*. On the post-Fire City, Pepys, Reddaway, also John Evelyn's Diary. Immediate demands for labour: comment 13 September 1666 at Custom House quoted in Survey of London, *All Hallows Barking Part II*, 1934, p. 39.

2. On Bethlehem Hospital, Victoria County History, *London*, 1909, pp. 495ff, and *Calendar of State Papers Domestic*, 1667, p. 21; company accounts 1666–8, 1668–70, pp. 174, 212 on company payments there, Burial register St Michael's, Ms 11,367.

3. Committee minutes September 1666 in Ms 6762.

4. Plate sold to Vyner: accounts 1666–8, p. 158; same page, record of purchase of the salt by 'this Accomptant' (Prime Warden Trattle), also court minutes 24 August 1669, p. 203. Trattle leases, list in front of court minutebook 1666, and n. 11 below; *Loyal London*, accounts 1666–8, pp. 160, 172, 176; timber to Trattle and Hawes, the same, p. 160.

5. Receipts for timber and related payments to Jerman: accounts 1662–5, pp. 86, 87, 93, 125, 126, 132; court minutes 22 April, 11 September 1662, pp. 1001, 1028.

6. Accounts 1670–2, p. 243.

7. Later, a Mary Jerman died in the Jesus Hospital, Bray, c. early March 1681 (court minutes 15 March 1681, p. 675); Mary Jerman, widow of Edward's brother Roger, died c. early March 1681 (admin. Roger Jerman's will, PCC Reeve 128); Edward's widow was Rose.

8. Edward Jerman's will, PCC Coke 72; burial register, St Giles Cripplegate, Ms 6419 vol. 8, GL. Court minutes, 8 October 1668, p. 145; accounts 1672–4, p. 272.

9. *Wren Society* (ed. A. T. Bolton), vols. X, 49, 51, 55; XIX, 27.

10. Isaac Foster: court minutes, 5 December 1667, p. 99; Beaven; Dame Agnes Foster as riverside tenant 1474, deed in Ms 6707, as Mayor's wife, Stow I.40 and Beaven, any connection with Isaac Foster unproven; loan of £500: court minutes 25 November 1668, p. 153 on repayment.

11. Trattle leases, Ms 6973; court minutes 5 December 1667, p. 100, 11 February, 11 November 1669, pp. 170, 221. Warren leases, court minutes, 21 October 1670, pp. 277–8; accounts 1670–2, p. 224.

12. Chap. 2, n. 32. On Lamott, see Woodhead; Hooke's *Diary* (chap. 8, n. 19 below).

13. Plan on vellum in GL collection; fees in April 1656 for unspecified surveys, accounts 1654–6, p. 426; court minutes 25 August, 21 October 1670, pp. 273, 278.

14. Leases, White Lyon, Thames Street, in St Martin Orgar parish to Michell/Mitchell in 1665 and 1667, Ms 6973.

15. Court order 5 December 1667, pp. 95–6, referring to committee report of 16 April (not preserved but preceding also the court order for a 'modell' in June).

Chapter 8
Rebuilding the Hall, 1668–9, 1669–71

Principal sources: court minutes March 1668–October 1671 (Ms 5571, vol. 1, 1666–83); prime warden's accounts 1668–72 (Ms 5561, vol. 2, 1658–82); Reddaway.

1. Other City livery companies queried report no Jerman drawings, but I have not done a systematic survey of all possible holdings.

2. Reddaway, pp. 200–1, 221–43 on Thames Quay.

3. Surveyors' reports, Ms 5862-A, 23 March 1820, Alexander on enclosure of portico 'similar to the Windows of the Entrance to the Library of Trinity Coll. Cambridge' (if he meant the Neville's Court side); and auction sale catalogue 13 January 1830, Ms 5845, file 2, includes 'circular-headed' window-frames from that enclosure.

4. Foundations: Joseph Moxon, *Mechanick Exercises* (1678ff), pp. 127–8, describes the process.

5. Probably mainly in the summer of 1670, see court minutes 18 May 1670, p. 254, site of (former) Stockfishmongers' Hall to be measured; but by July, pp. 267–8, they were discussing the roof.

6. Basement plan on vellum (with two later plans based on it), inscribed with names of occupiers of 1770s–80s, company drawings collection GL.

7. Court minutes 1 August 1751, p. 540, 16 May 1753, p. 24; committee minutes 17 December 1762, p. 220.

8. C. C. Knowles & P. H. Pitt, *History of Building Regulations in London*, 1972, p. 37.

9. J. Seymour, 'Edward Pearce: Baroque Sculptor of London', *Guildhall Miscellany*, vol. 1, no. 1 (January 1952); M. Whinney in Oxford History of Art, 1957, and Giant Pelican History of Art, 1964; Colvin; Gunnis; n. 30 below. Peirce was the more usual, but not invariable, spelling in this company's records. On plans for stone statue of Queen Elizabeth at Royal Exchange, court minutes 30 May 1684 and 18 June 1685, and p.w. accounts 1684–6, p. 44; payments for chimneypiece and for Walworth statue, n. 30 below and chap. 9, n. 12; also p.w. accounts 1670–2, p. 233.

10. Accounts 1670–2, p. 233; known to have been a Turkey merchant and in the timber trade (Woodhead).

11. Freedom register, Ms 5576, vol. 1, 1635, so this William Allington probably born c. 1621. *The Architecture of Sir Robert Pratt from his Note-books*, ed. R. T.

Gunther, 1928, pp. 121, 129. Lock, chap. 3, n. 35 above.

12. Planbook no. 1, Ms 5860, p. 4; probably an old trade joke: somewhere in Pepys or his editors is a bit of folklore that most houses in Chatham were built of chips from the Navy Yard.

13. Court minutes 19 September 1672, p. 380.

14. Chamberlain's Foundations Posting Book in vol. 1 of *Mills-Oliver Survey of Building Sites* (London Topographical Society, 1967), Thames Street, p. 75; and court minutes 8 April 1669, p. 180.

15. In Ms 6762, sheet endorsed '27 May 1669 Coppy of Dr Wren's certificate for ye Hall'. Accounts 1668–70, p. 209: 'Paid to Doctor Wren his Majties Surveyr for his Certificate to the Lord Maior concerning this Companyes building of their Hall tenne peeces of Gold £10.5.0'.

16. The 'several plats of the ground of several houses annexed to the lease thereof' in Lock's accounts (court minutes 19 September 1672, p. 380) might include four plans on vellum for Porter's Quay, Thames Street at Water Lane, Queenhithe, and Fish Street Hill, though these may well be later (and any plan by Lock likely to have been redrawn); also two sheets, Thames Street elevation and plan of house built by him beside the Gully Hole, may be his: company drawings collection GL.

17. Drawings of 1691 and 1802, *Architectural History*, 1971, Fig. 26–7.

18. Colvin.

19. *Diary of Robert Hooke,* ed. H. W. Robinson, 1935; Colvin.

20. Summerson, *Architecture in Britain 1530–1830*, 1970, pp. 152–3. *Vitrurius Britannicus*, vol. III, elevation of Horseheath.

21. First reliable view of rebuilt City, at base of William Morgan's map published 1682 (shown to this company in October 1681, see p. 87 below).

22. Strype in 1720, Maitland in 1739, Noorthouck in 1773, and others described the Hall river-front in glowing terms.

23. Pratt notebooks (n. 11 above) pp. 121, 123.

24. John Soane, *Lectures in Architecture* (delivered to Royal Academy 1809–36), ed. A. T. Bolton, 1929, p. 136.

25. Colvin.

26. Pratt notebooks, p. 195.

27. O. Hill & J. Cornforth, *English Country Houses: Caroline 1625–85*, 1966, p. 110, fig. 163.

28. E. Croft-Murray, *Decorative Painting in England*, vol. 1, 1962, p. 233.

29. Colvin lists, under Wren, 32 City churches with decorative plasterwork by Grove and/or Doogood. On the Groves, G. Beard in *Country Life*, 22 March 1973, p. 788, also Beard's *Georgian Craftsmen and Their Work*, 1966.

30. Accounts 1672–4, p. 264 (in addition to £157 paid him 'for carving work', 1670–2 p. 233 and 1672–4 p. 264, perhaps all outdoor work).

31. See Alice Clark, *Working Life of Women in the Seventeenth Century*, 1919, pp. 150–235 on crafts and trades.

32. Musicians hired then were all trumpeters, under 'Mr Walker the Trumpeter' in 1701 as in 1660. See p. 93 on instruments in the 1730s.

Chapter 9
From Lodgers to Affluence

Principal sources: court minutes and prime warden's accounts 1670-1770 (Ms 5571, vols. 1–6; Ms 5561, vols. 2–7); committee minutes 1712–70 (Ms 6243 and Ms 5573, vols. 1–4).

1. On aldermen in this chapter, Beaven, Sharpe and, on the earlier ones, Woodhead.

2. Ms 6973 contains three leases to Shepherd of vaults under the Hall, 1681–9. See Sharpe, Woodhead.

3. Court minutes 6 October 1681, p. 685. *DNB* quotes a comment of 30 October 1681 that Barbon 'hath set up an office for it'. Largest-scale building speculator of his day, he was developing Essex Street, Strand, at the time. The Hall was insured with the Friendly Society 1687–1728, with the Hand in Hand Fire Office 1728–65, and others including the Phoenix and Union Fire Offices thereafter.

4. *Wren Society* index volume, and information from John Newman.

5. Company drawings collection GL.

6. The same; and chap. 8, n. 6 above.

7. Moorage rights, citing similar case between coal merchants and Society of Middle Temple: court minutes, 2 October 1794, p. 349; 3 December 1795, p. 397; 18 June 1801, pp. 115–6; committee minutes 25 March 1801, pp. 356–8, citing long-forgotten Thames Quay legislation (cf Reddaway as in chap. 8, n. 2 above).

8. A recent summary of Leybourn(e)'s career is in Betty R. Masters, *The Public Markets of the City of London Surveyed by William Leybourn in 1677* (London Topographical Society, 1974), pp. 9–10 with references.

9. Darlington & Howgego, p. 22, no. 28.

10. Committee minutes 1762 (as chap. 8, n. 7 above): apparently this 'upright post in the yard . . . intended to support the northwest corner' of the riverside block's roof had not been clothed in brickwork; Price now brought up a brick pier 'from the ground through the floor of the flat of the yard', placed a stone base on it, cut off the lower part of the post and fixed the post on the base with oak wedges, Mary-Ann-behind indeed.

11. Ms 5856 contains extracts made in 1830 from court minutes 1592ff on the company burial ground. On protests, court minutes 8, 19 June, 24 October 1683, pp. 729, '733, 739; agreement with Archbishop, 4 January 1684, f. 4v.

12. Court minutes 4 January, 18 February 1684, 9 March 1685; p.w. accounts 1682–4, p. 21 first £15 paid, before end of period ending mid-June 1684; 1684–6, p. 44, £15 more paid in March 1685.

13. Plasterer's charges 1789: Ms 5829, billbook 9, p. 6, April 1789. Auction sale 1827: Ms 5845, file 2, catalogue 17 July 1827, lots 71, 75.

14. P.w. accounts, e.g. 1694–6, pp. 182–3; 1696–8, pp. 212–14; 1698–1700, pp. 242–3, etc.

15. Trees at waterside: court minutes, 30 March 1683, p. 722; p.w. accounts 1684–6, p. 44; 1698–1700, p. 245; Canaletto pen drawing, View of London Bridge, British Museum Print Room.

16. Papers concerning company barge and bargehouse property at Vauxhall in Mss 5861, 6911–17, 7263, 10,141 at GL. Edward Bird: Croft-Murray (chap. 8, n. 28

above) I. 217. Jonathan Mayne: Gunnis, and Colvin under Wren.

17. A plan for water-stairs, kept with the Marquand drawings of 1753 (chap. 10, n. 8 below), seems not to have been used. In 1768, e.g. Old Swan stairs was still 'this Company's usual place of landing', committee minutes, 20 September 1768, p. 12. But references in 1814–16 to 'new steps' and 'iron gate' to the water before Fishmongers' Wharf imply replacement of existing steps and gate: court and committee minutes, June–October 1814, March 1815, May 1816.

18. George Holmes: Croft-Murray I. 222.

19. Disadvantages of lodgers summarized, court minutes 6 April 1720, p. 298.

20. Court minutes 3 June, 7 October 1702, ff 273, 278; p.w. accounts 1700–2, 1702–4, pp. 278, 307. The pair by Murray were given by a liveryman, William Blackburn, in 1779 (company pocketbook).

21. In 1790 a plasterer charged for 'Making good to Prime Wardens Shields in Cove of Great Hall', i.e. by that time these also ornamented the curved frieze under Grove's ceiling: Ms 5829, Willats' billbook, p. 34.

22. 'Company's arms to be set up in the middle of the shields there placed' ordered from Wade 13 April 1732 (court minutes), shield now over great hall's central door bears date 1732. Besides the shields now hanging in great hall, courtroom, corridors and offices, the company has a further collection in store; none made before 1727 though dates on some would be older, as dates of office or benefaction: court minutes 14 June 1727, consideration deferred from April 1701 and December 1722, shields ordered for Lord Mayor's day 1720 perhaps temporary; also accounts 1728–30, 1730–2, pp. 74, 112. Shields 1815: instructions dated 6 June 1815 and endorsed 'Orders given by Mr T. Bodley as to Colours etc', concerning shields and banners, in Ms 7263 with barge papers.

23. J. A. Knowles, 'The Price Family of Glass Painters', *Antiquaries Journal*, July–October 1953, p. 184.

24. Undated elevation in company drawings collection GL, on paper with Villedary watermark, probably dated 1730–1 by court order of 3 October 1730, p. 577.

25. Bateman, who became Prime Warden in 1710 only a year after admission to freedom and election to livery and court, had the use of the Hall in 1716–17 for his mayoralty; he acquired the carcase of Monmouth House on Soho Square only in February 1717 after which much finishing was done, probably by Thomas Archer (Survey of London, *Parish of St Anne Soho*, XXXIII, 109).

26. J. Fowler & J. Cornforth, *English Decoration in the 18th Century*, 1974, p. 205.

27. Contract 6 February 1734 in Ms 6917.

28. As in 1761, when the Royal Family came to Guildhall: committee minutes 28 October, 5 November 1761, pp. 156–8.

29. Easton family: Gunnis. Order for chimneypiece, committee minutes 10 August 1741, p. 139. Stages in appearance: original state, drawing A.16, probably early 1834, company drawings collection GL; mounting of surviving panel (after stay in St Peter's Hospital), Austen Hall drawings 1936 and war-damage photograph 1940 kept at Hall; remounting as now in courtroom. Originally about 9′ 8″ wide (shelf and consoles), two feet wider than now; original parlour wall was about 47′ long. History after 1834: pp. 174–5.

30. Court minutes 20 December 1749, 14 February, 17 October 1750, 7 February, 27 October 1752; committee minutes 7 February 1750, 21 January, 13 February, 25 March, 17 July, 13 October, 21 November 1752, esp. pp. 102–3; renter warden's account, Ms 5825, vol. 59, 1751–2, pp. 23, 26. On William Gould, J. P. Fallon in *Antique Dealer & Collector's Guide*, November 1974, pp. 100–5, a reference kindly given by Miss Susan Hare, Goldsmiths' Company Librarian, who has also pointed out the episode's interest in relation to early methods of silvering copper; and that Gould, after serving time in gaol and returning to the trade, actually applied, unsuccessfully, for the post of Assay Master to the Goldsmiths' Company.

31. P.w. accounts 1766–8, p. 224, bought from a Thomas Bennett (possibly a 'merchant & insurer' of Wapping, trade directories) as by Van Hacken, who is also known for a view of Billingsgate. In 1790 a Thomas Bennett (possibly a brazier of Wapping,

trade directories) was paid for 'new Gilding the Dagger' (Ms 5566, vol. 1, p. 29), perhaps the earliest reference in surviving company records to Walworth's alleged weapon, though it is mentioned in Strype's edition of Stow's *Survey* (1720, book V, p. 183) as hung up in one of the rooms of the Hall then; and Ms 5829, carpenter's billbook, p. 51, says the second Bennett also provided a scabbard. The wooden dagger held by Peirce's carved figure was painted a bloody red (Strype as above).

32. GL has an early state of the first view, dedicated to the Fishmongers' Company by B[ernard] Lens, probably published 1700–1 in honour of the Fishmonger Lord Mayor, Sir Thomas Abney. *Fontange*: C. & P. Cunnington, *Handbook of English Costume in the 17th Century*, 1972, p. 181; —, *...18th Century*, 1972, p. 156. Trees, n. 15 above. Sutton Nichols may have drawn both views (Pl. 6, 7) but little is precisely known about his career or the altering of his plates.

33. Sash-windowed bar: W. A. Pantin, 'Medieval Inns' in *Studies in Building History*, ed. E. M. Jope, 1961, pp. 188–9. Committee minutes 18 March 1754, p. 255; and six-year lease from 1748 to William Smith, Ms 6973 at GL and transcripts vol. 68 at Hall, of vault 'being that under the Hall & next the Wharff in his Possession'.

34. W. Herbert, *History and Antiquities of the Parish of St Michael's Crooked Lane*, 1831, pp. 105ff; K. Rogers, *Signs and Taverns round about Old London Bridge*, 1937, pp. 35–6.

Chapter 10
The Return of the Company Surveyor

Principal sources: court and committee minutes 1710–1822 (Ms 5571, vols 3–12; Ms 6243 and Ms 5573, vols 1–11), prime wardens' accounts to 1784 (Ms 5561 to end); office ledgers 1784ff (Mss 5565–6, 5826–7); craftsmen's billbooks 1788–92 (Ms 5829); auction particulars 1827–31 (Ms 5845); surveyors' reports 1791–1821 (Ms 5862–A).

1. James Gould: D. Stroud, *George Dance, Architect, 1741–1825*, 1971, pp. 29, 30, 32. He seems to have developed Gould or Gold Square, Coopers Row (1730s–

1880s), where the father of Henry Roberts (chap. 13, n. 18 below) was to have his office.

2. George Sampson: Colvin; Summerson, *Architecture in Britain 1530–1830*, 1970, p. 366; H. R. Steele & F. R. Yerbury, *The Old Bank of England*, 1930.

3. John Price Jr: Colvin, under Price Sr; Alford & Barker, *Carpenters' Company*, list of masters, 1753; court minutes 29 August 1739, pp. 168–9; committee minutes 24 August 1739, pp. 90–1, 12 December 1740, p. 117, 14, 21 January 1741, pp. 119–20, 5 June 1741, p. 134. B. F. L. Clarke, *Parish Churches of London*, 1966, p. 263 on Porter (the company bricklayer 1716–42, p.w. accounts).

4. Bower: court minutes 7 January 1741, pp 229–30; p.w. accounts 1740–64; 1718–20, p. 179; freedom lists, Ms 5576, vol. 3, 1719.

5. Court minutes 29 April 1743, p. 311.

6. On Gibbs, etc., see Colvin; also Stroud (n. 1 above) p. 37 on Mansion House.

7. Samuel Bennet Smith: trade directories GL; p.w. accounts 1754–6, p. 303, when his most recent large work had been at the Hall, but in 1750–2 in Lombard Street, rebuilding two company houses, for which surviving plans and elevations in company collection GL may be his.

8. Foundations, see chap. 8, nn. 4, 7 above. On floods, Brazell. Marquand: Colvin; pamphlet in GL; court minutes, 27 October 1752, p. 12, 9 February 1753, pp. 17–18, 16 May 1753, pp. 24–5, 29 May 1754, p. 55; three sheets plans and sections for piling under south front, with Clerk's note 'by Marquand and others 1753', company drawings collection GL.

9. Series of drawings for alterations to Beadle's and Clerk's and Thames Street tenants' houses, not necessarily as executed (court minutes 8 October 1765, p. 538), company drawings collection GL. Silverside (not in Colvin's first ed.): court minutes 6 December 1765, p. 3.

10. George Gwilt Sr: court minutes 8 January 1771, p. 272; committee minutes 3 May 1771, p. 109; Colvin.

11. John Gorham Jr. Colvin; D. Olsen, *Town Planning in London*, 1964, p. 183; Stroud, *Dance*, p. 101; Survey of London,

St James's South of Piccadilly, XXIX, 37, 39, *St James's North of Piccadilly*, XXXI, 292, *Covent Garden*, XXXVI, 160; information from Drapers' Company, kindness of Mr Brown; committee minutes Fishmongers' Company 21 June 1771, p. 113, and p.w. accounts 1770–2, p. 30. A small planbook by Gorham, 1772, is at the Hall, and see n. 16 below.

12. Ms 5829: billbooks of James Gubbins, carpenter (n. 21 below), William Hobson, bricklayer, Thomas Piper, mason, John Woodall, smith, Hayward & Cope, glaziers, Thomas Jones, painter, Moses Willats, plasterer; those of John & William Poynder, plumbers, and various roofing people do not now survive. The £18,000 would be about £144,000 in, say, 1972.

13. Plan southwest basement endorsed 12 September 1816 in surveyors' reports. Ms 5862–A.

14. A. Clifton-Taylor, *The Pattern of English Building*, 1972, pp. 383–4.

15. Two anonymous watercolour views of Hall river-front, and one by E. W. Cooke of 1826 in GL collection.

16. Drawings in company collection probably by Gorham 1788–90: one for a screen of four columns, two for plasterwork ceiling and frieze details, and one for alterations to Peirce's Thames Street gateway, probably none executed as drawn; these resemble signed drawings by him in the Drapers' Company collection.

17. There are only unitemized payments for Hall and wharf repairs in p.w. accounts 1752–4 and 1754–6, totalling c. £4400, half of which went to the carpenter for unspecified work 'in & at the back of the Hall', including piling. We must owe the preservation of craftsmen's billbooks for 1788–92 and sale particulars of 1827–31 after demolition of their work to J. D. Towse (born 1760, entered office 1775, Clerk 1809–39), as well as to committee caution about compensation.

18. *Walpole Society* vol. 32, 1951.

19. A receipt for 50 guineas signed by Eleanor Coade for this piece existed until recently; on this and other Coade work bought, Gunnis' figures suggest that he saw other records besides the accounts Mss 5565–6, 5826–7 (totals less than his). On

'Charity' in the present century, see p. 150. It will stand in the Hall again.

20. Mss 5826–7, three payments to Van Gelder 1789–92 totalled £296 for carving and statutory work, specified by Gunnis, who may have seen Van Gelder's receipts.

21. Ms 5829 in both billbook A, July 1788–Christmas 1790, and billbook B, Christmas 1790–Christmas 1792 (other papers with them are roughs for A and an abstract by Gorham, also a letter from Samuel Wyatt as outside assessor). Billbook B also has furniture bills of 1790, e.g. wine cistern, f. 3v.

22. Ms 5829, Gubbins' billbook B, f.13v, and Gorham's abstract, note at end. Survey of London, *St Mary's Lambeth, Part II*, pp. 67, 71.

23. L. Wright, *Clean and Decent*, 1960, p. 107.

24. Ms 5837 vol. 1, committee 26 April 1827, pp. 82–3, a list of 18th-century tavern fixtures of some interest. (Clerk's rough notes in Ms 5846 file 1 also include 'small lead cistern for washing glasses').

25. River views of the Hall showing lateral flights of steps to great-hall door date before 1788–90; with only a walled terrace above the wharf, after 1790. Legal point, wharf railing; case by company solicitor January 1862, Ms 6279, papers relating to proposed pier at Old Swan Stairs. Descriptions of Shades and wharf: *Chronicles of London Bridge: by an Antiquary*, 1827, p. 3; Herbert, *Parish of St Michael's Crooked Lane*, 1831, p. 105. On company barge in Nelson's funeral procession, court minutes 1 January, 14 February 1806, pp. 441–4.

26. Alexander: Colvin; country-house work consisted mainly of partly-realized ambitious additions to Longford Castle, Wilts. Portrait by John Partridge belongs to the Port of London Authority.

27. I'Anson: Colvin; father of Edward I'Anson, PRIBA 1886–8.

28. Report by I'Anson, 24 June 1813, Ms 5862-A. Subsequent lease, e.g. court minutes 27 February 1817, p. 281.

29. Court minutes 1 August, 30 October, 12 December 1822, pp. 339, 349–52, 363.

30. Court minutes 11 April 1867, p. 206, 'after 50 years uninterrupted performance

of the duties', that is, in fact, since 1817. Certain drawings at GL show that Suter was more at home with working details for the new embankment than with classical façades: e.g. a weak Palladian elevation, with plan, unsigned and undated but probably for a 'Metropolitan Horse & Carriage Repository' exhibited R.A. 1854, and court minutes, building on company ground at Elephant and Castle. For some years Suter shared an office in Fenchurch Street with Annesley Voysey, architect and engineer, grandfather of the architect C. F. A. Voysey. Suter's origins are obscure: directories 1803–11 give Thomas Suter, builder of London Street, Greenwich; Richard Suter in will proved 1883 left property in London Street, Greenwich. He retired to Maidenhead after 1867; one of his sons became Bishop of Nelson, New Zealand. See also Chap. 13, n. 11 below.

Chapter 11
A Sacrifice to the Bridge

Principal sources: court and committee minutes 1825–7 (Ms 5571, vol. 13; Ms 5573, vol. 12); auction particulars 1827–31 (Ms 5845).

1. A set of eight printed London Bridge Acts, 1823–34, is bound in vol. 1 of building committee minutes Ms 5837 (minutes duplicating Ms 5573 until mid-1832).

2. *Chronicles of London Bridge*, 1827, pp. 636–66. City Corporation Pocketbooks 1824ff, CLRO, lists of officials and committees (C. for Building the New London Bridge, C. for Letting the Bridge-house Estates, C. for Letting City Lands) with which this company was much concerned.

3. See chap. 2, n. 5 above.

4. List of furniture reserved. May court order as per committee 26 April 1827, p. 66. Sale catalogue, building contents 4 July, building materials 16–17 July 1827, Ms 5845 file 2. E. W. Cooke drawing no. 203, GL, shows demolition of roof. Regrets: *The Mirror of Literature, Amusement, and Instruction*, 14 January 1832, excerpt mounted with views of Hall in GL prints and drawings collection.

5. No. 115 Upper Thames Street, sale

15 April 1828; remainder of Hall, sale 13 January 1830; Nos 113–14 Upper Thames Street, sale 18 February 1831 (catalogues Ms 5845); Nos 110–12 came down in March or April 1832 (committee minutes March 19).

6. Ms 5852, 3 files papers, Aldermanbury premises 1829–35; and 2 plans by Suter in company drawings collection GL.

7. John Locke, freeman of Painter-Stainers' Company and son of an Edmonton coal merchant, married a sister of Thomas Cartwright the Fishmongers' Company bricklayer (Cartwrights and Lockes living from c 1805 at Nos 135–6 Upper Thames Street opposite the Hall as company tenants); the Lockes' son was a future QC, MP for Southwark and Recorder of Brighton: Painter-Stainers' apprentice-binding book at GL; City Corporation Pocketbooks; Boase, *Modern English Biography*, and *DNB*.

8. On the Margrave and Margravine, court minutes 14 February 1793, p. 259; 3 April 1794, pp. 321–2; 8 February 1798, p. 490; committee minutes 15 May 1826, p. 153. No payment to Romney appears in company accounts for the 1790s, and the portraits may have been gifts, but the painter's own records should be consulted.

9. 'To take the Company's barge in tow from Kew': the results, since this was not repeated, are reading between the lines; when a steamboat accompanied the barge later, e.g. to Wandsworth in 1849, each proceeded separately under its own power. Instructions 1825: committee minutes 16 July, pp. 60–2. On Rogers: P. W. Clayden, *Rogers and His Contemporaries*, 1889, I.290, also Clayden's *The Early Life of Samuel Rogers*, 1887.

Chapter 12
The Circumstances 1827–31

Principal sources: court and committee minutes 1827–31 (Ms 5571, vols. 13, 14; Ms 5573, vols. 12–14, special committee also in Ms 5837, vol. 1); loose papers relating to relocation of Bridge (n. 8 below).

1. J. M. Crook, *The Greek Revival*, 1972; J. Summerson, *Architecture in Britain*

1530–1830, 1970 ed., chap. 29; H. H. Bellot, *University College, London 1826–1926*, 1929; Survey of London vol. 21, *Tottenham Court Road and Neighbourhood* (Parish of St Pancras, Part III), 1949, section 63.

2. On building-committee members: freedom registers and livery lists, Mss 5576, 5584; London street, trade, and court directories; Beaven; *DNB*; Boase, *Modern English Biography*; on Towgood, Clayden's *Rogers* cited chap. 11, n. 9 above, and on Sturch, A. Saunders, *Regent's Park*, 1969, pp. 105, 141, 160, 184.

3. *DNB* under Banks; a portrait of Banks is in the Guildhall Art Gallery, no. 69 in 'To God and the Bridge' exhibition, 1972, catalogue pl. viii; Jolliffe's son became first Baron Hylton.

4. Court and committee minutes 24 December 1827; Ms 5846, file 1, papers on embankment, Suter's reports and sketches. Working drawings signed by Suter are in GL's own collection and others are in the company collection.

5. Cockerell married Rennie's sister in 1828: D. Watkin, *Charles Robert Cockerell*, 1974, p. 51. Levels: Rennie finally gave Suter precise figures early in 1831, the Clerk noting that Suter was ready 'to lay before this Committee the Bridge levels' (Ms 5849, agenda 1831, also Clerk's notes on 'sundry heights' in Ms 5843, file 2).

6. Five small pencil sketches, thought to date 1829–31, RIBA Drawings Collection; Watkin, p. 252; Rennie, *Autobiography*, 1875, p. 197: Rennie's opinion of the approaches as built, 'a more unworthy set of buildings was never designed', may or may not include Fishmongers' Hall.

7. On Knight at No. 112, court minutes 25 August 1831, and letter from him in Ms 5843, file 1, as from 'London Bridge Works 112 Thames Street'; for his plan of the neighbourhood see Fig. VII; receipt for rejected design, motto Pont, Ms 5843, file 15, no. 65; competition drawing signed Pont in company collection; Colvin.

8. On company properties affected: Mss 5843 (file 5), 5847–8, 5855 (envelope of letters re Three Tuns tenant's claim), 6253–4, 6257–9; special committee minutes Ms 5837, vol. 1, e.g. on Three Tuns arbitration 8 February 1831 and on another claim

taken to law August 1829–January 1830, etc. On Hardwick, Wilkins: Colvin. GL, Prints and Drawings, have a large rolled plan from Rennie's office showing properties affected by northern bridge-approach, and both old and new bridge-sites. The former Guildhall (new London) Museum has a model of the approaches.

Chapter 13
The Competition of 1831

Principal sources: court and committee minutes August 1831–March 1832 (Ms 5571, vol. 14; Ms 5573, vol. 14); loose papers 1831–2 (Ms 5843, files 1, 2, 7, 8, 10, 14, 15, 17); competition drawings in company collection at GL and in GL's own collection.

1. Deeds and abstract of title 1666–1863, No. 109 Upper Thames Street, Ms 6276; on close-knit community of cheese trade, R. C. Jarvis, 'Eighteenth-century London Shipping', *Studies in London History*, ed. Hollaender & Kellaway, 1969, pp 418–19. Deeds 1828–82, Shades tavern, Mss 6742–4, 6759; it appears that the post-Fire pair of houses visible in the Morgan and Buck views were rebuilt after a fire of 1820 by John Garratt, wholesale tea dealer, alderman of Bridge Ward, Lord Mayor 1824–5 (Beaven, and see chap. 11 above).

2. Unsigned and long unidentified, soft-pencil perspective view as from Bridge, in company collection GL.

3. *Architectural Magazine*, vol. II, 1835, p. 326; the Hansom-Welch correspondence ran from January to July, pp. 16, 18, 20–3, 238, 325–6.

4. Loose papers including instruction sheets, Ms 5843, file 2. Suter's master-drawing delineating site between Bridge and Shades as seen from north and south, company collection GL.

5. Ms 5843, file 2, notes by Towse endorsed 18 May 1829, 'sketch of Hall', with notes added in 1831 (chap. 12, n. 5 above).

6. P. Metcalf, 'The Fishmongers' Hall Competition 1831', based on the company's drawings and papers, listing everyone known to have been interested, *Guildhall Studies in London History*, probably 1977.

7. Clerk's lists, Ms 5843, files 2, 7, 8, 15. Mamhead design of 1822 (before Salvin was brought in): C. Hussey, *Late Georgian Country Houses*, p. 194.

8. But J. W. Johns (admitted to R. A. Schools 1833, Colvin) signed the receipt only as clerk to No. 60.

9. Roberts' model, with 'glass shade & stand' was kept in the court waiting-room at first (Ms 6242, inventories up to 1860). A letter of 29 April 1834 from the well-known model-maker Stephen Salter of Hammersmith, estimating for a paper model of the great-hall interior (Ms 5843, file 6, for planning decoration) may imply that he made the, doubtless wooden, competition model. See *Marble Halls*, Victoria and Albert Museum catalogue, 1973, on the use of models.

10. Ms 5843, files 2, 14.

11. R. A. Summer Exhibition catalogue, 1832, no. 959, as having been 'submitted to the court in 1828, and used by the building committee during the years 1829, 1830, and 1831'. Letters from Suter to court, Ms 5843, files 14, 15. A model 'of the Hall', probably of Suter's design, was offered to the company in his will proved in 1883 and declined.

12. Cottingham: 7 sheets of drawings (2 plans, 2 elevations, 1 section, 2 interiors) with Tobit mark in company collection GL, and perspective in GL collection (exhibited 1975, 'London as it might have been', no. 102), probably that returned to him and exhibited R.A. 1832, no. 993; title sheet 1827 for set of drawings by him of old Hall (other 5 sheets now lost) in company collection; Ms 5843, file 2, his letter identifying Tobit, no. 84; file 14, his letters to court in February–March 1832, and Clerk's 'Notes on hearing Mr Cottingham' 5 March 1832; Colvin, esp. on Cottingham's restorations and publications. GL has some unexecuted drawings by him for Salters' Hall.

13. Davies: Ms 5843, file 14, his letters to court in February–March 1832, and Clerk's 'Notes on hearing Mr Davies'. An engraving of his Highbury College is in J. Elmes's *Metropolitan Improvements*, 1827, the plate respectfully inscribed to Thomas Wilson Esq. Davies is in Colvin. His model for the Hall was shown at the R. A. in 1832,

no. 963. GL has some drawings by him, but none for Fishmongers' Hall.

14. John Soane, *Lectures in Architecture* (delivered at R.A. 1809–36), ed. A. T. Bolton, 1929, p. 146, saying that windows in both principal storeys were of similar height in the Whitehall Banqueting House, in Fishmongers' Hall 'and in many other of Inigo Jones's best works': it is hard to believe that Soane thought the post-Fire Hall was by Jones, but that is how he put it. The court gave him permission, 5 May 1808 (Ms 5571, vol. 10) 'to take drawings' of the Hall; a watercolour drawing at the Soane Museum (pl. 88 in the *Lectures*) was probably done by one of his students, according to the Curator, for (pre-slides) use with the lectures.

15. Summerson, *Architecture in Britain*, p. 501: the first 'to give clubland its sense of architectural consequence'.

16. Clerk's comment 1829 (n. 5 above) with sketch-plan on verso: 'space as at present for an Area (of about 17 feet wide) . . . will afford an opportunity of having Windows . . . on the West side'.

17. Lewis Vulliamy, *The Bridge of the Sta Trinità over the Arno at Florence*, 1822. By late 1831 measured engravings of London Bridge were available, and measured drawings probably on hand in Smirke's office well before that.

18. Henry Roberts (1803–76) from information in Colvin, London directories, article by A. M. Foyle, *Builder*, 2 January 1953, Architectural Association dissertation by Anthony McIntyre, 1974: born a British subject in Philadelphia, Pa, USA (census 1851) sometime between April and November 1803 (R. A. Schools register, age 22 in November 1825; census, 47 on 30 March 1851), son of Josiah Roberts, of 4 Gould Square by 1806 but not in directories 1802, of Fen Court, Fenchurch Street by 1819, of Fen Court and Camberwell by 1822, died 1846; Henry's brother Charles was a drug, spice and salt-petre broker, first office 1826 at 110 Fenchurch Street (Fishmongers' Company property, incidentally) and various City addresses to 1860. Henry's birth in the United States suggests that their mother may have been American. Roberts' competition entry: sheets 3–12 (3

elevations, 2 sections, 5 plans; no. 1 probably a perspective view, no. 2 perhaps a warehouse plan) are at GL; model (n. 9 above) does not survive; 'Description of the Accompanying Design', Ms 5843, files 10, 17; pseudonym (with seal-stamped goat symbol) *Mihi cura futuri*; identifying letter 31 December 1831 in Ms 5843, file 2; also his letters February-March 1832 and Clerk's 'Notes of answers by Mr Roberts' in interview 1 March, file 14; court minutes 4, 24 February, 5 March 1832. On Roberts see also chap. 14, nn. 41, 42 below.

19. Letter of 31 December 1831 (n. 18) accompanying his design.

20. On Smirke: J. M. Crook, 'Sir Robert Smirke: a Pioneer of Concrete Construction', *Transactions of the Newcomen Society*, vol. 38 (1965–6), 1968, pp. 5–22; Crook, *The British Museum*, 1972, chap. 3; Colvin. Roberts' 'Description' (n. 18 above) on the need for correspondence with other buildings at the two bridgeheads was what someone familiar with Smirke's responsibility for their character would say. On the Athenaeum building committee 1824–30, Survey of London, *St James's South of Piccadilly*, vol. 29, 1960, p. 387.

21. Illustrated in C. Stewart, *The Stones of Manchester*, 1956, p. 19, where it is dated 1819–34; the central façade is now re-erected in Heaton Park.

22. Rude comments by William Ross (a competitor, no. 14 per receipts, Ms 5843, file 15, as from Bristol, initial enquiry in file 1 as from Bury Street, St James's Square), *Architectural Magazine*, vol. 2, 1835, p. 329, as late of Bristol but now of New York, also p. 526; and T. Hamlin, *Greek Revival Architecture in America*, 1944, pp. 154–5, on Ross's part in Customs House, now Sub-Treasury, New York, possibly suggesting the nature of his design for the Hall. The fact that Smirke in his private work was mainly a Tories' architect, and the Fishmongers' Company an outstandingly Whig and Radical group at the time, would have had nothing to do with it, as it was under one of his public hats that Smirke oversaw the bridge-approaches. On Scott, chap. 14, n. 6 below.

23. An advertisement for a water-filter in 1830 quoted a number of London doctors

condemning Thames drinking-water, advertisement section, Robson's London directory, 1830.

24. William Smith (1756–1835) to Prime Warden, 23 February 1832, Ms 5843, file 14.

Chapter 14
Rebuilding, 1832–5

Principle sources: court minutes March 1832–August 1835 (Ms 5571, vols. 14, 15); committee minutes March-July 1832 (Ms 5573, vol. 14) and building committee minutes July 1832–July 1836 (Ms 5837, vol. 2); loose papers 1832–5, including architect's reports, Clerk's comments, incomplete specifications, tenders, draft contracts, and correspondence on fixtures, fittings, and furniture (Ms 5843, files 1–17); accounts 1832–5 (Mss 5834, 5841, 5843 file 2 with Roberts' summary 1835, file 8 with table of estimates 1831, Ms 7287 with loose sheet Clerk's summary, Ms 7288 summary 1831 of money from auctioneer); inventories 1835–60 (Ms 6242); drawings: nos. 1–22 for carcase 1832, with 3 for alterations 1832, 11 sheets details 1833, 7 sheets exterior details 1834–5; 88 sheets 1834–5 and 68 undated sheets for interior work, some for fittings (total, with 10 surviving competition sheets, and including 6 damaged sheets surviving only as photographs: 209 sheets of drawings from Roberts' office); J. C. Loudon's *Architectural Magazine* (1834–9).

1. During 1815–49, London brickmaking, an index of building-activity, was at its lowest in 1832: H. Hobhouse, *Thomas Cubitt*, 1971, p. 318.

2. Ms 5843, file 14, rough minutes 31 March 1832 (not in the fair copy).

3. Crook, *Newcomen Society* (chap. 13, n. 20 above); early articles on concrete, *Architectural Magazine*: Charles Reed in 1836, III, 79–86, George Godwin in 1838, V, 304ff, adding to his article in *Transactions RIBA* 1836; *Architectural Publication Society Dictionary*.

4. G. G. Scott at an RIBA meeting in 1857, *Transactions RIBA*, 1857–8, p. 43.

5. Committee minutes 2 April, 21 May 1753 (Ms 5573, vol. 2).

6. Roberts to Clerk from Camberwell, 28 May 1832, Ms 5843, file 14; Scott was presumably hired after that, in time to see the ground open. Scott (1811–78): *Personal and Professional Recollections*, 1879, pp. 73–5; *DNB*; n. 19 below. Kempthorne was mentioned as Suter's assistant at the court's spring 'annual view', 1830, 1831.

7. James Noble, *The Professional Practice of Architects*, 1836, p. 26.

8. Clerk's list of names, 14 July 1832, Ms 5843, file 14 (also including Jolliffe & Banks, crossed out).

9. Draft contract for carcase, 24 August 1832, Ms 5843, file 3. For William Cubitt (1791–1863), future M.P. and Lord Mayor (not to be confused with Sir William Cubitt, 1785–1861, civil engineer) and Lewis Cubitt (1799–1883), see Hobhouse, n. 1 above.

10. Hobhouse (n. 1 above), pp. 27–9. We don't know who the quantity surveyors were, since they were not paid by the company.

11. Draft specifications for carcase, Ms 5843, file 17. The structural drawings nos. 1–22 make it clear that this included only the brick shell, iron and timber membering, and outer stonework, and no internal wall-finishing, pilasters, stairs etc.

12. Kyan's broadside sheet, sent by Roberts to the Clerk 10 September 1832, is in Ms 5843, file 14; agreed, building committee, 6 October, pp. 14–16. *Architectural Magazine*, vol. II, 1835, p. 236.

13. Letter from secretary, Haytor Granite Co. (endorsed 17 March 1832, Ms 5843, file 14), saying they had furnished much granite used in the Bridge including pedestals at both approaches, the Pitt pedestal in Hanover Square, much of new General Post Office, and the granitework of Goldsmiths' Hall, and inviting direct contract with them, but it was decided in July that the granitework would be part of the Cubitt contract, they dealing with the Haytor people.

14. Hollow bricks and pot-tiles: Henry Roberts, *The Dwellings of the Labouring Classes*, 1850, p. 11n; *Builder*, 17 May 1851, pp. 311–12; *Architectural Publication Society Dictionary*, 'Pot construction'; H. R. Steele & F. R. Yerbury, *The Old Bank of England*, 1930, p. 12; Hobhouse, *Thomas Cubitt*, pp. 308–9; H-R. Hitchcock, *Archi-*

tecture Nineteenth and Twentieth Centuries, 1971 ed., p. 171.

15. Hitchcock (as n. 14), p. 171; also A. W. Skempton, 'Samuel Wyatt and the Albion Mill', *Architectural History*, vol. 14, 1971, p. 53.

16. Roberts drawings, sections and ironwork details (nos. 1–22 for carcase). J. M. Crook & M. H. Port (H. M. Colvin, ed.), *The History of the King's Works 1782–1851*, 1973, p. 416 on cast-iron beams at British Museum, p. 436 at General Post Office. When Roberts designed his two 39′ 6″ 'bearers' and others at first-floor level and his '½ Brick Arches in Cement between Iron Bearers' at entrance-floor level, the world's first iron-framed buildings, at Shrewsbury and Salford (Hitchcock, n. 14 above), were only some thirty years old.

17. Roberts' reports 9 February, 20 May 1833, Ms 5843, file 11. J. Gwilt, *Encyclopaedia of Architecture* (1842, rev. ed. 1912), section 1671e on Aberdeen granite, forming and polishing practical from *c.* 1822; J. V. Elsden & J. A. Howe, *The Stones of London*, 1923, pp. 117, 119: 'Notable examples are the fine columns of Fishmongers' Hall'.

18. Smirke on Messrs. Kepp, *King's Works* (n. 16 above), p. 415. On the previous Hall's copper roof, p. 104 above. As for the timber roof-trusses, Roberts did not envisage war from the air.

19. Rough draft specifications for internal finishings, Ms 5843, file 17. Most of the dated interior drawings are inscribed 31 January 1834 (date of meeting when tender accepted) and these will have been the ones young Scott (n. 6 above) mainly worked on. He was with Roberts until the spring of 1834. On the Cubitts' attitude to a second tender, building committee minutes, 29 November, 10 December 1833, also 31 January 1834.

20. *Architectural Magazine*, vol. II, 1835, pp. 308–9.

21. Statues, see pp. 160, 166, 174. Athenaeum entrance hall (for those unable to step inside), Survey of London, *St James's South of Piccadilly*, vol. 30, pl. 80.

22. Rider clause, draft contract, 12 February 1834 (signed in April), Ms 5843, file 16. Mallcott to Roberts, 27 September 1834, file 6.

23. *King's Works* (n. 16 above), pp. 138–9, 271, 281–5, 295–6.

24. It has not been previously known (the Department of Ceramics, Victoria and Albert Museum, tell me) that Hancock & Rixon dealt not only in lamps and chandeliers, but in ornamental glass windows; these, according to Roberts' descriptions, were a mixture of stained, painted and enamelled glass (Ms 5843, file 6). An inventory of *c.* 1843 (Ms 6242) includes '4 lanterns for painted glass windows & stands for ditto', for illuminating the great-hall pair during dinners.

25. Roberts' specifications, Ms 5843, file 17. *Architectural Magazine*, I, 1834, 319 on superiority of dowelled floors; II, 1835, 237 on Canada timber. *King's Works* (n. 16 above), p. 436.

26. On Mona marble, A. Clifton-Taylor, *The Pattern of English Building*, 1972, p. 188. That chimneypiece from Brown & Co. was replaced after the last war.

27. Roberts showed in a drawing of December 1832 how Peirce's armorial stone panel could be mounted on the Hall's west face. Richardson asked for the remaining posts (shown in Cottingham title drawing for lost set, chap. 13, n. 1 above) as a 'Relic . . . to form an entrance to the Garden Walk' behind his house, no. 8 Saville Row on the Walworth Road (letter in Ms 5843, file 6); on history of that house and company's Walworth Estate, a rural area (e.g. committee minutes November 1836) before railways came there, see court minutes 14 March 1861. Gate taken to Wandsworth, committee minutes 16 January, 10 April 1861, no further mention of it.

28. D. Wiebenson, *Sources of Greek Revival Architecture*, 1969, p. 67, citing this Hall as an example. At the gallery end, the upper halves of the central pair become piers.

29. *King's Works* (n. 16 above), p. 284, for the King's and Queen's staircases, balustrading of 'hard white metal painted bronze'.

30. Roberts' specifications (file 17) included two corridor doors 'each to have four Squares of plate looking Glass of the very best description', that is, the mirror panels removed in 1898 were original fixtures, not added in 1840 or 1865.

31. Inventories, Ms 6242. Samples of crimson tabaret and brown holland are in Ms 5843, file 12.

32. Roberts' undated courtroom plan, showing platform, wall-seating, and partition, was water-damaged in the last war, surviving now in a photograph taken at GL after these were rescued.

33. W. H. Leeds in his expanded edition of Britton & Pugin's *Public Buildings of London*, 1838, p. 24. Leeds' account there of the Hall, pp. 21–32, with two elevations and first-floor plan, seems to have been the first substantial account of the new Hall to be published.

34. Noble (n. 7 above), p. 61. Candidus, *Architectural Magazine*, III, 1836, 560.

35. Watkin, *Cockerell* (chap. 12, n. 5 above), pp. 73–4.

36. A. E. Richardson, *Monumental Classic Architecture*, 1914, p. 67. Unlike many contemporary buildings, e.g. Smirke's west side of Trafalgar Square, the Hall has no decorative ironwork (railings originally at the Thames Street entrance were entirely practical); the Hall's character is wholly three-dimensional.

37. *Athenaeum*, February 1836, in an article on the new Houses of Parliament, pp. 358–63, refers to a City company whose costs were far above the estimates (Dr Michael Port kindly gave me this reference).

38. Roberts estimate, 14 August 1832, Ms 5843, file 14, and his comparative statement of estimated and actual cost, 29 October 1835, in file 2. The value of the pound sterling was seven or eight times that in, say, 1972.

39. Ms 7287, loose sheet.

40. Survey of London, *St James's South of Piccadilly*, 1960, vol. 29, p. 411.

41. McIntyre (chap. 13, n. 18 above), p. 26. On Roberts' Sailors' Home, 1835, where he also later built the church, in Well Street and Dock Street, his own essay (n 14 above) read to the RIBA in 1850, p. 15n. So in the summer of 1835 in Roberts' office, drawings for the Sailors' Home and for the London & Croydon Railway Co. jostled heavy correspondence about the Hall's holland covers.

42. Graves; Society of Antiquaries minutebook, vol. 37, 1835–9; *Architectural Magazine*, IV, 1837, p. 360. Another of his

proposers for the Antiquaries in 1838 was J. A. Giles (*DNB*), headmaster of the City of London School, Cheapside, and earlier head of the Camberwell Collegiate School designed by Roberts. His election as Fellow of the Institute of British Architects in May 1837 followed five years as 'principal' architect in his own office since his appointment at Fishmongers' Hall. He also became a member of the Athenaeum (will of 1873 with addresses, Athenaeum in London and Villa Romana San Gaggio in Florence). His will mentions testimonial silver given him in 1853, probably honouring his unpaid pioneering housing work. He left about £25,000 in 1876, having apparently been in independent circumstances since his father died in 1846.

Chapter 15
Victorian Gilding and Riverside Smoke

Principal sources: court minutes and committee minutes (Mss 5571, 5573 to 1870, thereafter at Fishmongers' Hall); annual summaries of accounts in court minutes; Hall building accounts 1827–47 on decoration of 1840–1 in Ms 5834; loose papers relating to decoration 1894–1903 in Ms 7278.

1. Tenders for wharf and warehouse, Ms 5843, files 6, 11; building committee minutes February–April, November–December 1834, and court minutes 18 December 1834.

2. On 'Nuisance occasioned by Smoke arising from the Steamers', court minutes 13 August, 31 October 1835, 7 March, 11 July, 1 August 1840, 25 March 1841, and committee minutes 22 July 1839, etc.

3. Herman Melville's travel journal 1849, edited by E. M. Metcalf for Harvard University Press, 1949, contains the germ of this description, later developed in his novel about the 1770s, *Israel Potter* (chap. xxv, standard edition, 1923, pp. 210–13), grafting impressions of the Victorian bridge on to its predecessor; on 'carts, coaches, drays' he may have been reading Stow (p. 9 above). A photograph of 1895 of the traffic on London Bridge is in Dyos & Wolff, eds., *The Victorian City*, 1973, fig. 135, and an engraving of the crowd in 1872 as seen

from Fishmongers' Hall is in my *Victorian London*, 1972, fig. 33.

4. G. A. Sala, *Twice Round the Clock* [1859], p. 88.

5. The surviving 'barge deckings' of carved and painted or gilded wood probably date from 1734 (figure of St Peter) and 1773 (heraldic sternpiece, figures with trumpets): barge papers, Mss 6917, 7263. After St Peter's Hospital moved to new buildings, designed by Suter in minimal Tudor at East Hill, Wandsworth, part of the ground at Elephant and Castle was sold in 1859 to the trustees of Spurgeon's Tabernacle. Mattresses for the new almshouses were bought in 1851 from Messrs Heal & Son, already of Tottenham Court Road.

6. Sources on the Hall decoration of 1840: court minutes 12 March–22 June 1840 (certain other contractors refusing to tender, p. 465, 'being unwilling to prevent . . . the parties who built the Hall from the pleasure of finishing it'); accounts, Ms 5834, June 1840–January 1841 (Roberts' fee for superintending 'completion of painting and decorating Hall' £135; Cubitts paid £1831; to a clerk of works £2.12.6 per week for 16 weeks; and various extras); also committee minutes on bills audited 2 September 1840, p. 405; no specifications, drawings, or bills survive. The committee in charge were two, the Prime Warden J. K. Hewson and Samuel Boddington (the latter, ship-owner, a director of the London Dock Co., and a collector of pictures, sometime resident in St Helen's Place, Bishopsgate, and in Upper Brook Street).

7. Woodington: Boase, Graves, Gunnis; from his two models, Bielefeld presumably prepared moulds. Bielefeld: review, *Architectural Magazine*, IV, 1837, 538, of his book on papier mâché ornament and his recent enrichment of Grocers' Hall with this material (the fibre-glass of its day); like plaster it was then painted. Woodington and Bielefeld were each paid £60. There is no record of the overdoor reliefs in the court dining room until in 1865 they were ordered 'to be tinted' (committee minutes, 30 October 1865, p. 605).

8. Loft: Survey of London, *St Anne Soho*, vol. 33, pp. 140–1 on his separate plaster-cast business (Gunnis on his own sculpture).

9. On Beechey portraits, court minutes 22 June 1840. On the Queen's portrait, 28 May, 9 July, 1 August, 10 December 1840, 14 January, 25 March 1841; accounts (Ms 5834) February–July 1841. Smith received £115, plus £10 for expenses while staying at Windsor. On him, *DNB*, Graves. In 1840 Colnaghi & Puckle of 23 Cockspur Street advertised as 'printsellers & publishers to Her Majesty' (Tallis view no. 84, *John Tallis' Street Views*, ed. P. Jackson, 1969); on Dominic Colnaghi, 1790–1879, *DNB*.

10. Samuel Birch (1757–1841, see Beaven, *DNB*), Lord Mayor 1814–15, head of the Cornhill caterers (shopfront in Victoria and Albert Museum), playwright and poet, sold the family business in 1836 to his chief assistant John Ring (later Messrs Ring & Brymer), ancestor of the Lord Mayor 1975-6. Samuel Birch held the appointment of Cook (i.e. caterer for big dinners) to this company, with his brother Lucas, from 1800, preceded by their father Lucas Birch; predecessors early in the 18th century included Baines to *c*.1712, followed by Inwood.

11. After 1840, Roberts had no further connection with the Hall.

12. Dr Neil Arnott (1788–1874), a progressive physician and scientist, invented a smokeless grate known as Arnott's Stove, the principles of which he published in 1838. Various hoists and lifts long in use for shiploading and warehousing were being improved in the 1830s–40s, as for building materials at the Houses of Parliament, for heavy ledgers in Lombard Street, and for visitors to the Regent's Park Colosseum, in some cases substituting steam engines for manual operation.

13. No. 7 Billiter Lane with vault below was subleased to Messrs Ruskin, Telford & Domecq in 1815; in 1827 a new lease was granted to Messrs Ruskin & Telford only, Mr Domecq 'always residing Abroad', in 1848 the lease was renewed for another 21 years, and by 1868 assigned to a Henry Ritchie.

14. Frederic Tudor, known as the Ice King, was the pioneer in this Yankee export sent by clipper ships as far as India (American Guide Series, *Massachusetts*, 1937, pp. 420, 424, and personal knowledge).

15. Information from Michael Darby,

and committee minutes 19 May 1865, p. 481, Peto requested to consult Jones.

16. Ms 6279, loose papers relating to proposed Old Swan Pier, esp. Suter's report of February 1860 and legal opinions of January–February 1872, also with papers of 1844 on company's encroachment on bridge-stairs, all relating to ancient rights to 'free plying places', wharf-owners' rights to work directly from barges, and fears of hindrance from the recently-founded Thames Conservancy's proposals for steamboat piers lying out in the stream.

17. Jones Sr, as antiquary, is in the *DNB*. On his son the architect, pending publication by Michael Darby, see *Marble Halls* exhibition catalogue, Victoria and Albert Museum, 1973, and R. McLean, *Victorian Book Design and Colour Printing*, 1963, pp. 56ff, 89ff; the two Alhambra folios in the RIBA library were given by Jones. He was born at 148 Upper Thames Street, on the north side just east of Suffolk Lane.

18. Handbooks to the second Crystal Palace in 1854 included, as an addition to the one on the Greek Court, Owen Jones's *An Apology for the Colouring of the Same*.

19. Sources on Hall redecoration of 1865: Jones's drawings, Victoria and Albert Museum; committee minutes 29 April–29 November 1865; newspaper cuttings, January 1866, mounted at end of court minutebook no. 24; and *Building News*, 23 February 1866, pp. 121–2. The presence on the committee of George Moore, who lived at no. 15 Kensington Palace Gardens, as well as Sir S. M. Peto of no. 12, and also on the court Russell Gurney of no. 8, not to mention Owen Jones's earlier commissions in the neighbourhood (Survey of London, vol. 37, *North Kensington*), all suggest the Kensingtonian cultural background to City ideas of decoration at this period.

20. Kershaw had been paid £500 on account in September 1865, and his balance authorized by the accounts committee was £1475 (architect's fee £208, both rounded to nearest pound). Jones not only prepared designs for repainting but for new grates, carpets, curtains, and various fixtures. Jackson & Graham, whose chief designer Jones was, in this instance having been underbid by Kershaw for the main rooms, were employed under Suter in decorating the lesser

rooms and also provided some fixtures to Jones's design, including door handles, and renovated some furniture.

21. Fire Brigade: committee minutes 31 March, 18 August 1855, pp. 55, 92; court minutes 13 May 1869, p. 40; committee minutes March, May 1881, pp. 660, 706, 709.

22. Report on Architectural Association's visit to the Hall, *Architects' Journal*, 27 February 1924.

23. Court minutes 8 October 1885, p. 367, connecting Hall with system of United Telephone Company Ltd.; later they had National Telephone Company's apparatus. Telephone directory 1897–8 at GL. Jones Bros in 1882 (court minutes 22 June) were early birds.

24. Court minutes 20 December 1894, 9 May, 6 June 1895. There was flooding in November 1894 (not serious below Richmond, according to Brazell), there had been floods the previous winter (company surveyor's drawing relating to basement flooding in December 1893), and earlier, in November 1874 the wine cellars were 'again flooded from the sewers', with aspersions from the surveyor upon 'the bad construction of the new Low Level Sewer' of London's new Main Drainage.

25. William Etty (1787–1849) the painter, whose uncle was partner in the firm of Bodley, Etty, & Bodley, lacemen, returned from Venice in 1824 when Thomas Bodley was Prime Warden; the portrait was bequeathed to the company in 1939 by the architect's son as of 'his grandfather', although the architect's father was William Hulme Bodley, physician, old George's son. That George Bodley was admitted freeman by redemption in 1768; Thomas Bodley, his former apprentice, was admitted freeman in 1796, not by patrimony but by service to him, so probably a nephew: Thomas' report on banners and shields in 1815 (chap. 9, n. 22 above) suggests a family eye for colour. William Hulme Bodley was admitted freeman by patrimony in 1801 while his father was Prime Warden, when the family lived in Clapton; both W. H. and Thomas later lived in Brighton, where W. H.'s son G. F. Bodley the architect did some of his early work (addresses in livery lists, Ms 5584).

26. Bodley's report, committee minutes 20 February 1894, pp. 621–9; also privately printed copy with papers in Ms 7278.

27. Sources on Hall decorations of 1898: surveyor's report, committee minutes 13 February 1894, pp. 614–18, and Bodley's advice (n. 26); electric-installation proposals and drainage-works, committee minutes 1894–5; loose papers 1898, Ms 7278, including joint report by H. Chatfeild Clarke and J. D. Crace, specifications, and agreement; committee minutes throughout 1898 (Bodley not on committee); *Architect*, 10 February 1899, pp. 101–2; *Architectural Association Notes*, vol. 14, 1899, p. 64. Later alterations to courtroom etc., committee minutes October, November 1899, March, June, July 1900, July 1903, May, July, September, November 1904, February, April, May 1905.

28. W. S. Frith the sculptor acted as consultant about the commission to Turner, R.A. student gold-medallist 1898, court minutes 9 February, 9 March 1899. Turner's other works included statuettes of Justice, Labour, Maternity etc. for the thrones of Queen Victoria Memorials at Delhi and Sheffield (Graves); allegory then was the sculptor's best friend.

29. Plans 1900 by Bodley in Ms 7278.

30. Drawing at the Hall.

31. No. 6 Martin's Lane, in rate books and directories, was occupied until about 1799 by an oil, hop and seed merchant, thereafter by unspecified merchants who may have been vintners; but until 1882 the Old Shades on its second riverside site, next to the Hall, was the original tavern of that name in the neighbourhood.

32. T. C. Barker & M. Robbins, *A History of London Transport*, vol. 1, 1963; and court minutes 13 May, 10 June 1886, pp. 472, 485ff. The Pearl Assurance Company's architect for Seal House (in brick with free-range Mixed-Tudor touches) was H. P. Monkton; their main office in the City was at Adelaide Buildings until the present building in Holborn was erected *c.*1912.

33. Holman Hunt's painting of London Bridge decorated for the royal wedding in 1863 is in the Ashmolean Museum (illustrated in Wolff & Dyos, *The Victorian City,*

fig. 352). On the Diamond Jubilee, special scrapbook 1897 at the Hall.

Chapter 16
Beside the Bridge, 1901–75

Principal sources: court and committee minutes at the Hall.

1. In the company collection are engraved plans assembled by the Clerk from parliamentary reports, Committee for the Improvement of the Port of London, e.g. 1800, pl. IX by Messrs Telford & Douglass, pl. XVII by George Dance. At GL are imaginative views by George Allen and Peter Jeffery. On Col. (later Sir) F. W. Trench (1775–1859), *DNB*. *British Architect*, 14 October 1910, pp. 253ff on Town Planning Exhibition and various plans.

2. On affairs of 1902–4, newspaper cutting scrapbooks at Hall. The bridge balustrades that went to Arizona are no older than 1902; the set in front of the centre bay of the Hall dates from 1833 (p. 146); those north of the Hall front steps have had to be renewed.

3. The Earl also gave to the company the colours of the captured ship, *Ville de Paris*, part of which survives.

4. On the Hall as hospital, court minutes 6 August 1914–10 April 1919; newspaper cuttings in Hall scrapbooks. Other ranks in the City had a hospital on Finsbury Square.

5. Memories of May 1915 obtained for me by Dr Timothy Wood from Mr M. Bryce-Smith, to both of whom I am most grateful,

6. *British Architect* (n. 1 above) on Caröe's design. Strong English sentiments notwithstanding, almost nothing medieval survived the Great Fire here (parts of no. 6 Martin's Lane are thought to be pre-Fire), and except for St Magnus and the Monument, buildings in this historic locality dated mainly after *c.*1825–31.

7. On the Three Tuns, p. 123 above. On effects of Adelaide House on Steam Packet Hotel, newspaper cutting scrapbooks, esp. *Evening News* 4 November 1922, *Times* 22 November 1922. On height of Adelaide

House, *Times* 14 March 1924, *Observer* 5
October 1924, *Builder* 17 October 1924.
About a third of Adelaide House was built
on ground reclaimed from the river.

8. Sources on Hall redecoration of 1926–
7: committee minutes 18 May 1926–21
April 1927; *Times* 2 August 1927 on the
'restoration'; *Country Life,* 19 January 1929,
article by C. Barman.

9. On its earlier history, p. 95, and
chap. 9, n. 29 above.

10. Nos. 14–16 on the east side of Wood
Street, just south of the present Gresham
Street.

11. This was at Shenley Church End,
near Bletchley.

12. Howard Chatfeild Clarke (p. 165
above), a President of the Surveyors' Institution like his father, died in 1917 and was
succeeded briefly as company surveyor by
Edwin T. Cooper, architect to the Port of
London Authority, followed by H. C. Web-
ster in 1922, P. C. Tuckett in 1926, and
(Sir) Edward Gillett in 1936. The present
company surveyor Mr R. A. S. Brock is the
sixteenth holder of that title since Jennings
had it around 1600 (but with long gaps in
the line, as explained in chapters 3 and 10).
The present Clerk, Mr Earl, is the seventeenth since Glover was appointed *c.*1579,
with no gaps; names before that unknown
(before 1547 the clerks to this company may
have been chaplains).

13. One of the original two court dining-
room chimneypieces, of 'black & gold
[veined] marble' according to an early inventory, is shown in a snapshot photograph
at the National Monuments Record.

Index